Third Edition

The High Performance Toolbox

SPENCE ROGERS
& SHARI GRAHAM

Succeeding with
Performance Tasks, Projects, and Assessments

PEAK
LEARNING
SYSTEMS

PEAK LEARNING SYSTEMS, INC. • EVERGREEN, COLORADO

The High Performance Toolbox

Succeeding with Performance Tasks, Projects, and Assessments

3rd edition

By

SPENCE ROGERS

SHARI GRAHAM

Published by
Peak Learning Systems, Inc.
6784 S. Olympus Drive
Evergreen, CO 80439-5312
(303) 679-9780
e-mail: Peaklearn@aol.com

Peak Learning Systems books may be purchased for educational or business use. For information, please call or write: Order Department, Peak Learning Systems, Inc., 6784 S. Olympus Drive, Evergreen, CO 80439-5312. Telephone: (303) 679-9780; Fax (303) 679-9781.

Portions of this book are based on an earlier resource titled *The Performance Learning & Assessment Toolbox* from Peak Learning Systems.

Clip art courtesy of Phil Frank Megatoons and CorelDraw 7.0
Cover Design by Dani Burke

Publisher's Cataloging in Publication
(Prepared by Quality Books Inc.)

Rogers, Spence.
  The high performance toolbox : succeeding with performance tasks, projects and assessments / Spence Rogers, Shari Graham.
  --3rd ed.
  p. cm.
  Includes bibliographical references and index.
  Preassigned LCCN: 98-67970
  ISBN: 1-889852-07-4

  1. Competency based education. 2. Curriculum planning. 3. Education--Evaluation. I. Graham, Shari. II. Title.

LC1032.R64 1998   371.2'7
                                                  QBI98-1368

To Mike, to whom I owe more than he will ever know; to Roz, who has always been there and whose love, understanding and commitment have made all this a reality; to Chris who is a light that still shines; and to my father who provided the direction, love, and inspiration.

Spence Rogers

To Dan for his unending love and support; to my parents for their guidance, love, and devotion; and to Spence for his constant challenge to question and seek.

Shari Graham

Table of Contents

Chapter 3   An Overview of Performance Design   71

This chapter provides an overview of performance design. Included in this chapter:

Chapter 4   Designing Performances   89

This chapter develops in significant detail the beginning steps in performance design. Included in this chapter:

Chapter 5   Performance Task Design Templates for People in a Hurry   171

When time for inservice is severely restricted, it is helpful to have these short, easy to use designers to help teachers get started. These designers are also helpful for teachers who are working on their own and already know what they should be including in their designs.

Chapter 6   Aligning Curriculum, Instruction, and Assessment   179

Complex performances and projects require careful attention to curriculum, instruction, and assessment alignment in order to ensure rigor. Included in this chapter:

Chapter 7   Rubrics   193

Rubrics are the key to high quality performances and learning. This chapter provides extensive coverage of rubrics including:

x

About the Authors

SPENCE ROGERS

Spence Rogers is the coauthor of numerous articles and books supporting educational reform. He coauthored *Motivation & Learning: A Teacher's Guide to Building Excitement for Learning & Igniting the Drive for Quality* (1997) and *Quick Tips & Strategies to Improve Student Motivation and Learning* (1996) which preceded it. Spence also coauthored *The Performance Learning and Assessment Toolbox* (1995) which is the predecessor to this book. In addition, he worked with Bonnie Dana to produce a Phi Delta Kappa Fastback.

As a classroom teacher, Spence received awards on four occasions for excellence in teaching mathematics and science. In addition, he was recognized for excellence by his Board of Education in Glendale, Arizona.

In the Glendale Union High School District, Spence served as math teacher and department chairperson, math curriculum coordinator, staff-developer, and co-facilitator of the mastery learning implementation initiative.

Spence has consulted with schools and districts across the United States and internationally in the areas of Performance Tasks and Assessments, Mastery Learning, Outcome-Based Education, Mathematics Education, Motivation, Leadership, and Effective Instructional Practices and Strategies for Improving Student Learning, Utilizing Block Schedules, and Teaching for High Performance for all. In addition, he has presented thousands of keynote addresses and breakout sessions at national, international, state, and local conferences.

Currently, Spence is the Director and a senior consultant with Peak Learning Systems. As such, he continues to present highly acclaimed sessions at conferences and conduct effective staff-development for schools and districts across the continent. His commitment to custom tailoring every workshop to the needs of the participants and his modeling of what he teaches continually result in praise for making a difference for teachers, administrators, and students alike.

SHARI GRAHAM

Shari Graham is the 1993 teacher of the year for East Grand Rapids, Michigan where she served as a language arts teacher for twenty two years. She served as Assistant Director and a senior consultant with Peak Learning Systems for two years. During this time, Shari conducted highly acclaimed staff-development workshops across the United xii

States and Canada in the areas of performance assessment and effective instruction. She is currently the Professional Development/ Assessment Consultant with the Muskegon Intermediate School District in Muskegon, Michigan and a senior consultant with Peak Learning Systems.

Shari is the coauthor of *Motivation & Learning: A Teacher's Guide to Building Excitement for Learning & Igniting the Drive for Quality* and *Quick Tips & Strategies to Improve Student Motivation and Learning* which preceded it. She also coauthored *The Performance Learning and Assessment Toolbox,* the predecessor to this book.

CONTRIBUTING MEMBERS OF THE PEAK LEARNING SYSTEMS TEAM

JIM LUDINGTON

Though Jim is not a coauthor of this book, he has been instrumental in its development. He is an award winning math teacher and staff-developer in the Gananda Central School District in Walworth, New York. On two occasions, Jim was honored by the University of Rochester with their *Excellence in Teaching* award. He has also been named Employee of the Year by his district. Jim was a key player in the development of Gananda's Graduation Project praised by educators from around The United States and Canada.

In addition to being a practicing classroom teacher, Jim serves as a senior consultant with Peak Learning Systems. With over twenty years of classroom experience, he brings a sense of day to day reality to his writing and his workshops.

Jim is a coauthor of *Motivation & Learning: A Teacher's Guide to Building Excitement for Learning & Igniting the Drive for Quality, Quick Tips & Strategies to Improve Student Motivation and Learning* and *The Performance Learning and Assessment Toolbox.*

SUE TOMASZEWSKI

Though Sue has not served as a coauthor of this book, she has been so important to our staff-development efforts and thinking that it is appropriate to recognize her here. She is a coauthor of *The Performance Learning and Assessment Toolbox.* She is also a staff-development specialist with the Professional Development Center of the Orleans/Niagara BOCES in Lockport, New York. In this capacity she has become a recognized expert in the areas of effective instruction, assessment, cooperative learning, motivation, classroom discipline concerns, shared decision making, and group facilitation as well as Choice Theory and Reality Therapy.

Sue has worked with inner city, suburban, and rural school districts in multi-age, self-contained, and resource room settings. She has specialized in working with the "more difficult" students and began her staff-development work as a training specialist for the New York State Special Education Training and Resource Center Network.

Currently, in addition to serving as a senior consultant with Peak Learning Systems, Sue is recognized as a faculty member of The William Glasser Institute as a Basic and Advanced Practicum Supervisor in Choice Theory and Reality Therapy.

Acknowledgments

We would like to thank all those people who have contributed to our professional development and to the essence of this book. There have been so many people who have played a role that it would take most of this book to list them all and their contributions.

First and foremost we would like to express our appreciation to our families for their patience and unwavering support. The strength of their convictions and their contributions to the production of *The High Performance Toolbox* have helped to make it a reality.

We would also like to thank George Sisemore. His leadership, commitment, standards, and support provided the catalyst to help Spence open doors that eventually made this book possible.

The President of National School Conference Institute and former Superintendent of the Glendale Union High School District, Jerry George, has continued to provide inspiration and unparalleled encouragement for professional development. His continued support have been invaluable.

Bill Spady unselfishly and relentlessly has struggled for significant reform in education. His commitment to curriculum and assessment based on high level application of essential knowledge and skills has been a driving force in making performance learning and assessment a significant issue today. Bill's belief in us and the opportunities he provided for us to grow professionally have been a major factor in the development and completion of this resource.

John Booth has been a friend, team teacher, colleague, and inspiration since the day he joined the staff of Apollo High School. Without his support, ideas, energies, contributions, and friendship, this book never would have happened.

We would also like to thank Roz Rogers for her limitless energy and commitment to the publishing of this book. Without her expertise, understanding, and contributions, we would still be working on Chapter One.

A special thanks goes to Jim Ludington and Sue Tomaszewski for their endless support, contributions, editing, and using of the materials in this book.

Spence's son, Mike Rogers, was in Lynda Geames eleventh grade Language Arts classroom. During Mike's year with her, Lynda engaged her students in an outstanding, rigorous performance that became a lasting and important memory for Spence and Mike. We would like to offer a special thanks to Lynda for her inspiration, courage, and leadership. Lynda, we thank you as the representative for all the other teachers like you, for the positive differences you make in peoples' lives.

We would also like to thank the following people who have contributed either directly or indirectly to the concepts and ideas in this book or to our development as professionals. Judy Aaronson, Kris Baca, Suzi Barnett, Barbara Benson, Janet Berry, Ken Blanchard, Jim Block, Benjamin Bloom, Ron Brandt, David Briggs, Dani Burke, Helen Burz, Robert Lynn Canady, Ricki Chowning, Susan Close, Karin Cordell, Stephen Covey, Ceil Critchley, Patrick Cwayna, Willard Daggett, Bonnie Dana, Cristi Davis, Doug Deever, Debra DeWeerd, Roxanne DeWeerd, Jerry and Heavia Doyle, Margaret Dugan, Lynne Fletcher, Howard Gardner, Kathy Gardner, Margery Ginsberg, William Glasser, Rick and Shelly Grothaus, Tom Guskey, Stephanie Harris, Jan Hicks, Mary Kay Hoffman, Sid Holodnick, Heidi Hayes Jacobs, Judy Jamieson, Bena Kallik, Amy Karbula, Jim Kieffer, Giselle Martin-Kniep, Judy Krohn, Doug Krug, Paul LeMahieu, Suzi Loya, Kit Marshall, Robert Marzano, Kay McKernan, Iris McGinnis, Jay McTighe, James Morse, Christine Neal, Mark Pellegrino, Jim Pfieffer, Debra Pickering, Sharon Pollice, Linda Powell, Sue Powell, Chuck Schwahn, Wendy Shannon, Gary Soto and the staff at Southridge Middle School, Rick Stiggins, Rebecca Swanson, Roger Taylor, Michael Tillmann, Kathy Tocco, Teresa Tracy, Christine Vettese, Mary Walker, Sherrelle Walker, Tim Waters, Sue Wells-Welsh, Jo Sue Whistler, Grant Wiggins, Gary Wilson, Raymond Wlodkowski, and Pat Wolfe. In addition, we would like to thank the entire Lockport City School District Design Team and the staff of the Center for Systemic Educational Change of The District of Columbia Public Schools. Their hard work has contributed to the refinement of many of the materials included in this book.

There are thousands more who have contributed to the development of the concepts in this book. We apologize for not listing all their names, but still wish to extend our thanks for their contributions.

SPENCE ROGERS

SHARI GRAHAM

Introduction

Educators are finding themselves bombarded with pressures to reform, demands to return to the basics, desires to provide the best for all students, regional and national standards, and a plethora of outstanding innovations. The purpose of this toolbox is not to provide another new and improved approach to solving every problem in education. Instead, the purpose is to provide teachers (practicing and student), staff-developers, and support personnel in the areas of curriculum, instruction, and assessment with proven templates, procedures, support documentation, numerous ideas, and evaluation instruments necessary to be successful with performance tasks, projects, and assessments.

How to Use *The High Performance Toolbox*

The Toolbox is just what its name implies – a toolbox. Like any good toolbox, it contains numerous *tools* with overlapping, but different uses. Use these tools to …

- increase student learning;
- improve the significance of what students are learning;
- increase student motivation toward learning and school; and
- improve student results with local, regional, state/ provincial, and national assessments.

The High Performance Toolbox (*The Toolbox*) should be used much the same way one uses good computer software "how to" books. Some people are most comfortable reading them "cover-to-cover." Others have enough background knowledge to jump around – studying those parts that are needed at any given time. *The Toolbox* is designed to accommodate either of these approaches.

The Toolbox has been prepared with both classroom and system needs in mind. Where applicable, there are different templates, documentation, and guides to accommodate these two similar, but different sets of needs.

Systems will want to use the templates, or adaptations of them, to be certain to address each detail. Classroom teachers quite often are so busy on a day-to-day basis that the thought of completing endless templates is almost more than can be tolerated. The templates are not the issue. Classroom success will be determined more by adherence to the principles and concerns prompted by the templates then by a dedication to creating reams of completed templates.

A Guide to The Chapters

Chapter 1 – Performance Learning develops the foundation for using performance learning (tasks and projects). In Chapter 1, you will learn ...

- the essential terminology used with performance learning efforts;
- how performance learning is different from traditional approaches;
- what performance learning looks like in a classroom and how deadlines and quality expectations still play an important role;
- why performance learning is important for students today;
- the beliefs and principles that form the basis for performance learning;
- the critical differences between performance learning and performance assessment; and
- 15 essential considerations to be addressed when using performances.

Chapter 2 – Assessment and Evaluation develops the essential concepts surrounding the multiple forms of assessment and evaluation that are critical for teaching and assessing or evaluating learning in today's world. In Chapter 2, you will learn ...

- terminology critical to understanding and using assessments and evaluations effectively;
- the 3 major categories for assessments and evaluations and the advantages and disadvantages of each;
- how to improve assessment and evaluation alignment and validity;
- 5 crucial considerations in performance assessment and evaluation design; and

- how to use practical templates for designing and implementing either system or classroom level performance assessments and evaluations.

Chapter 3 – An Overview of Performance Unit Design overviews the essentials for designing performance-based units. In Chapter 3, you will learn …

- how 12 common starting points for designing performances differ;
- the 10 essential facets to performance design; and
- a 10 point checklist for managing performance design.

Chapter 4 – Performance Designs - The First 3 Performance Design Facets provides extensive, detailed guidance and templates for addressing the first 3 facets of performance design. In Chapter 4, you will learn …

- how to develop the overview and the primary learning and assessment focus for a performance unit;
- how to craft a performance scenario from any one of several common and effective perspectives; and
- how to develop the essential performance action structure that ensures performances replicate or simulate "real-life" performances.

Chapter 5 – Quick Designers provides a quick, 2 page designer for designing performance tasks. This designer is best used for short, introductory inservice sessions or by teachers who are familiar with what they are doing and want quick reminders.

Chapter 6 – Aligning Curriculum, Instruction, and Assessment focuses on ensuring that performance tasks and units effectively address desired curriculum. In Chapter 6, you will learn …

- how to differentiate declarative and procedural knowledge as desired learning within a performance; and
- how to use a set of practical templates for carefully planning the desired learnings and the essential aligned instructional and assessment strategies.

Chapter 7 – Rubrics develops the philosophical foundation and common understanding for the effective development and use of rubrics. In Chapter 7, you will learn …

- what rubrics are and what distinguishes effective rubrics from ineffective ones;
- how to help students and parents develop an understanding of rubrics;
- how to develop rubrics that are effective for scoring assessments or coaching students to high levels of quality in their work;
- how to use both dynamic and static criteria in rubrics to create standards challenging to all students;
- how to use quality terms to improve the effectiveness of your rubrics; and
- how to develop rubrics that go beyond assessing essential components to assessing quality results.

Chapter 8 – Learning Events, Checkpoints, and Logistics – Getting the Details Under Control identifies the details that must be adequately addressed to be successful with any performance. In Chapter 8, you will learn …

- what details must be addressed to succeed with performances;
- how to use a set of practical templates to plan the learning events involved in complex performances;
- how to plan and use checkpoints to improve performance results; and
- how to use project planners to facilitate the successful implementation of performances.

Chapter 9 – Assessing Performance Designs provides tools for evaluating performance designs so that you can avoid unnecessary, predictable problems.

Chapter 10 – Launching Initiatives and Staying Afloat develops premises, principles, and strategies for successfully implementing performances tasks, projects, and assessments. In Chapter 10, you will learn …

- essential, underlying principles for being successful with initiatives;

- basic beliefs that significantly increase the likelihood that your initiatives will be successful;

- tips for building the foundation for success;

- tips for succeeding with students;

- tips for succeeding in earning the parents' trust and support with your initiatives; and

- ways to earn the trust and support of your colleagues.

Appendices – Resources, Resources, Resources!

Use the resources available in the appendices to …

- learn practical ways students can show their learning through products and performances;

- use an extensive list of performance verbs to strengthen performance task designs;

- choose from powerful ideas for performance tasks and projects;

- gain performance frameworks of long-term, transferable value;

- choose from rich performance contexts;

- select from authentic life-roles;

- choose from easy-to-obtain audiences for student performances;

- pick from important, universal concepts for connecting subject matter information, skills, and concepts to prior learning through universal concepts important throughout life;

- draw from self-assessment prompts to facilitate self-directed learning;

- check definitions and usage of over 38 related terms; and

- choose from over 123 resources for information regarding implementing performance tasks, projects, and assessments.

Suggestions for People Who Want to Jump Right in

If you're the type of person that is very happy avoiding structure and just jumping into your projects, then jump around throughout the toolbox, and ...

Find and use *templates* to design ...

- classroom and district performance assessments;
- rubrics and performance checklists for coaching and scoring;
- aligned curriculum, instruction, and assessment within extended performances;
- performance implementation plans; and
- system assessment administration plans.

Find and use *documentation* to develop an understanding of ...

- the principles behind performance learning and assessment;
- the multiple types of assessment and their best uses; and
- performance tasks and assessments - their strengths and weaknesses.

Find and use step-by-step *procedures and guides* to develop system or classroom level ...

- tasks, performance assessments, and projects;
- rubrics, scoring guides, and checklists;
- procedures for administration of system level performance assessments; and
- performance implementation plans including learning events and management of logistics.

Use any of the evaluation tools to assess your performances or those provided by publishers, other educators, or governmental agencies. Gain insights into how to refine or adapt others' performances through the insights provided by these instruments.

Build support, understanding, and skills by using the 85 tips for earning the support and having success with students, parents, and fellow educators.

And use the appendices to gain literally hundreds of ideas and additional resources.

Copyrights and Our Commitment to You

Individual classroom teachers who own a copy of *The High Performance Toolbox* have full permission to duplicate any portion of their book to support their efforts (only) with their students. In order to support these classroom teachers, this book has been designed to be easily duplicated. Staff-developers, teacher teams, and others using this book for the purpose of instructing or coordinating others are asked to obtain individual copies of this book for each person with whom they are working. (Site Licenses and both system and quantity discounts are available by calling or writing Peak Learning Systems.)

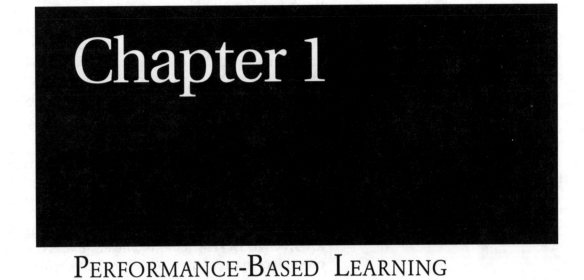

Chapter 1

PERFORMANCE-BASED LEARNING

Performance-Based

What is Performance-Based? Why should we get involved? Why is it important to so many people? What are the basic beliefs and principles on which the approach is built? What are some essential considerations if we are to be successful with it? These are but a few of the questions that will be addressed by the following overview and the helpful tools provided throughout *The Toolbox*.

A Performance-Based Approach Adds "Give, Use, and Learn" to "Know and Do"

In the simplest sense, we look at traditional curriculum as a *KNOW AND DO* curriculum. The emphasis has been strongly on subject matter . . .

- concepts and information (The *KNOW*); and
- skills (The *DO*).

What distinguishes a Performance-Based approach is that it is the best of the old combined with the beyond subject matter abilities that people outside of school also need – the abilities to . . .

- communicate what they know and can do to others (*GIVE*);
- apply what they know and can do as it is needed (*USE*);
- learn new information, concepts, and skills as they are required (*LEARN*).

> Simply, but mathematically stated,
>
> **PERFORMANCE-BASED = KNOW & DO + GIVE, USE, & LEARN**

Performance-Based Learning is an approach to education based on the commitment to lead and support the development of *the students' abilities to actively acquire and utilize* applicable content knowledge (information, skills, and concepts) in various contexts that can vary from simulated to authentic. This implies the students are taught to function effectively in settings that continuously require acquisition and application of knowledge, skills, and concepts while identifying, developing, assessing, and adhering to quality standards and expectations. These standards and expectations include timelines, deadlines, and quality levels for performances and products that cannot be compromised, but may certainly be exceeded.

In a performance-based approach, clearly identified performance abilities and content standards are established and combined to create active learning experiences (performance learning units) and associated assessments (both performance-based and non performance-based) for students in which they show their continued development.

Standards-Based

Standards-Based is similar to performance-based because in each case, what is planned and done is based on a predetermined foundation. With standards-based, the predetermined foundation is a set of standards for what the students are to learn or achieve. In most instances, the standards are content area standards, and often reflect a commitment to the students being able to apply the subject area knowledge and skills (performance-based).

Terminology

With respect to current educational terminology, a few patterns worthy of recognition seem to be surfacing:

1. There are almost as many definitions for current educational terms as there are implementors.

2. There seem to be an endless number of beliefs, premises, principles, and guidelines that, in many cases, seem to be saying the same things in a million different ways.

3. Members of the public and educators are becoming increasingly confused by terminology they either don't understand or that seems to lack a common definition.

Consequently, we have decided to keep our language as simple and consistent with common usage as possible. The following are a few definitions we need to establish up-front due to the numerous definitions that are in the world of education:

- A **Performance** is an event in which people are *doing* things according to prescribed expectations such as writing, speaking, persuading, teaching, building a model, or acting out a script. In chapter 2, we will split student performances into four categories to facilitate efforts to improve alignment and validity. These four performance categories are constructed response, product development, performance, and process.

- A **Performance Task** is a learning experience that replicates or simulates situations in which people are faced with a complex situation that needs to be resolved. These situations can include the need to have a real-life problem resolved, the need to have a group learn something, or the need to formulate a hypothesis and test it in a scientific manner. Performance tasks result in the students being engaged in the purposeful production or creation of something that is communicated, shared, or used with others for some observable purpose. Performance tasks are like excellently designed "projects" in which the students are engaged in meaningful, real-life like actions. In these tasks, the students are learning, using their learning, and being assessed in multiple ways for everything from knowledge and skills to their abilities to communicate, apply, and learn both independently and cooperatively.

- A **Performance-Based Unit** (also referred to as a performance learning unit or a performance unit) is an instructional unit that is designed as a performance task.

- **Performance Assessment** is a "checking experience or event" in which educators assess (check) the students' abilities to actually do or produce something that shows predetermined, well-defined criteria. These criteria are the type that are best observed and measured while students are engaging in a performance task. During a performance-based assessment, one might check for constructed response abilities, product development abilities, performance abilities, or abilities to execute a process. (This concept is developed to much greater depth in Chapter 2.)

- **Performance Evaluation or Performance Assessment?** A performance task is a performance assessment if the resulting data is used to make decisions as to how to improve performance. It is a performance evaluation if the student scores are recorded and used in the computation of a grade.

Students Are Seen Using and Communicating Their Learning in Performance Learning Environments

In Performance Learning Environments, the students are actively engaged in the learning process. They are working side by side with their teachers in various capacities designing and engaging in active, hands-on learning situations that are designed to accomplish a beneficial result that certainly includes, but goes beyond the learning of the subject matter. These tasks require both the gaining of and the application of specified "content."

- We might see students building and using museums to learn and teach valuable information and concepts to other students, parents, or members of the community.

- We might see the students using what they're learning to help members of the community with a project such as having sidewalks or streetlights approved and built, creating and publishing authentic voters' guides, or designing needed hospital additions.

- We might see students trying to replicate the results of a scientist's experiment rather than just following the procedures in a totally pre-planned science experiment. Or maybe they'll be designing and conducting experiments to test scientific, or other, hypotheses that interest them and that will necessitate learning the prescribed curriculum.

Deadlines and standards? Yes, and in very real-life ways. Students are engaged in researching, setting, and adhering to deadlines and standards of performance.

Accountability? Yes, like never before. When the students are engaged in demonstrating their learning or its application before an audience or to achieve a significant purpose, they are forced to meet quality standards and deadline realities at levels far beyond most traditional school situations. In addition to the audience and the performance's intended effect, the students' commitment to excel is built through involving them in the establishment of ...

- the design and development of final performances and projects;
- the timelines; and
- the performance standards.

A Performance Learning Approach Teaches Skills Essential in Today's World

Research of current trends is clearly showing us that being "knowledgeable" is no longer sufficient for success as careers come, change rapidly, and go. Our students will encounter an explosion in ...

- the amount of knowledge available;
- the availability of knowledge to everyone;
- the scrambling of accurate and inaccurate information now available through sources like the Internet;
- the increasing dependence on "sound bites" as a major communication vehicle;
- the expectation that they can and do access knowledge as it is needed;
- the need to work in regularly changing teams to solve complex problems; and
- the expectations that they apply their knowledge in new and rapidly changing situations.

A performance-based approach to learning is one that specifically targets each of the above trends combined with the essential academic knowledge, skills, and concepts the students will need. In a nutshell, performance learning is an approach in which the students are taught to function in ways consistent with current and expected future demands that are and will most likely be placed upon them.

A Performance Learning Approach Is Based on Fundamental Beliefs about Schooling

It is the obligation of the schools to teach every student the essential knowledge, skills, and abilities they will need both during and after their formal schooling. This certainly includes . . .

- academic knowledge and skills;
- effective methods for the continual acquisition of knowledge and skills; and
- effective methods for application of knowledge and skills.

Performance Learning, Evaluation, and Assessment Initiatives Are Based on 5 Premises

1. All students can, need, and want to learn.
2. Students learn at different rates and in different ways.
3. Learning achievement is maximized by meaning, application, high standards, and support being present.
4. Various portions of essential curricula are best addressed through varied approaches.
5. Schools, educators, parents, students, and community members all impact learner achievement; they all share in the responsibility.

Performance Learning, Evaluation, and Assessment Are Driven by 5 Principles

1. Focus on Desired Results with respect to performance capabilities and curriculum standards (including essential academics) in all planning and associated actions.
2. Balance Needs of students, parents, educators, and community members.
3. Maintain Highest Standards for growth and achievement.
4. Utilize Best Known Practices for curriculum design, instruction, assessment, and earning and maintaining stakeholder support.
5. Adhere to Values established within the community.

CAUTION: Performance learning, evaluation, and assessment are necessary, but NOT sufficient!

Performance Tasks

Performance tasks provide essential opportunities for students to learn and practice high level abilities. They provide a rich and motivating context in which to teach and assess such learnings as the ability to . . .

- build consensus;
- debate issues;
- actually communicate information and concepts to others;
- utilize the subject matter being learned;
- resolve complex problems; or
- persuade someone or a group.

For abilities such as these, it is important to teach and assess them in multiple contexts (to achieve what is referred to as multiple validations). It is also important to note that performance tasks, particularly if they are collaborative, are not effective means for assessing knowledge, comprehension, or many level skills that may become buried or not observable within the performance. These are all best assessed through other methods.

Performance tasks facilitate hands-on, integrated, contextualized learning when the "content" expectations lend themselves to a task. If we use a performance task to teach and assess "content" that does not lend itself to a task, we create a contrived situation that will probably not be effective. Therefore, we believe that students will be best served by an appropriate *combination* of performance learning tasks and more traditional means of teaching and assessing *in each classroom*.

15 Essential Considerations When Using Performance Tasks

Effective performance tasks have certain characteristics about their design and implementation. What follows is a brief identification and explanation of what we consider to be the most important of these characteristics.

Consideration 1: Design performance tasks to address significant learning purposes (content standards).

The performance task has a clearly and precisely defined educational purpose that is to be taught and assessed as part of the entire performance task process. This purpose can be multi-faceted and include *performance abilities, content standards, and behaviors.*

By *performance abilities* we mean that each performance task, whether in or out of school, typically should incorporate 5 distinct, yet interwoven, performance ability areas:

1. Information, skill, and concept **ACQUISITION** abilities for accessing information, skills and concepts (e.g., interviewing, reading, researching, questioning, listening, observing, and surveying);

2. Knowledge and situation **INTERPRETATION** abilities for effectively determining what needs to be learned and mentally processing accessed information and concepts to determine their importance, meaning, and applicability for achieving a desired impact or result (e.g., organize, prioritize, evaluate, judge, compare, contrast, decide, and resolve);

3. **PRODUCTION or CREATION** abilities for actually producing, building, creating, making, or assembling plans, designs, products, solutions and performances;

4. **COMMUNICATION, DISSEMINATION, or UTILIZATION** abilities for communicating, disseminating, utilizing, expressing, portraying, or persuading in order to achieve some predetermined result or impact; and

5. **EVALUATION & IMPROVEMENT** abilities for continuously evaluating (or assessing) processes, accessed information and concepts, and results in order to plan and make necessary and appropriate refinements.

By *content standards*, we mean a clear identification of the specific discipline related information, skills, or concepts that are to be accessed, utilized, learned, and assessed. These should be consistent with the best thinking and research available.

By *behaviors* we mean those behaviors that have been identified by the community and school as important to be learned.

Consideration 2: Design performances that have a purpose, result, or impact the students are to achieve as a result of their efforts.

Each performance task should be designed with a pre-identified result or impact that the students' work should have. In other words, each product, performance, or process should have an identified, observable, and assessable result or impact that is to be achieved through its use or dissemination. For example, the performance, product, or process is done in order that ...

- information, skills, or concepts are learned by others;
- someone or some group is persuaded; and
- people become aware of a situation or a series of events.

(Refer to Chapter 4 for a more in-depth presentation regarding performance purposes.)

Consideration 3: Earn and maintain stakeholder support.

It is essential to have the support of the parents, students, and educational staff for the performance tasks. Great care and effort should be devoted to earning and maintaining this support. Refer to Chapter 10 for a more in-depth presentation regarding stakeholder support.

Consideration 4: Adhere to basic local values.

The performance should be seen as worthwhile by the students, parents, community, and other educators. It should also be consistent with the shared values and expectations of the students, parents, and community. For example, we do not believe that young people should be taking positions on issues that are considered to be inappropriate by them, their parents, the community, or the school. Under no circumstances should situations be created that will turn parents and students against one another.

Consideration 5: Involve students, parents, colleagues, and community members.

The most effective performance tasks depend heavily on the active involvement of students, parents, other educators, and community members. These people can serve as audiences, learners, evaluators, judges, and providers of information, materials, and other resources. Involvement also takes the form of participation in the development of the performance tasks and the standards for evaluation of the various performance abilities, products, and final performances.

Consideration 6: Maintain both high standards and high expectations.

The highest standards must be established and expected for all students. However, this can only produce high levels of learning and performance if we also hold the highest expectations for all students. The expectations and standards need to be clear, precise, accompanied by examples, co-developed with students wherever possible, and known by all.

The most effective standards tend to be a combination of static standards (fixed/non-movable) and dynamic (not fixed/continuously moving) standards. Neither type is sufficient by itself. The difference between static standards and dynamic standards can easily be seen through a sport's analogy. In high jumping, the coach may establish a static standard such as "the height that must be jumped in order to be on the team" and a dynamic standard such as "each high jumper is expected to improve in form and height jumped throughout the season." Without this addition of dynamic standards into the academic environment, we continue to have standards that are too difficult for some and not challenging enough for others.

One additional complicating factor is the confusion with the word "standard." In some contexts, such as with rubrics, the word criteria is being used. Whichever word, standard or criteria, the need for both static and dynamic still exist.

Consideration 7: Use multi-faceted, thorough assessment.

Performance tasks are excellent contexts or vehicles in which to assess performance abilities providing adequate care is taken to develop the appropriate criteria/standards. However, they are not as effective, and certainly not as efficient, as selected response and oral or written presentation/essay for assessing knowledge. The converse is also true. Therefore, specific assessments need to be developed and utilized with each specific, identified, essential learning that is a part of the intended educational purpose for the performance task. (Chapter 2 provides more information about this topic.)

Consideration 8: Use multiple validations.

Complex abilities such as persuasive speaking, problem solving, and designing valid experiments cannot be adequately assessed in a single assessment. Therefore, when targeting complex abilities, develop numerous opportunities in varied contexts in which the students are expected to learn and demonstrate the targeted abilities.

Consideration 9: Develop and use rubrics effectively.

Performance, product development, and process abilities are most effectively coached and assessed through the use of rubrics. Rubrics are clearly and precisely identified criteria/standards for a given performance, product, or process that are in a logical, easy to read format with clear, precise, and observable components. For the rubrics to be truly effective, they must address both the breadth (Is all the "stuff" there and at a high enough level?) and the depth (Is this collection of excellent components really having the effect it should?) required for the given performance or product. Rubrics should differentiate between as many levels of quality as appropriate for the given purpose. The number of levels used tends to vary from two (Does "it" meet the quality expectations or not?), to four for most scoring uses, to ten or more for a process in which we are tracking growth over an extended period of time. To be effective, rubrics need to be based on exemplars of actual student and/or professional work, have examples (anchors) to support the descriptions of the various quality levels, and be thoroughly understood by the students and teachers. (Refer to Chapter 7 for more in-depth information about rubrics.)

Consideration 10: Plan thoroughly.

Performance tasks are like any other major undertaking. Each one requires thorough "project planning" that addresses a careful analysis of the task, determination of associated timelines, identification of responsible parties, and development of "scaffolding" necessary to support the efforts of the people involved. (Refer to Chapter 8 for more information about this topic.)

Consideration 11: Effectively use audiences.

Every coach knows when students perform before an audience, the quality of their efforts and performance results tend to increase. The same is true with performance tasks in a more academic environment. It is important to expand the scope of the audience by getting the students out of their classroom environment or by bringing an audience into the educational setting. The more the audience is valued by the students, the greater the impact will be.

Consideration 12: Use sound and stakeholder supported grading and documenting practices.

Performances, products, and processes that are associated with performance tasks are not easily scored or graded by traditional means, and yet the system expects documentation of results. Not all aspects of a performance lend themselves to typical grading procedures, and in many aspects of a performance, typical grading procedures will be counter productive. Separate the components of the performance into those that lend themselves to grades and those that do not. Grade, as always, that which is grade-able, and document that which does not lend itself to grading. Document what has occurred and to what level through narratives, portfolios, and other forms of evidence.

Consideration 13: Design feasible and manageable performances.

The resources associated with a given performance task need to be within our material, space, financial, and time limitations. They also need to be within the students' developmental levels and our abilities to teach and facilitate. Plan the performance carefully - think it through first. If necessary, it is better to tone down plans rather than to set ourselves and our students up for failure.

Consideration 14: Design performances that merit the time and energy – avoid flurries of empty activity.

Performance tasks involving students, just like projects in life, take a lot of work and time. They need to result in learning that is meaningful enough to justify the time and energy expended by those who are involved or affected. Performance tasks should be designed in such a way that they are effectively addressing local and/or state/provincial curriculum for which the students are to be accountable. "Canned" performances that have been developed by outside resources tend not to result in high levels of commitment and performance due to a lack of ownership and in-depth understanding on the part of the students, teachers, and parents.

Consideration 15: Continuously re-evaluate and improve your designs.

In today's world, the focus is on quality, and a large part of many reform movements is dedicated to improving the students' ability to evaluate and refine their own efforts until quality expectations have been met. Performance designers need to "walk-the-talk" and engage not only in evaluating their own efforts, but also in submitting them for peer and outside review.

Summary

In summary, entering into a performance-based approach does not require the abandonment of everything currently being done. It requires building upon what has been done well to this point and adding a commitment to have the students also know how to "Communicate (give), Use, and Learn."

PERFORMANCE-BASED = KNOW & DO + GIVE, USE, & LEARN

Note: This transition needs to be done in a way that matches best known practices in quality performance design and collaboration as members of a total community.

Chapter 2

An Overview of Assessment and Evaluation

Basic Terminology – Laying the Foundation

What is an assessment? Unfortunately, depending on whom one asks, the answer may be quite different. Based on our commitment to stay consistent with common usage, we define assessment this way:

An assessment is any effort through which the specific value, worth, or quality level of a student action, or purposeful combination of actions is determined in order to adjust instruction to improve learning and performance. This may be an action or actions that show the students' …

- retention of information, facts, or concepts;
- ability to perform subject matter skills in isolation;
- conceptual understanding of specified concepts;
- ability to utilize subject matter skills, information, or concepts in subject related tasks;
- ability to utilize subject specific or universal concepts and skills in diverse, unexpected contexts; or
- ability to utilize broad, transferable abilities such as debate, problem solving, consensus building, persuasion, teaching, or translation across communication modalities while drawing on specific information, skills, and concepts.

At the current time, many educators are separating the concept of assessment from that of testing. Though we see strong rationale to support this separation, we also see the potential for compounding the level of confusion and suspicion that can result with our many publics. Educators need clear and precise technical language for effectively communicating with fellow experts in the field. However, educators also need effective language for communicating with non-educators and educators who are new to the complexities of assessment. Unfortunately, all these necessary languages are not the same.

To the public, *to assess* means to determine the value, worth, or amount. It is a word that members of the public tend not to associate with education. The public tends to think of *testing* as the procedures that educators use to "check" (assess) the students' knowledge and skills. When many members of the public hear us making fine distinctions in the use of words such as tests and assessments, they become confused or suspicious at best. This is particularly true if they are led to believe that testing is not good anymore – after all, they believe it worked for them when the schools were still good and standards were high!

The bottom line in assessment terminology is to use the language that will be effective in the given situation. In Stephen Covey's words, "Seek first to understand." Learn the language that will best accomplish the desired effect and avoid confrontations over nuances in language that go far beyond the intent of the conversation. When a parent asks, "Do you mean a performance assessment is how you *test* how well my daughter can use arithmetic in situations like at the bank or in a store?" – Please just say, "Yes." And when the parent then asks, "Why all the fancy language? Why not just call it a test?" — Consider seriously saying, "That's a really good idea!" Agreement over precise nuances in language is not the critical issue. The issue is whether or not educators and members of the public reach a common understanding of the concepts.

Throughout *The Toolbox*, we will use the word "assess" to refer to *any* effort in which educators "check for" a student's knowledge, skills, understanding, or ability. We will differentiate between the types of assessment by using descriptive terms and phrases that are rapidly gaining popularity.

Distinguishing Between Assessment and Evaluation

As assessment is gaining attention, it is getting more and more confused with evaluation. This type of confusion is caused by people tending to make concepts that are new to themselves fit what they are already doing. The unfortunate result can be the loss of advantages of the new concept and the gradual re-labeling of former practices. This not only leads to the loss of the new concept, it also leads to the continued deterioration of vocabulary, which then leads to resentment and confusion.

Assessment is the gathering of information so that changes can be made in order to improve performance. This implies that when we use the word assessment as a part of school improvement efforts, we're probably doing just fine. But as soon as the word "assessment" gets brought into the classroom for performance tasks that are having "grades" recorded in the book, we are creating confusion between assessment and evaluation.

Evaluation differs from assessment. Evaluation is the gathering of information in order to score, label, grade, judge, or document. This implies that most of what is being called classroom assessments are actually classroom evaluations, and the power of "monitor and adjust" is being lost.

The Assessment and Evaluation Wheel – A Metaphor to Support Going Full Circle

For many years, assessment in school has been incomplete compared to assessment efforts outside of school. Multiple choice, true/false, matching, short answer, "show-your-work," and essay tests make up a huge proportion of the assessment in school. And yet, even all together, these most common assessment methods can only provide a very limited picture of a student's *total knowledge*. (By total knowledge we mean the knowledge and skills along with the ability to use them effectively and appropriately as needed.)

To help clarify the need for *Thorough Assessment and Evaluation*, consider all the multiple assessment methods used before young drivers are entrusted with the family car. The state administers a multiple-choice test (selected response assessment) to check for knowledge regarding traffic laws, and other bits of important information. Most parents engage their children in oral quizzing (selected and constructed response) to check for knowledge of information and perspectives considered important. The state and the parents both use performance-based assessments to check for performance and process abilities. And the parents typically use personal communication-based assessment to get at the attitudes and beliefs their children have regarding difficult issues and driving situations that are so dangerous they cannot be tested in real conditions. As the new drivers proceed through instruction and their early years with a license, the state, drivers' training instructors, and parents continue to use the different forms of assessment – almost the way the points along a wheel come in contact with the road over and over again as it rolls down the highway.

The Assessment and Evaluation Wheel

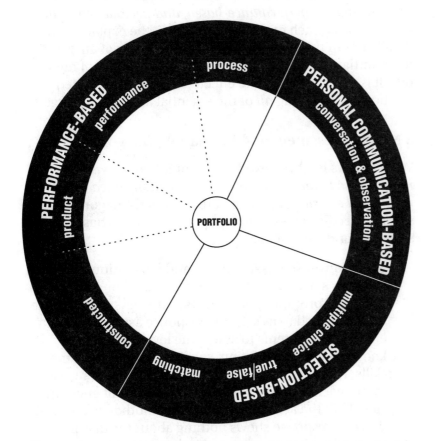

When using assessment to determine the extent of students' knowledge and their ability to use it, one is faced with clarifying all the specific, desired assessment targets. Common assessment targets include …

- information;
- skills;
- conceptual understandings;
- application of knowledge, skills, or understandings;
- product development abilities;
- performance development and execution abilities;
- process abilities; and
- attitudes/states of mind (not to be scored or graded).

We define *thorough assessment* as the combination of assessment methods that will best assess all the relevant assessment targets. Seldom is one method adequate. Each of the assessment targets can be addressed with varying levels of effectiveness through the three major assessment methods of *selection-based, performance-based, and personal communication based.* (Each of these methods will be explained in detail later in this chapter.) The thoroughness of an assessment initiative is not determined by the selection of methods; it is determined by the effectiveness of the selected methods in assessing *all* of the essential assessment targets.

3 Major Assessment and Evaluation Categories

What follows is a brief explanation of *selection-based, performance-based, and personal communication-based assessments and evaluations.* Each of these broad categories has several specific assessment types, and each one has its own strengths and weaknesses.

1. **Selection-Based Assessments and Evaluations** in which students select from available responses for given questions and prompts. Selection-Based assessments (sometimes referred to as selected response assessments) are efficient for systems to assess the level of students' knowledge of information, some concepts and some skills. However, they offer several drawbacks for classroom teachers – one of which is the fact that guessing can affect the accuracy of the data. Another, is the selection of a response shows nothing about the depth of knowledge or the processes used to determine the response. Example selection-based assessment and evaluation methods include the following:

    - multiple-choice,
    - true/false, and
    - matching.

2. **Performance-Based Assessments and Evaluations** which include . . .

    - **Constructed Response Assessments** in which the students create short responses to given prompts or questions – an excellent means of assessing information and some skills.

Examples of constructed response assessment and evaluation methods include ...

- fill in the blank tests with words and phrases;
- short answer tests – sentences and paragraphs;
- show-your-work tests – as with many math tests;
- organizers and visual representations (depictions) such as concept maps, pattern maps, webs, flow charts, graphs, tables and matrices, and illustrations and depictions.

- **Product (Development and Usage) Assessments and Evaluations** in which students plan, produce, and possibly use a product to meet given criteria and/or needs – an excellent means of assessing product development skills. It is important to note that a completed product is not necessarily solid evidence of a student's product development ability or knowledge information. Typically, additional methods are required. Refer to Appendix A for a list of product, performance, and process ideas. The following are but a few example products:

  - art exhibits,
  - articles,
  - audio tapes,
  - books,
  - dioramas,
  - editorials,
  - essays,
  - journals,
  - logs,
  - models,
  - museum displays,
  - plays,
  - poems,
  - process logs,
  - research papers,
  - science projects,
  - spreadsheets,
  - stories, and
  - video tapes.

- **Performance (Development and Execution) Assessments and Evaluations** in which students plan and carry out a performance that meets given criteria and/or needs - an excellent means of assessing performance skills and any imbedded information and/or skills. Refer to Appendix A for a list of product, performance, and process ideas that the students can create and/or perform to use and/or disseminate information. For clarification, several example performances from the list are ...

  - athletic or artistic skill demonstrations,

  - dances,

  - dramatic readings,

  - enactments,

  - individual athletic performances,

  - oral presentations,

  - recitals,

  - scientific demonstrations, and

  - speeches.

- **Process (Usage) Assessments and Evaluations** in which students use a process according to specific criteria and/or needs – an excellent means of assessing process skills. Because a process provides for numerous decisions and changes in direction, process assessments tend not to be efficient means for assessing content specific information, concepts, and skills. Again, refer to Appendix A for a list of product, performance, and process ideas. This list includes numerous ideas for processes in which the students can engage. When assessing processes, it is helpful to have the students record their efforts through the use of *process logs*. A few example processes are listed below:

  - competitive athletic games,

  - conferencing,

  - consensus building,

  - debating,

  - dialoging,

  - interviewing,

- problem solving (process focused),
- process "think out loud" assessments,
- questioning,
- researching,
- resolving conflicts,
- teaching, and
- using the scientific method.

3. **Personal Communication-Based Assessments** which entail conversations with the students or observations of students' efforts to determine attitudes or perspectives.

It is important to devote a few words to the assessment of attitudes, states of mind, or perspectives. *Respect the rights of the students.* Most teachers use continuous, on-going assessment of the students' thoughts regarding the content and the effect of the instructional methods. Also, most teachers want their students to like/appreciate the subject matter/discipline being taught, and thus constantly are monitoring how the students are feeling about it. Under no circumstances should students' attitudes, states of mind, perspectives or beliefs be graded, scored, or marked. If they are, the students will quickly learn not to share them. This is not to say that as teachers we should not be striving for students to appreciate learning or school, be honest, or have integrity. Nor is it implying that we shouldn't be teaching and expecting honest behavior. It's just saying, *"Don't grade attitudes, beliefs, states-of-mind, or perspectives – students have the right to have the thoughts that they have."* We have the obligation to require that students act with honesty and show respect for others' property. We don't have the right to require that they like, value, or appreciate anything. Besides, once people learn that their thoughts will be scored, graded, or used for or against them, the assessor loses the ability to accurately perform an assessment anyway.

Sample assessment targets for personal communication-based assessments include the students' ...

- appreciation for a particular piece of literature;
- respect for the right of others' to have their own beliefs;

- beliefs about the merits of different forms of government; and

- personal value placed on classroom rules or procedures.

Performance Learning Is Not Performance Assessment or Evaluation

One last major distinction – projects, performances, performance tasks, and units that provide active, hands-on, authentic or simulated learning opportunities for students will not be referred to in this book as assessments nor evaluations. We will refer to these as the "performance learning" that is used to support multiple, varied, and rich opportunities in which intended learning and aligned assessment can occur.

Portfolios: A Brief Introduction

Portfolios are purposeful collections of work. Many people refer to portfolio assessments, however, in themselves, portfolios are not *true* assessments – they can be assessment vehicles. Portfolios are the vehicles through which much assessment can occur or be presented. They may contain any combination of the assessment methods mentioned previously. Portfolios also are an excellent vehicle for assessing the students' abilities to self-evaluate their work or progress.

A student's portfolio should have a "letter" from the student that serves as a "road map" to explain the contents of the portfolio, justify each selection, and present the supported direction and procedures targeted for growth. It is through this letter that the student's ability to assess or evaluate his/ her own work and/or see patterns or trends in it can be assessed. It is also through this letter the student's ability to develop and present effective and appropriate improvement plans based on the careful assessment of his/her work, strengths, and weaknesses can be assessed.

Portfolios, like any other approach to assessment, should be based on clearly identified criteria.

Several of the more common types of student portfolios include:

- **Best Work Portfolios** – Students and their teachers select pieces of student work that best illustrate the students' varied best achievements. These selections are to be made based on specific, predetermined criteria that is aligned with the purpose of the portfolio.

- **Growth Portfolios** – Students and their teachers select those pieces of work that best illustrate past, present, and probable future improvement. These selections are based on, and justified with, specific, predetermined criteria.

- **Scrapbook Portfolios** – Students include selections they think best illustrate or represent what they consider to be important or exemplary work. They also include rationale for each selection.

- **Introduction Portfolios** – Students select those things that will best introduce or support an introduction of themselves for some particular purpose in a given context.

CAUTION: Do not score, grade, or mark students' attitudes, values, beliefs, or states of mind that may be expressed in portfolios.

Match Assessment and Evaluation Targets with Aligned Methods—to Improve Alignment and Validity

The Assessment Matching -- Tool I chart on page 26 and The Assessment Matching -- Tool II chart on page 27 provide some basic guidance for matching targeted learning with appropriate assessment. The assessment targets listed are . . .

- Information and Facts
- Skills
- Application of Information or Skill
- Understanding of a Topic or Concept
- Product Development
- Performance ability
- Process Ability
- Attitudes/Perspectives

Assessment and Evaluation Matching -- Tool I

Targets	Methods
Information (facts)	Say; circle; list; match; select; find; true/false; multiple-choice; fill-in-the-blank; present in essay or oral presentation.
Skills (write, listen, speak, paint, perform mathematical operations, scientific procedures, isolated athletic skills, or structured problem solutions)	Do it (showing procedure) and describe or explain how it was done.
Application of Information or Skill (using arithmetic to determine change, using writing to describe how to find or make something, using welding to repair something)	Use it to achieve a purpose; describe and/or explain its use.
Understanding of a Topic or Concept (equations, literature, animals, change, force, evolution, conflict)	Explain; generalize; create examples; find examples; apply it in varied contexts; & draw conclusions in new contexts.
Product Development (essay, lab report, book, story, painting, model, video/audio tape, portfolio, research paper)	Create it and describe and/or explain how it was done and why it was done the way it was.
Performance Ability (singing, dramatic reading, science demonstrations, oral presentations, individual athletic performances such as figure skating)	Do it and describe how it was done and explain why it was done the way it was.
Process Ability (interview, debate, build consensus, teach, dialogue, communicate, compete in athletic games, research, solve un-structured problems)	Work through it in varied/unexpected contexts; explain how it was done and why it was done the way it was.
Attitudes/Perspectives (appreciation for something, liking or disliking something)	These can be assessed by observing behavior or engaging in open conversation – providing trust has been developed. (Do NOT score or grade.)

Assessment and Evaluation Matching -- Tool II

Each methodology included in the table below can provide us with valuable information regarding what the students know and/or can do. It is important to select the methodology that provides the best possible combination of effectiveness and efficiency for the intended purpose and targeted learning. In the table below, the following codes are used to indicate best matches between methods and targets.

3   This is an excellent method for the targeted learning in most circumstances.

2   This may be a good method for the targeted learning (depending on the specific targeted learning and the actual vehicle being used). Depending on the assessment data desired, additional methods may be necessary.

1   This is usually an ineffective and/or inefficient methodology for the targeted learning.

Learning Target	Selection-Based Selected Response	Performance-Based			Communication-Based
		Constructed Response	Product	Performance	Process	Conversation & Observation
Information & Facts	3	3	2	2	2	2
Conceptual Understanding	1	2	2	2	2	2
Skills	2	2	2	2	2	2
Reasoning	1	1	2	2	2	3
Product Development	1	1	3	1	1	2
Performance Ability	1	1	1	3	1	2
Process Ability	1	1	2	2	3	2
Attitudes & Perspectives	1	1	1	1	1	3

Note: For additional insight and depth regarding this topic, refer to the work of Rick Stiggins and Jay McTighe.

5 Essential Considerations with Performance-Based Assessments and Evaluations

Performance-based assessments and evaluations are purposeful, active experiences in which the students' abilities to do any of the following are assessed against specific criteria:

- use specific information and/or concepts;
- communicate specific information and/or concepts;
- perform specific skills;
- apply specific skills;
- execute performance abilities;
- utilize product design and/or development abilities; or
- use transferable process skills.

Each performance-based assessment or evaluation needs to have the following:

1. A clearly identified purpose which includes …

   - the type of data to be generated;
   - the intended use for the data; and
   - the audience for the data.

2. A clearly and precisely identified focus which includes …

   - specific skills, knowledge, and/or abilities to be assessed;
   - a clearly defined context in which these are to be demonstrated; and
   - clear, precise, and example supported criteria for evaluation.

3. A well designed task that includes …

   - a clearly stated task that will cause the students to demonstrate the targeted learning focus in assessable ways; and
   - a structure that addresses the five actions associated with quality performances (access, interpret, produce/create, disseminate/use, evaluate).

4. A clearly and precisely identified administration context
    which includes ...

    ■ nature and extent of coaching permitted;

    ■ nature and extent of student preparation prior to the
      assessment;

    ■ time and other resources needed and to be provided;

    ■ clear and precise directions for both the assessment
      administrator and the students; and

    ■ conditions of the assessment site.

5. A clearly identified evaluation and reporting procedure
    which includes …

    ■ criteria with models for evaluation;

    ■ adequate preparation for the scorers to produce
      consistent evaluation results;

    ■ established procedures for multiple readings as
      needed; and

    ■ a plan for what, how, and for/to whom.

Templates for Designing Classroom Performance Assessments and Evaluations

What follows is a set of templates that can be used to facilitate the development of classroom performance-based
assessments and evaluations.

These templates consist of four pages. When used, they will
result in …

■ a task overview identifying the task developers, the task
  reviewers, the targeted standards, and the appropriate
  grade level(s) and subject area(s);

■ a task to be given to the students;

■ limits (parameters) that define the task's level of difficulty;

■ clear identification of the learning being assessed; and

■ a scoring rubric.

The components in these classroom templates are selected
ones from the system performance templates presented on
pages 39-54. Therefore, please refer to these pages for directions
to complete the templates.

On the following pages, you will find ...

- a completed example set of templates. The completed example is a modification of the example provided for the system performance assessment; and

- a set of blank templates.

Classroom Performance Assessment or Evaluation

The Overview – Page 1 of 4

Subject Area(s):	Grade Level(s):
mathematics	2

Development Team Member(s)

Jan Hicks and Lynne Fletcher

Peer Reviewer(s)

Shari Graham and Spence Rogers

Standard(s)/Indicator(s) Targeted

The students will demonstrate an understanding of statistics by gathering, interpreting, and graphing data.

Resources Needed for Administration

Pre-prepared graph paper with half inch squares, colored chips (about half inch) in five different colors, crayons and color pencils.

Estimated Required Time:	45 minutes
Estimated Total Administration Time:	1 hour

Classroom Performance Assessment or Evaluation

Targeted Student's Knowledge of … (facts)

Factual information is not the target of this assessment.

Targeted Student's Ability To … (skills or processes)

- sort by color/shape
- count
- determine comparative data regarding more/less than
- construct a bar graph from data

Limits for the Targeted Skill/Process:

- For primary age students …
  - colors will be common and easily distinguishable.
  - objects will be easy to grasp, manipulate, and see.
- There will be no more than 10 in any category and no more than 30 objects total.
- Only one set of two of the five objects will have the same characteristics. (Example: only the red and green will be equal in number.)

Primary Scoring Criteria:

- Accurate graph
- At least two correct comparisons

Targeted Student's Understanding of … (concepts)

Understanding of comparison is being assessed by the students finding and relating comparisons as identified above.

Limits for the Targeted Understanding:

Not applicable

Primary Scoring Criteria:

Not applicable

Classroom Performance Assessment or Evaluation

THE ASSESSMENT TASK TO BE GIVEN TO THE STUDENTS – PAGE 3 OF 4
(Attach any required resource material.)

The situation is (if applicable) … Not applicable

Your task is …

… to construct a graph and write a letter about what your graph shows.

- Each of you has been given a bunch of colored chips. The chips are red, blue, green, black, and white.
- Sort your chips into piles according to color. Be sure each pile of chips has only one color of chip.
- Count the number of chips you have of each color.
- Make a bar graph that accurately shows the number of each color chips you have.
- Write a letter to someone you like telling him/her how many of each color chip you have. Also tell him/her about which you have more of, … less of, … and equal numbers of.

An excellent performance (the primary criteria) …

- Your graph will be excellent if it is accurate and easy to read.
- Your letter will be excellent if it is complete, accurate, and understandable.

The amount of time you will have to complete this task is   … 1 hour.

(Note: Because of the nature of this example task and the format of *The Toolbox*, a package of colored chips and a sheet of lined paper is not attached.)

Classroom Performance Assessment or Evaluation

THE RUBRIC – PAGE 4 OF 4

Rubric		
	Graph	**Letter**
Exemplary (4)	The graph is accurate and easy to interpret.	The information is complete and accurate.
Proficient (3)	The graph is accurate and interpretable.	The information is not complete or contains minor errors, but there is enough to see understanding of counting and comparing.
Developing (2)	The graph has minor errors but is still interpretable.	The information is not complete or contains minor errors, but there is enough to see understanding of counting. The ability to compare is not detectable.
Emerging (1)	The graph has conceptual errors or is not interpretable.	The letter shows some connection to the task, but counting and comparing are not addressed.
Not Score-able (0)	Blank or nothing is related to the task.	

Classroom Performance Assessment or Evaluation

THE OVERVIEW – PAGE 1 OF 4

Subject Area(s):	Grade Level(s):

Development Team Member(s)

Peer Reviewer(s)

Standard(s)/Indicator(s) Targeted

Resources Needed for Administration

Estimated Required Time:

Estimated Total Administration Time:

Classroom Performance Assessment or Evaluation

THE ASSESSMENT'S TARGETS – PAGE 2 OF 4

Targeted Student's Knowledge of … (facts)

Targeted Student's Ability To … (skills or processes)

Limits for the Targeted Skill/Process:

Primary Scoring Criteria:

Targeted Student's Understanding of … (concepts)

Limits for the Targeted Understanding:

Primary Scoring Criteria:

Classroom Performance Assessment or Evaluation

The Assessment Task to be Given to the Students – Page 3 of 4
(Attach Any Required Resource Material.)

The situation is (if applicable) …

Your task is …

An excellent performance (the primary criteria) …

The amount of time you will have to complete this task is …

Classroom Performance Assessment or Evaluation

THE RUBRIC – PAGE 4 OF 4

Rubric

Templates for Designing Blueprints and Models for System Performance Assessments

What follows is a set of templates that can be used to develop performance-based assessments and their associated models for the future development of parallel assessments for system use. (Parallel assessments are assessments that are different in surface detail but identical in targets, structure, and level of difficulty.) These templates are very similar to the classroom templates on the previous pages – classroom teachers functioning independently would not typically address several of the prompts in the system templates. An assessment model is used by educators the same way home builders use blueprints, a model home, and a list of acceptable parameters for a given subdivision. Builders can use all this to build numerous houses that appear different on the surface, but are fundamentally the same when it comes to value and use. Similarly, with an assessment model, educators can design numerous assessments for a given target that are varied and yet equal in difficulty.

These templates for facilitating the development of system performance-based assessments consist of five pages. When used, they will result in …

- a sample assessment;

- a statement of how it is structured;

- limits (parameters) that define its level of difficulty;

- clear identification of the learning being assessed; and

- sets of directions for students and assessment administrators.

On the following pages, you will find …

1. a guide for using the templates;

2. a completed example; and

3. a set of blank templates.

System Performance Assessment Model

THE OVERVIEW – PAGE 1 OF 5

Template Guide

Subject Area(s):	Grade Level(s):
Indicate targeted subject area(s).	Indicate the targeted grade level(s).

The Purpose for the Assessment

Indicate how the assessment is to be used. (For example: classroom assessment or program evaluation.)

Development Team Members

Indicate the names of the assessment's developers.

Peer Reviewers

Indicate the names of the assessment's peer reviewers.

Standards/Indicators Targeted

Indicate the content or other standards and/or indicators targeted by the assessment.

By … (The Task's Frame)

Indicate the assessment frame which is the expression of the task without the specifics.

Example

The students are to summarize the main points found in a standard news article (as found in a common news magazine) that is at an eleventh grade reading level. Notice that with further clarification in this example, many parallel assessments could be created using numerous articles. Each parallel assessment would assess a student's ability to summarize a new article of a certain type at a certain level.

Resources Needed for Assessment Administration

Indicate the resources needed for the assessment.

Estimated Assessment Time:	Indicate the time the students will need.
Estimated Total Administration Time:	Indicate the total time.

System Performance Assessment Model

THE ASSESSMENT'S TARGET(S) – PAGE 2 OF 5
Template Guide

This Assessment Is To Assess A Student's Knowledge of ... (facts)

Indicate the specific facts students are expected to show they know as a part of this assessment.

Every performance assessment may NOT target factual knowledge.

This Assessment Is To Assess A Student's Ability To ... (skills or processes)

Indicate the specific skill(s) or process(es) students are expected to show they can do as a part of this assessment.

Every performance assessment may NOT target skills or processes – though most will.

Assessment Limits for the Targeted Skill/Process:

Indicate the limits as to the level of difficulty for the targeted skill(s)/process(es).

Primary Scoring Criteria:

Indicate the major criteria that are to be scored.

This Assessment Is To Assess A Student's Understanding of ... (concepts)

Indicate the understanding students are expected to demonstrate as a part of this assessment.
This may NOT be addressed by every performance assessment.

Assessment Limits for the Targeted Understanding:

Indicate the limits as to the depth of understanding to be shown.

Primary Scoring Criteria:

Indicate the major criteria that are to be scored.

System Performance Assessment Model

SAMPLE ASSESSMENT – PAGE 3 OF 5

Template Guide

By … (Sample Assessment Task)

Present a sample assessment task exactly as it would be presented to students. Be certain to attach any materials the students might need to complete the task such as readings, charts, pictures, or graphs.

Note: Districts/Systems develop sample, parallel assessments so teachers can use them to prepare their students for the secured system assessment.

Attach Any Required Resource Material.

System Performance Assessment Model

DIRECTIONS FOR STUDENTS AND TEACHERS – PAGE 4 OF 5
Template Guide

Appropriate Prior Instruction

Indicate the prerequisite learning that is to be taught prior to the assessment.

Appropriate Coaching During the Assessment

Indicate the nature and extent of coaching that is appropriate while the students are doing the assessment. Be certain to allow enough coaching so that the target of the assessment can be seen. However, be certain to limit the coaching so that the assessment results provide credible evidence of the students' actual ability levels with respect to the assessment's target.

Directions to the Students

Provide any directions that are to be given to the students that are not directly a part of the statement of the assessment task itself.

System Performance Assessment Model

SCORING RUBRIC – PAGE 5 OF 5

Template Guide

Scoring Rubric

Include a scoring rubric along with anchors.

A Completed Example
System Performance Assessment Model

THE OVERVIEW – PAGE 1 OF 5

Subject Area(s):	Grade Level(s):
mathematics	2

The Purpose for the Assessment
program evaluation

Development Team Members
Jan Hicks and Lynne Fletcher

Peer Reviewers
Shari Graham and Spence Rogers

Standards/Indicators Targeted
The students will demonstrate an understanding of statistics by gathering, interpreting, and graphing data.

By … (The Task's Frame)

The students will be asked to sort manipulatives that represent different colors, shapes, or types of objects. They will then be asked to graph their findings in a bar graph. They will also be asked to express in writing (orally is acceptable) their findings including relative comparisons.

Resources Needed for Assessment Administration
colored chips in 5 different, easily discernible colors, shapes, or type; a prepared graph with half inch squares; crayons (same colors as chips); pencils, and lined writing paper.

Estimated Assessment Time:	45 minutes
Estimated Total Administration Time:	1 hour

A Completed Example Continued …
System Performance Assessment Model

THE ASSESSMENT'S TARGET(S) – PAGE 2 OF 5

This Assessment Is To Assess A Student's Knowledge of … (facts)

Factual information is not the target of this assessment.

This Assessment Is To Assess A Student's Ability To … (skills or processes)

- sort by color/shape
- count
- determine comparative data regarding more/less than
- construct a bar graph from data

Assessment Limits for the Targeted Skill/Process:

- For primary age students …
  - colors will be common and easily distinguishable.
  - objects will be easy to grasp, manipulate, and see.
- There will be no more than 10 objects in any category and no more than 30 objects total.
- Only two of the five objects will have the same characteristics. (Example: only the red and green will be equal in number.)

Primary Scoring Criteria:

- Accurate graph
- At least two correct comparisons

This Assessment Is To Assess A Student's Understanding of … (concepts)

(Note: Understanding of comparison is being assessed by the students finding and relating comparisons as identified above.)

Assessment Limits for the Targeted Understanding:

Not applicable

Primary Scoring Criteria:

Not applicable

A Completed Example Continued ...
System Performance Assessment Model

SAMPLE ASSESSMENT – PAGE 3 OF 5

By ... (Sample Assessment Task)

Each of you has been given a bunch of colored chips. The chips are red, blue, green, black, and white.

Sort your chips into piles according to color. Be sure each pile has only one color of chip represented.

Count the number of chips you have of each color.

Make a bar graph that accurately shows the number chips you have of each color.

Write a letter to someone you like telling him/her how many of each color chip you have. Also tell him/her about which you have more of, ... less of, ... and equal numbers of.

Attach Any Required Resource Material.

(Note: Because of the nature of this example and the format of *The Toolbox*, a package of colored chips and a sheet of lined paper is not attached to this page. However, within a system, these examples would be attached.)

A Completed Example Continued ...
System Performance Assessment Model

Appropriate Prior Instruction

Teach the children . . .

- the different colors
- how to construct a bar graph
- how to detect and express comparative data

Appropriate Coaching During the Assessment

It is acceptable to help the children with the names for the different colors.

If expressing their findings in writing is a problem, it is acceptable to have them express their findings orally.

Clarify directions as necessary.

Don't tell the students such things as how high their bars should be.

Directions to the Students

No additional directions are needed.

A Completed Example Continued ...

System Performance Assessment Model

THE RUBRIC – PAGE 5 OF 5

Scoring Rubric		
	Graph	**Letter**
Exemplary (4)	The graph is accurate and easy to interpret.	The information is complete and accurate.
Proficient (3)	The graph is accurate and interpretable.	The information is not complete or contains minor errors, but there is enough to see understanding of counting and comparing.
Developing (2)	The graph has minor errors but is still interpretable.	The information is not complete or contains minor errors, but there is enough to see understanding of counting. The ability to compare is not detectable.
Emerging (1)	The graph has conceptual errors or is not interpretable.	The letter shows some connection to the task, but counting and comparing are not addressed.
Not Score-able (0)	Blank or nothing is related to the task.	

System Performance Assessment Model

Subject Area(s):	Grade Level(s):

The Purpose for the Assessment

Development Team Members

Peer Reviewers

Standards/Indicators Targeted

By ... (The Task's Frame)

Resources Needed for Assessment Administration

Estimated Assessment Time:

Estimated Total Administration Time:

System Performance Assessment Model

This Assessment Is To Assess A Student's Knowledge of ... (facts)

This Assessment Is To Assess A Student's Ability To ... (skills or processes)
Assessment Limits for the Targeted Skill/Process:
Primary Scoring Criteria:

This Assessment Is To Assess A Student's Understanding of ... (concepts)
Assessment Limits for the Targeted Understanding:
Primary Scoring Criteria:

System Performance Assessment Model

By ... (Sample Assessment Task)

Attach Any Required Resource Material.

System Performance Assessment Model

DIRECTIONS FOR STUDENTS AND TEACHERS – PAGE 4 OF 5

Appropriate Prior Instruction

Appropriate Coaching During the Assessment

Directions to the Students

System Performance Assessment Model

THE RUBRIC – PAGE 5 OF 5

Scoring Rubric

Performance Assessment or Evaluation Task Design Checklist

Use the following scale and criteria to evaluate your design and implementation plan:

Exemplary: Yes! There is no doubt!
Close: This needs more work.
Not Yet: This needs to be addressed.

___ 1. The task is designed to assess a standard addressed by state/district/national standards and assessment efforts.

___ 2. The task provides credible evidence of its target.

___ 3. The task provides usable data.

___ 4. The task is valid. (It truly assesses what it's claimed to.)

___ 5. The task is reliable. (It provides consistent results over time.)

___ 6. The task has a tight focus. (The limits are sufficiently defined.)

___ 7. The task is worthwhile. (It's an effective and efficient use of time.)

___ 8. The task is do-able.

___ 9. The task is clear to its targeted audience.

___ 10. The task is score-able.

___ 11. The task expects accuracy, depth, rigor, logic, and support.

___ 12. The criteria are well understood by the students.

___ 13. The criteria and identified quality levels are based on challenging exemplars and actual examples of student work.

___ 14. Anchors for all criteria and levels are available for teachers and students.

___ 15. The assessment has been adequately tested by its designers and *non-biased others* and found to meet the standards expressed in items 1 -14 above.

Templates to Assist with the Administration of System Performance-Based Assessments

If a performance assessment is to be used to gather data for making either instructional or programmatic decisions from a team, school, or district perspective, then the assessment context needs to be stabilized. If this is not done effectively, conclusions cannot be drawn with confidence as to what the data is or means. Factors that need stabilizing include ...

1. prior instruction regarding prerequisite knowledge and skills;

2. prior instruction in performing tasks similar to the assessment;

3. coaching during the assessment;

4. administration of the assessment;

5. conditions during the assessment;

6. scoring of the assessment; and

7. security of the assessment.

The purpose of the four templates on the following pages is to support items 1 through 5 above. Any assessment that is to be used by more than one teacher needs to have these items stabilized. Item 6 is addressed on a classroom level as part of Chapter 7. Item 7 is beyond the scope of this book.

Templates Supporting Performance Assessment Administration

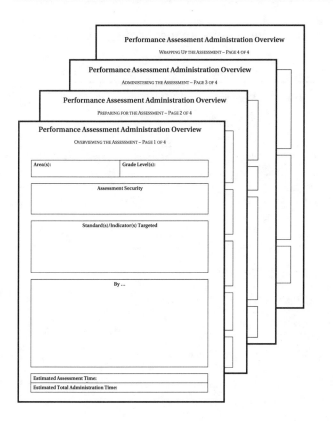

The four templates used to support the administration of performance assessments are …

1. Overviewing the Assessment,

2. Preparing for the Assessment,

3. Administering the Assessment, and

4. Wrapping Up the Assessment.

Directions for completing these templates are presented one at a time on the following pages.

Note: The information being provided to people who will be administering the system assessments cannot be too clear or precise. If one is to err, err on the side of clarity and precision.

How to Complete Template 1 "Overviewing the Assessment"

This template is to provide a quick snapshot of the assessment.

Performance Assessment Administration Overview

OVERVIEWING THE ASSESSMENT – PAGE 1 OF 4

Area(s):   Grade Level(s):

Assessment Security

Standard(s)/Indicator(s) Targeted

By ...

Estimated Assessment Time:
Estimated Total Administration Time:

Area(s) – Provide the subject area or areas to be addressed by the assessment. Examples include Language Arts, Science, Choral Music, and Math.

Grade Level(s) – Enter the specific grade levels for which the assessment is designed. Examples include first, third through fifth multi-age, ninth, and pre kindergarten.

Assessment Security – Provide a statement as to the level of security for the assessment. For example:

- Secured Assessment - Do not duplicate, or
- Unsecured Assessment.

Standard(s) / Indicator(s) Targeted – Indicate the content standard(s) and indicator(s) that are being specifically assessed with this assessment. Example: New York Math Standard 3 – "The students use measurement in both metric and English measure to provide a major link between the abstractions of mathematics and the real world in order to describe and compare objects and data."

Indicator: "Use trigonometry as a method to measure indirectly." *By . . .* Indicate briefly what the performance task is that the students are to do in order to show the targeted standard(s) and (indicator(s). Example: writing a note to an imaginary friend (who has been absent from math class for a week) explaining to her how to apply the trigonometric functions to determine distances that cannot be directly measured.

Estimated Assessment Time – Indicate the estimated time it will take the students to complete the assessment task. Examples include:

- two, ninety minute periods;
- one hour; and
- five class periods.

Estimated Total Assessment Time – Indicate the estimated time that the entire assessment will take, including reading directions and collecting materials.

How to Complete Template 2 "Preparing for the Assessment"

This second template is to provide the assessment administrators (most likely the classroom teachers) with information regarding what they need to do and know prior to the administration of the assessment.

Performance Assessment Administration Overview

PREPARING FOR THE ASSESSMENT – PAGE 2 OF 4

Early Directions for the Assessment Administrator

Supplies to be Obtained in Advance by the Assessment Administrator

Prerequisites Assumed Taught Prior to the Assessment

Appropriate Preparation of the Students for the Assessment

Inappropriate Preparation of the Students

Early Directions for the Assessment Administrators – Complete this box with any directions the assessment administrator will need *before* the day of the assessment. Examples include:

- supplies the students are to be told to obtain before the assessment date; and

- methods to use for informing the students as to the importance of doing their best.

Supplies to be Obtained in Advance by the Assessment Administrator – List any supplies the teacher needs to obtain before the assessment is to be administered. Examples include:

- pencils,
- measuring tools,
- tape,
- scrap paper, and
- chart paper.

Prerequisites Assumed Taught Prior to the Assessment – List any relevant grade, course, or subject level prerequisites upon which the assessment is dependent. Examples include:

- paragraph construction,
- arithmetic operations,
- measures of central tendency,
- character analysis, and
- compare/contrast processes.

Appropriate Preparation of the Students for the Assessment – Present what is appropriate preparation of the students for the assessment. With any assessment, there are preparatory things that when done facilitate the students' abilities to demonstrate the target of the assessment. Examples include:

- teach the students the concepts and skills listed as prerequisites;
- have the students practice doing _____ while using the *rubric* that will be used to score their actual assessment(s);
- practice the targeted problem solving process in multiple contexts; and
- teach and have the students practice in a number of contexts a compare/contrast process - the focus of the assessment.

Inappropriate Preparation of the Students for the Assessment – Present what is considered inappropriate preparation because it will undermine the assessment's effectiveness. For example, if the target of the assessment is problem solving as a process, then it is inappropriate for the students to practice problem-solving in the same context or situation as that presented in the assessment.

How to Complete Template 3 "Administering the Assessment"

The purpose of this template is to provide information that the assessment administrator needs during the administration of the assessment.

Directions for Administering the Assessment – Indicate the directions that the Assessment Administrator is to follow when administering the assessment. Examples include …

- advise the students to clear their work area;

Performance Assessment Administration Overview

ADMINISTERING THE ASSESSMENT – PAGE 3 OF 4

Directions for Administering the Assessment

Materials to be Provided by the Students

Directions to be Given to the Students

Appropriate Coaching During the Assessment

- distribute to each student a pencil, scrap paper, a copy of the assessment, and the map set;

- read the directions aloud to the students while they read silently along with you; and

- double-check for the students' understanding of their directions before they begin the assessment.

Materials to be Provided by the Students – List any supplies the students are to supply themselves. (We recommend having backup supplies for those students who forget theirs.) Examples include:

- paper,

- pencils,

- calculators,

- newspaper articles, and

- library research.

Directions to be Given to the Students – Indicate the directions that are to be read to the students. Examples include:

- "As I read aloud the directions found on the second page of your assessment package, please read silently along with me."

- "In groups of three, check to see if you all have the same understanding of what you will be asked to do as a part of the assessment – in a few moments, I will ask several of you to clarify the task for me."

- "Clear your work area of everything except …"

- "Work quietly until you are done."

- "When you are done, you may …"

Appropriate Coaching During the Assessment –Clarify the coaching that is appropriate during the assessment. Include cautions as necessary for clarity. Examples include:

- You may read a passage aloud for a student.

- You may provide factual information if asked.

- You may clarify the directions.

- You may ***not*** provide any help other than to clarify the directions.

How to Complete Template 4 "Wrapping Up the Assessment"

This template is to provide guidance and directions for the administrator as to what can be done and what needs to be done at the completion of the assessment.

Performance Assessment Administration Overview

WRAPPING UP THE ASSESSMENT – PAGE 4 OF 4

Classroom Scoring & Usage

Directions for Assessment Collection

Number of students enrolled:
Number of completed assessments attached:
Number of incomplete assessments attached:
Number of blank/unused assessments attached:

Additional Comments

Classroom Scoring & Usage – Clarify the options available to the classroom teacher regarding how he/she may use the assessments. The level of desired assessment security can impact options considerably. Examples for this box include:

- The scoring rubrics have been provided for your use if you wish to score the students' work before sending it to the district/school office.

- If you wish to score and review the assessments with your students, the scoring rubrics have been provided and you have one week until everything needs to be received by the assessment coordinator's office.

- Because the assessments are to remain secure, you may review and/or score them yourself, but do **NOT** review the assessments with your students.

Directions for Assessment Collection – Provide the directions the assessment administrator is to follow to be certain the assessments, the student work, the supplies, etcetera are all in proper order and in the proper place to facilitate the collection process. Examples include:

- Verify that you are returning the same number, _____, of assessment bundles that you received.

- Use rubber bands to bundle the assessments and the student work separately.

- Please alphabetize the students' assessments – complete and place the assessment cover sheet on the top of the bundle of student assessments.

- Return the assessments and the student work, bundled and arranged as noted in the directions, to the front office by 3:00 PM on the day of the assessment.

Additional Comments – Complete this box with any additional comments you have for the assessment administrator. An example is: Thank you for your time and energy in supporting this effort to gather solid data to support our decisions and plans to improve student learning.

Performance Assessment Administration Overview

OVERVIEWING THE ASSESSMENT – PAGE 1 OF 4

Area(s):	Grade Level(s):

Assessment Security

Standard(s)/Indicator(s) Targeted

By …

Estimated Assessment Time:
Estimated Total Administration Time:

Performance Assessment Administration Overview

PREPARING FOR THE ASSESSMENT – PAGE 2 OF 4

Early Directions for the Assessment Administrator

Supplies to be Obtained in Advance by the Assessment Administrator

Prerequisites Assumed Taught Prior to the Assessment

Appropriate Preparation of the Students for the Assessment

Inappropriate Preparation of the Students

Performance Assessment Administration Overview

Directions for Administering the Assessment

Materials to be Provided by the Students

Directions to be Given to the Students

Appropriate Coaching During the Assessment

Performance Assessment Administration Overview

WRAPPING UP THE ASSESSMENT – PAGE 4 OF 4

Classroom Scoring & Usage

Directions for Assessment Collection

Number of students enrolled:

Number of completed assessments attached:

Number of incomplete assessments attached:

Number of blank/unused assessments attached:

Additional Comments

Reflection Questions

1. What are the important points in this chapter?

2. How do I feel about what I've read?

3. What questions do I have?

4. How can I use what's here?

Chapter 3

AN OVERVIEW OF PERFORMANCE DESIGN

12 Common Starting Points for Designs

Creating designs for performance tasks, units, and assessments is a complex task in itself. This chapter will focus on 12 common design starting points and 10 major design facets. The entire discussion is based on the assumption that an effective plan for earning and maintaining stakeholder support has already been developed, and the assumption that a solid curriculum has been developed or a model is available for initial efforts.

The ten design facets are presented in an order that supports the concept of "designing back from the end." However, it is important to note that not all people who design outstanding performances start at the end (with a clearly stated standard to be demonstrated). There just does not seem to be one approach or order to designing performances that is the definitive, end-all, right approach. However, in our work with schools, we have noticed the following starting points to be the most common:

- Some successful designers start with important subject matter to be learned and ask, "How do people in outside of school roles use this?" (Our experience has shown that most people who are in or close to classroom situations utilize this approach.)

- Many people begin with an idea for a performance, project, or complex activity and then ask, "How can I work this idea into a sound performance?"

- And still others start with a content standard or intended outcome statement and then ask, "How can I design a meaningful, rich task that incorporates this and significant subject matter into a quality performance unit and/ or assessment?"

In fact, we have actually observed the following 12 common starting points.

1. Content Standards – the subject area standards being developed at the national, regional, state, and local levels. In several areas, discipline area associations are involved in the development of these standards – one example is The National Council of Teachers of Mathematics has developed "The Math Standards."

2. Graduation Learner Outcomes – statements identifying "broad goals" for students to achieve as a part of an educational program. Examples:

   - perceptive thinkers
   - effective communicators
   - critical thinkers
   - cooperative workers
   - knowledgeable problem solvers

3. Transferable Processes – those processes that are essential across most, if not all, life roles. Examples:

   - categorizing
   - decision making
   - comparing
   - analyzing
   - organizing
   - problem solving

4. Essential Content Skills and Information – important topics, concepts, or skills from required curriculum. An example from Language Arts is, "summarizing nonfiction articles from common magazines and newspapers."

5. Product and Performance Abilities – such as writing books, plays, and stories; planning and building cabinets and furniture; creating works of art; and developing conceptual frameworks.

6. Student Interests – such as bikes, pets, dating, animals, or movies. These are best determined by asking the students how they would like to demonstrate targeted knowledge, skills, or conceptual understandings. Student interests can also be used as a vehicle for teaching many aspects of research, presentation, or product development.

7. National, Regional, and District Standardized Assessments – such as SAT, ACT, Michigan Educational Assessment Program, and The New York Regents Exams.

8. Themes and Universal Concepts – Examples include preservation, variation, conflict, deterioration, change, and force.

9. Focusing Questions and Major Issues – complex open ended questions (or issues) to focus the students' learning

while providing a rich, motivating basis for lessons and projects. An example: "How can one determine when a lottery ticket is a fair investment?"

10. Parental Desires for Student Learning – such as solid academics, preparation for a good job, and college preparation.

11. Documentation of Achievement – such as documenting student progress or evaluating school or program efforts.

12. Exciting Ideas for Projects/Activities – such as ideas learned from other teachers, conferences, workshops, or journals. Typical examples:

   ■ Design and build a game to teach younger students important concepts or skills.

   ■ Determine the relative popularity of colors for cars over the last five years in your area. Compare your findings with car orders placed by your local car dealers. Present a formal report to your local dealers advising them of any discrepancies and request they explain discrepancies to you.

   ■ Determine an order from a local restaurant that would satisfy five friends' specified tastes and that can be purchased for between $24.00 and $25.00. Explain a process for developing and testing alternatives.

The issue is not so much where one starts in a design process. The issue is whether one creates a performance that is worthy of the time and energy required and that is an effective and efficient means of teaching, assessing, and/or documenting the knowledge, skills, and abilities targeted in contexts that are rich and engaging. No matter where one starts, what's important is to address all 10 of the performance design facets while continuously evaluating and tightening the design until it reaches quality levels. (In Chapter 9, we present 3 tools for assessing performance designs.)

According to Dr. Deming, an excellent approach for achieving quality is to continuously cycle through "Plan – Do – Study – Act." What this means in our context is …

   ■ access the best available information and resources;

- evaluate everything you can find and put "the good stuff" into the best possible plan for a performance-based unit with appropriate performance and non-performance assessments;

- evaluate and refine your plans with the aid of design evaluation tools (see Chapter 9), parents, colleagues, administrators, and experts in the field;

- implement your performance unit while engaging the students' help in continuously evaluating the design and all its components; and

- finally evaluate the results and the overall design in order to not just improve it, but to also provide some concrete insights into designing the next performance even better.

A Metaphor for Designing Performances

We like to equate the process for designing performances to that of tightening the "lug nuts" when putting a wheel on a car. What follows should help to clarify the connection.

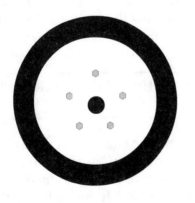

When a wheel is put on a car, we must remember that . . .

- there is not a particular lug nut that has to be put on first (though some are easier and more logical than others);

- there is no restriction as to which order the lug nuts should be started (though, again, there are some easier and more logical orders); and
- the lug nuts need to be tightened in small increments in a logical, jumping around, iterative order (based on which nut is "snugged up" first) until they're all well seated and the wheel sits snugly (aligned) on the car.

Similarly, when designing performances, keep in mind that there is …

- a set of quality standards by which the final design can be assessed;
- not an absolute right place to start;
- not a set order of steps that must be followed;
- a series of specific parts that must each be done well in conjunction with the others; and
- a necessity for an iterative approach of going around and around through the design actions until all the components have been brought into tight alignment.

In the next section, we describe the 10 facets of performance design. Each facet can be thought of as a "lug nut." We will describe them in a logical, design-back order, but feel free to start wherever it works for you, and be certain to continuously work your way around the design wheel until all the "lug nuts" are well seated.

A Quick Overview of the 10 Facets to Performance Design

Designing good performance tasks with their accompanying, multi-faceted assessments is an "iterative" process involving ten facets. Tight alignment to predetermined results necessitates going "over and over" the designs while at the same time, continuously making refinements that tighten the alignment to targeted learning(s). This "iterative" process is supported and driven by three focusing questions:

1. What is really important for the students to know and be able to do that is applicable in multiple contexts?

2. What evidence is necessary and sufficient to prove that this learning has occurred?

3. What is an authentic or at least simulated and rich way in which people outside of school use this learning?

10 Facets of
Performance Design

The performance facets that are overviewed in this chapter (and developed in depth with templates and other support tools in the following chapters) are represented as the two components of the hub and the eight major spokes of the above *Performance Wheel.* At the hub of the wheel are *Stakeholder Support* and *Curriculum Standards,* without which an effort to systematically use performance learning and assessment will struggle. In Chapter 10, numerous important tips for building and earning stakeholder support are presented. The development of curriculum standards is beyond the scope of this book.

In addition to the ten facets, without a strong commitment to on-going, effective staff-development and teacher support during change, any performance implementation initiative will have serious difficulties in the form of intense resistance, poor results, and consequently angry students, parents, administrators, and teachers.

What follows is a brief description of what needs to be addressed for each of the eight facets represented by the spokes of the wheel. Each of these facets will be developed to significantly greater depth in chapters four through eight.

Overview the Performance – In this facet, answers to the following two questions are determined and presented:

1. What is the general nature of what the students are to learn and do during the performance unit/task?

2. What does the unit/task look like and encompass as it unfolds?

These two questions can be answered through determining and presenting each of the following:

1. the title of the unit;

2. a brief description of the unit;

3. the open-ended, authenticating "essential question" that focuses the learning and the students' actions (hopefully enhancing motivation for doing the task);

4. the grade level;

5. the subject area(s);

6. the author of the unit;

7. the content and/or transferable standards and indicators taught and assessed within the unit;

8. the performance, product, or process assessment focus;

9. the criteria for the performance, product, or process assessment focus including the intended impact or result to be achieved;

10. the universal concept connections;

11. the essential subject area concepts and skills to be taught and assessed within the unit;

12. the student accountability plan (an overview of what and how grading will occur);

13. the performance context which includes location, audience, possible users or benefactors from the performance, the level of difficulty controlled by the context, and the evaluators;

14. the expected time frame for the unit;

15. special materials and resources needed; and

16. any additional comments.

The Performance Scenario – Develop a clear, aligned, and meaningful scenario or situation to serve as the performance task. This can be done in any of several ways …

- describe a role (such as an environmental engineer) and a corresponding point of view or perspective the students are to assume as they carry out a prescribed task;

- describe a task to be completed with any appropriate point of view or perspective to be assumed; or

- describe a situation or scenario in which the students are to function (or pretend they are functioning) and a problem or task that they are to resolve or complete as a result of the situation described.

As a part of the scenario description, a clear statement of how the students will know when they have been successful is made. For example, "You will know you have successfully finished when you have proposed a solution to the environmental dilemma that 60% of a random selection of community members find acceptable."

Also include in the scenario description statements that inform the students as to …

- the challenges and the resources they can expect;

- the resources they will need to obtain; and

- the expected timelines or due dates.

The Performance Structure – Successful, quality efforts as a part of complex tasks throughout both school and the rest of life tend to include five major, interconnecting and overlapping action categories. Take care to specify the primary ways (behaviors) the students are expected to perform each. The action (behavior) categories ...

- **access** information and skills needed to successfully complete the task;

- **interpret** or put meaning and order to what is known and discovered as a part of completing the task;

- **produce/create** whatever is prescribed or determined to be appropriate as a vehicle for successfully completing the task (examples: plans, presentations, voter guides, murals, museum displays, models, charts, or speeches);

- **disseminate, communicate, or use** whatever has been produced in order to achieve the intended effect, result, or impact (examples: awareness has been created, someone has been taught, a problem has been resolved); and

- **evaluate** the effectiveness throughout the performance. Within each of the above 4 action categories, design deliberate opportunities for student/peer/mentor/ teacher evaluation. With each of these planned evaluation opportunities, develop the expectation for refinement.

Clarification & Alignment of the Curriculum, Instruction, and Assessment – Identify the declarative and procedural learning objectives that are to be learned, effective instructional strategies for teaching them, and aligned assessment strategies for each.

The Rubrics and Scoring Guides – Develop the rubrics and other scoring guides to be used for ...

- developing understanding of expectations;

- facilitating student achievement of performance expectations; and

- final or interim scoring for official documentation of student efforts and achievements.

Chapter 7 addresses ways to develop effective rubrics and enhance student understanding and commitment with them.

The Learning Events – As with any complex project, carefully plan the specific activities that are to occur and their expected sequence. Examples of typical learning events include ...

- show a video tape to spark interest in the task and provide a basis for the importance of the task;
- lead a discussion around the "essential question" to further focus interest;
- utilize Dr. "So and So" as a guest speaker;
- use collaborative groups to isolate a problem to be resolved;
- brainstorm strategies for accessing needed background information;
- facilitate information acquisition; and
- test essential background information and concepts.

The Performance Management Logistics – "Best laid plans" can fail without adequate attention to detail. The keys to success in any complex endeavor lie in the details. Determine all the details that need to be addressed and develop plans for doing so. Examples include effective planning for ...

- guest speakers;
- parents who will observe final performances;
- other classes to serve as an audience or to peer assess; and
- needed materials and permissions.

Assessment of the Performance Design – Before implementing a performance unit, step back and assess its overall design, and then make any necessary modifications. Even after investing the energy to assess and evaluate the design, we know full well that as the performance is used with real students, it will need to be further evaluated and refined. (We strongly recommend the use of peers to assist in this review process.)

In the next several chapters, each of these eight design facets will be thoroughly addressed, one at a time, using templates, supportive documentation, and examples.

Performance Design Checklist

Whenever engaged in a complex task, checklists are always helpful to facilitate keeping track of the details. Therefore, what follows are two options for performance design checklists. The first is an abbreviated checklist, and the second is an extensive one.

When using the design checklists, it is helpful to have a means of identifying the applicability of each element of the list. Therefore, we have also include the following rating scale:

N.A – Not Applicable Check (√) if the particular item in the checklist is not necessary or applicable.

Yes — Check (√) if the particular item in the checklist has been fully completed.

I.P. — Check (√) (or leave the check boxes blank) to indicate, *"This is important, but it is still 'in progress.'"*

Abbreviated Performance Design Checklist

No.	Item	N.A.	Yes	I.P.
0.0	The Foundation			
1.0	The Performance Overview			
2.0	Major Targeted Learning & Assessment Focus			
3.0	Aligned Scenario/Task			
4.0	Specific Curriculum, Instruction, & Assessment Plans			
5.0	Rubrics & Evaluation Guides			
6.0	Learning Events, Checkpoints, & Logistics			
7.0	Performance Management Plans			
8.0	Evaluation of the Performance Design			
9.0	Effective Plans for Launching & Staying Afloat			

Performance Design Checklist

PAGE 1 OF 5

No.	Item	N.A.	Yes	I.P.
0.0	**The Foundation**			
0.1	Stakeholder support verified			
0.2	Curriculum standards used as base			
1.0	**The Performance Overview**			
1.1	Catchy, relevant title			
1.2	Connecting quote or illustration			
1.3	Authenticating & focusing essential question			
1.4	Grade level identified & matched			
1.5	Subject area(s) identified			
1.6	Author(s) identified			
2.0	**Major Targeted Learning & Assessment Focus**			
2.1	Curriculum standards & indicators identified and alignment checked			
2.2	Product, performance, or process focus established & alignment checked			
2.3	Product, performance, or process criteria established			
2.4	Impact/Purpose determined			
2.5	Product, performance, or process criteria established			
2.6	Universal concept connections established			
2.7	Essential subject area concepts & skills identified			

Performance Design Checklist

PAGE 2 OF 5

No.	Item	N.A.	Yes	I.P.
3.0	**Aligned Scenario/Task**			
3.1	Authentic, appropriate role determined			
3.2	"Authentic Like" task designed			
3.3	Student task responsibility clearly stated			
3.4	Performance purpose/impact stated in scenario			
3.5	Problem, issue, and/or perspective clarified			
3.6	Expected challenges identified			
3.7	Resources identified			
3.8	Completion date identified			

No.	Item	N.A.	Yes	I.P.
4.0	**Specific Curriculum, Instruction, & Assessment Plans**			
4.1	Declarative & procedural knowledge identified			
4.2	Aligned instructional strategies planned			
4.3	Aligned assessments planned			
4.4	Needed rubrics identified			

Performance Design Checklist

PAGE 3 OF 5

No.	Item	N.A.	Yes	I.P.
5.0	**Rubrics & Evaluation**			
5.1	Performance checklist included			
5.2	Analytic, holistic, primary trait, and checklists developed as needed			
5.3	Rubrics co-developed with students or effective conceptual understanding building strategies used			
5.4a	Exemplars used for models of the ideal			
5.4b	Anchors provided and used for all levels			
5.5	Quantitative & qualitative descriptors used appropriately			
5.6	The quality levels in the rubric are limited to those that are distinguishable and important for delineating quality			
5.7	The number of quality levels in the rubric matches the intended purpose			
5.8	Each defining characteristic or criteria is qualified for each quality level in the rubric			
5.9	Criteria are weighted appropriately for the task and its purpose			

Performance Design Checklist

PAGE 4 OF 5

No.	Item	N.A.	Yes	I.P.
6.0	**Learning Events, Checkpoints, & Logistics**			
6.1	Learning events planned and sequenced			
6.2	Performance checkpoints planned			
6.3	Necessary permissions obtained			
6.4	Resources planned for			
6.5	Evaluators planned for and invited			
6.6	Audience planned and arranged			
6.7	Outside experts and assistance is planned for and arranged, and appropriate people informed			
6.8	Project planning completed			
6.9	Parental involvement planned for and arranged			

No.	Item	N.A.	Yes	I.P.
7.0	**Performance Management Plans**			
7.1	Accountability plan developed			
7.2	Performance context determined			
7.3	Time frame established			
7.4	Required resources determined and planned for			

Performance Design Checklist

PAGE 5 OF 5

No.	Item	N.A.	Yes	I.P.
8.0	**Evaluation of the Performance Design**			
8.1	Design evaluated and refined for its curricular/academic value			
8.2	Design evaluated and refined for its assessment and scoring strengths			
8.3	Design evaluated and refined for its usability and feasibility			
8.4	Design evaluated for its perceived value by the stakeholder groups			

No.	Item	N.A.	Yes	I.P.
9.0	**Effective Plans for Launching Initiatives & Staying Afloat**			
9.1	Plan completed for successfully getting started			
9.2	Plan completed for earning student support and involvement			
9.3	Plan completed for earning parental support			
9.4	Plan completed for earning support of colleagues			
9.5	Plan completed for earning administrative support			

Chapter 4

DESIGNING PERFORMANCES
FACETS 1, 2, & 3

Introduction to the Process

Student performances, whether they are to last only an hour or up to an entire term, can all be designed using the same process. The differences will tend to be only surface differences. The process presented here for designing performances can be easily adapted for any of the following:

- performance-based units of instruction;
- performance-based assessments whether product, performance, or process focused;
- performances within a single discipline area;
- interdisciplinary performances; and
- problem-based performances.

In this chapter, we will focus on the first three facets of the performance design process. The first three steps are directed to the actual, overall design of the performance and the presentation of it to other educators.

Begin by Determining a Worthy Focus & Purpose

Throughout the design and implementation of a performance task, we need to continuously re-evaluate the implications of the question, "What is a really important ability or conceptual understanding that the students will continue to need throughout their lives?" For a performance-based task to be worth the amount of time and energy that it will take, it must effectively address the kind of significant learning that can manifest itself within a performance. Designing and implementing complex performance tasks that focus on isolated skills, information, and narrow concepts tends to expend too much time and energy for the return.

Performance tasks should address content information and skills that are best taught and assessed through application. However, they should also focus as much or more on transferable skills, abilities, and concepts in such a way that the students see the performance as achieving a purpose. Performance tasks can do this by being structured in such a way as to replicate the way people function throughout life – we tend to have a purpose for the things we do. Our purpose tends to be something we're trying to accomplish (rather than just do). To clarify, in school students tend to do things, outside of school, we tend to do things because they will accomplish some purpose. For example, in school, we write and/or present our research findings, outside of school we do research to find answers that we either personally desire or that we need to use to accomplish a further necessary task.

Therefore, performance tasks should be designed to have two major phases, 1) a preparation and production phase, and 2) an application or dissemination phase. The following is a list of common patterns that cause these two phases. We call them "performance frameworks" because they are the frames around which a performance is built. These frameworks are powerful, long-term, transferable focuses for performances in that they are applicable from elementary school through high school to life-role functioning. They are the powerful performance patterns in which successful people tend to continuously improve. They are the combination of preparation and application that people typically take in order to achieve a purpose.

Performance Designs Should be Based on Powerful Frameworks

Performance Frameworks are structures for performances that result in the students achieving an intended purpose. The following are 10 examples:

1. Clarify, research, and solve complex, meaningful problems.

2. Study the way experts do something in order to do it as well or better. (For example, study a number of very successful, persuasive speakers in order to determine what they do and how they do it. Use your findings to plan and present a persuasive presentation in order to achieve something you desire.)

3. Determine relationships, patterns, and interactions in order to beneficially apply your findings.

4. Create and use effective depictions and/or representations.

5. Research options in order to effectively make and execute decisions.

6. Function effectively in challenging, real-life scenarios that demand knowledge, skills, and abilities.

7. Independently or collaboratively learn required information, skills, and concepts in order to use them for beneficial purposes.

8. Assess your personal performance in order to develop and implement improvement plans.

9. Gather, interpret, and effectively present/teach needed and/or desired information, skills, and/or concepts.

10. Develop and effectively utilize a persuasive campaign in order to generate support for a position.

The above ten performance frameworks are the central framework within much of what people have to do consistently as a part of their lives. Performance tasks are the combination of the above, with meaningful and important content information, concepts, and skills done in relevant and demanding contexts.

An example of modifying one of the above frameworks into a performance is, "the students will develop and present an effective persuasive proposal in order to persuade others to some action or particular point of view."

Student Performances Should Have Purposes that Are of Long-Term, Transferable Importance

Each of the ten performance frameworks in the previous section serves as a basis for the development of student performances in which the students are expected to accomplish a pre-determined purpose (beyond the purpose of acquiring and demonstrating information, concepts and skills). Remember that one of the main reasons that we use performances is to teach and assess the ability to use content in order to achieve some purpose. It is this application purpose to which we are referring here. Example purposes that performances can be designed to achieve include ...

1. solve an important problem using a logical process;

2. teach people something important;

3. discern and use patterns or trends;

4. make others aware of an important situation or condition;

5. persuade people regarding an important matter;

6. create and use something to accomplish a predetermined purpose;

7. develop and conduct a service to accomplish a predetermined purpose;

8. draw and use and/or report conclusions;

9. read, interpret, and use nonfiction;

10. make and use generalizations for a predetermined purpose;

11. make and use/report summaries;

12. determine and use/report cause and effect for a predetermined purpose;

13. develop and us a plan of action for a predetermined purpose;

14. compare, contrast, analyze, organize, classify, prioritize, deduce, or categorize for a predetermined purpose;

15. develop a conceptual framework for a predetermined purpose;

16. learn, practice, and use content area skills for a predetermined purpose;

17. make and support recommendations; and

18. decide, predict, solve, resolve for a predetermined purpose.

This is not to say that students shouldn't be engaged in minor performances in which isolated content or process skill is the target. The foundation concepts and skills need to be learned and assessed somewhere. It is not uncommon to design performance tasks in which the focus is a single verb/action such as solve, decide, persuade, organize, prioritize, research, write, or sing. It is also not uncommon to design performance tasks in which the focus is a single, important content area skill. However, when we embed these important skills and concepts in performances in which the skills and concepts are then used to accomplish what the students, parents, teachers, and community see as a valuable purpose, we increase the authenticity, level of preparation for life-functioning, and student motivation.

The other essential component of the learning focus is the subject matter information and skills that are relevant to the situation being created and are essential components within the local, regional, and/or national curriculum.

Once the broad, transferable focus has been determined, an appropriate indicator of that "ability" needs to be identified. We address this by asking a question like, "What evidence is necessary to support the statement that the students have truly demonstrated that ability – at least in a particular context?"

Answering a question of this type requires the same approach that we may see in a court of law through the phrase "beyond a reasonable doubt." For example, if we are targeting "the students will demonstrate their ability to develop and present an effective persuasive proposal," we then ask ourselves questions like . . .

- What will truly show (prove) that they can do this?

- What evidence would be credible to show that they can do this?

- What are the different contexts in which this ability needs to be addressed?

- What are the appropriate levels of complexity and challenges that need to be successfully addressed?

From an instruction and assessment perspective, it is nearly impossible to teach and assess all that "develop and present a persuasive proposal" implies in a single performance task. But it is possible to isolate one of the several major performance "indicators" that most people would conclude have to be present for one to make the statement, "This student has demonstrated the ability to develop and present an effective persuasive proposal by doing (whatever he/she did)."

One of the most difficult tasks in designing quality performances is successfully identifying a worthy focus and then developing a task that will actually show it in a way that is supported as adequate evidence. It is because of this challenge that we cannot overemphasize the importance of "tightening the lug nuts" (the metaphor introduced in Chapter 3.) Whether one starts by identifying a targeted focus/standard or one starts with an activity or subject matter, without a commitment to an iterative refinement process, it is very common for the performance to be a flurry of activity without focus and accountability.

9 Questions to Help Focus Performances

There is a series of questions used for establishing and maintaining a worthy focus in performance designs. It's important to process the design efforts with focus questions like the ones listed below until we and our stakeholders can agree that the responses are solid and aligned.

1. What of long-term significance do the students need to know, be able to do, understand, or apply?

2. In what life-functioning performance abilities (performance frameworks mentioned earlier) is it essential for students to be strengthening their abilities?

3. How might they be imbedded in contexts that will increase their relevance and promote their development?

4. What evidence will it take to prove the students know, are able to do, understand, or apply them?

5. What can the students do that will provide the evidence?

6. How can what the students do be done so it achieves a student valued purpose for an audience?

7. How adequate is that evidence, and how might it have to be expanded to other means and other contexts?

8. What are the quality expectations (standards) necessary for us to conclude that the students do indeed possess the desired learning or ability?

9. What might be multiple levels of the quality expectations and how will they be documented?

The "Big Three" Focusing Questions

The above set of design focusing questions can be "boiled down" to what we refer to as the *"Big Three."*

1. What's most important for the students to learn?

2. What would truly prove they have learned it and that they can use it?

3. How can the students' performance be designed so that it accomplishes a purpose and has an audience?

Students' Interests Enhance Commitment

When student learning can be embedded in topics that are of interest to them, we encounter less resistance at worst and increased involvement, commitment and learning at best. It is worth the time to survey the students to determine those areas of interest that they have that are appropriate for and conducive to utilizing as a background for performances and instruction. What interests students changes over time and from region to region. The following are representative of interests many students have today.

Primary Students' Interests

- animals
- cartoons
- dinosaurs
- pets
- popular toys
- snakes

- ocean (sharks, whales, fish)
- other cultures
- snow
- the senses
- weather

Intermediate Students' Interests

- animals
- amusement & theme parks
- archeology
- books
- computers
- disasters/ catastrophes
- games
- movies
- space
- sports
- television
- video games

Middle Students' Interests

- amusement & theme parks
- clothes
- computers
- fashion
- friends
- games
- money
- movies
- music
- shopping
- sports
- video games

High School Students' Interests

- cars
- clothes
- college
- computers
- fashion
- friends
- jobs
- money
- music
- parties
- romance/ relationships
- shopping
- sports

Current Issues Enhance Student Commitment

Student interest can also be increased by designing performances to address current issues in the world. Some issues will interest the students more than others, and it's important to note that adults tend to become much more passionate about issues than young people. Current, real world issues can also be utilized to develop essential questions to be addressed by student performance tasks. An example essential question for focusing a performance is, "What are the impacts of homelessness on all of us in the community, and how might the situation be improved?" The following is a list of possible issues to address through performance designs.

- crime
- drug abuse
- environmental deterioration
- extinction of species
- health
- homelessness
- illiteracy
- injustices
- major disease threats
- national elections
- nutrition
- poverty
- racial, gender, and ethnic tensions
- violence

The Three Performance Focus Templates

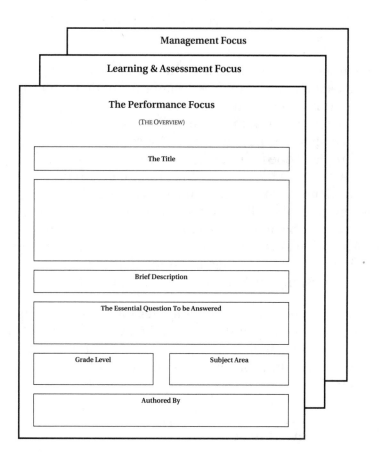

There are three templates for focusing the performance. Their use promotes alignment of the content standard, indicators, and performance actions while prompting the determination of essential contextual characteristics that have a significant impact on the performance. Briefly, these templates cause us to identify and clarify . . .

- how the performance is referenced;

- what the "content" and "cross content" learning targets are;

- what the essential question is that will focus and motivate the performance;

- what the students will be creating, and what they will be doing or trying to accomplish with it; and

- grade level, discipline areas, accountability plans, and other aspects of the implementation context.

CAUTION: Every performance does NOT require every box on every template to be filled.

The templates presented in this chapter are designed generically to facilitate performance design – from the simplest micro performance to the most complex authentic performance. Consequently, there are prompts in some of the templates that may not be relevant for some performances. For example, if one is designing a performance such as, "Write a note to a friend describing how to do your math homework problems," there probably is not an "effective question" that you will want to use to focus, authenticate, and motivate the performance. This does not mean the performance task is not a good one – in fact, we see immense value in it; it just means that an essential question for it would be pushing the issue and sound contrived.

An example set of completed templates for a language arts performance (Romeo and Juliet) can be found beginning on page 150. Refer to them at any point to help clarify specific template directions, concepts, or connections between templates.

The Overview Template

The first template is like the inside cover page in a book. Its primary purpose is to provide a quick insight into the performance.

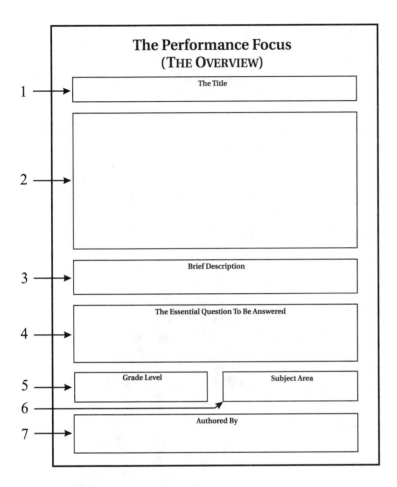

Box 1: Title of the Performance

Each performance-based unit or assessment should have a title that facilitates filing, recalling, and referencing. Titles tend to work best if they are . . .

- catchy and easy to remember;
- short;
- connected to the content, concept, or to the product, performance, or process that will be exhibited; and
- such that they facilitate filing and referencing.

  Example titles include …

  The Literary Looking Glass

  Endangered Species – Take 'em or Leave 'em

  In Search of Dinosaurs

  Courts in the Balance

Box 2: Picture, Drawing, or Quote

Like any book or booklet, people tend to relate to them better and grasp an overall picture faster if there is a picture, drawing, or memorable quote that helps to form connections to prior learning or experiences. The old adage, "a picture is worth a thousand words," best conveys the importance of this step. Example quotes include …

- "Ask not what your country can do for you, ask what you can do for your country." John F. Kennedy

- "History does not repeat itself. Historians repeat each other." Arthur Balfour

Clip art courtesy of Megatoons

- "Let no one ignorant of mathematics enter here." Plato

- "The louder he talked of his honor, the faster we counted our spoons." Ralph Waldo Emerson

Box 3: A Brief Description

At this point, we are still just providing a "quick snapshot" of what the performance is all about. Therefore, the description here should be very brief. An example is, "The students will create an informational video tape to inform members of the community of the pros and cons of having a proposed shopping center built in the neighborhood."

Box 4: The Essential Question to be Answered

This is the question that will focus the learning and activity throughout the performance – it is the question that will be answered by the students as they work through the performance. It should . . .

- focus the students' energies;

- help maintain focus and reduce "bird walks;"

- "authenticate" the performance by connecting the learning and activity to what people do in real roles outside of the role of student; and

- provide a framework for questions and discussions that continue to frame the performance, while at the same time building motivation and excitement for the effort.

An example essential question is, "How might judicial procedures be modified to better address the complexity of modern scientific evidence?"

Another example is, "What would we like to learn about dinosaurs that might be very important to us today and to our future?"

Box 5: Grade Level

Enter the grade level or levels for which the performance has been designed. If the performance can be utilized or adapted for other grades, parenthetically indicate this. Example: Grade 4 (easily adapted for grades 3 through 12 by changing the content).

Box 6: Subject Area

Indicate the subject area or areas for which the performance has been designed. If it is easily adapted to other areas, indicate the other areas parenthetically.

Box 7: The Author(s)

Proudly indicate the name of the person(s) who authored the performance, his/her/their school, address, and phone number. For example ...

- Dr. Karin Cordell, District of Columbia Public Schools; or

- Jim Ludington (Gananda High School), P.O. Box 403, Ontario, New York 14519

The Performance Focus

(THE OVERVIEW)

The Title

Brief Description

The Essential Question To be Answered

Grade Level	**Subject Area**

Authored By

The Learning & Assessment Focus Template

The purpose of this template is to identify the major focus for what the students are to learn and for what they are to be assessed.

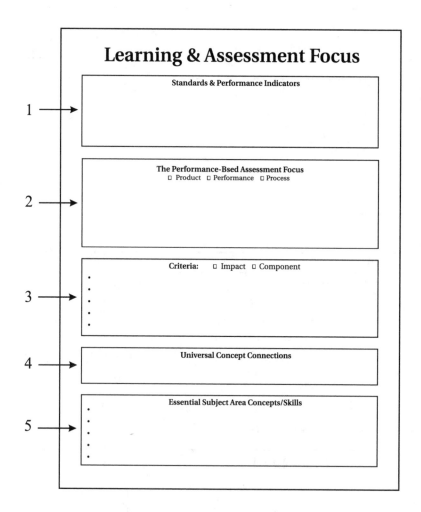

Box 1: Standards and Performance Indicators

In this box, indicate the targeted standards and indicators. These can be from your grade level or subject area team, your local school or district, or they can be state, provincial, or national. Regardless of the source, they should be statements of significant skills, abilities, or concept applications that have long-term, transferable value. They need to be specific enough that their alignment with the student actions is readily apparent to yourself and others. One key to assessing alignment is to verify that the verbs in the statements and the performance task match in meaning.

The following table should help to clarify what is meant by matching the verbs.

Verb in the Content Standard or Indicator	Verb in the Student Performance Need to Be an Associated Action
Analyze	Graph, Chart, Compare, or Contrast
Compare	Compare

The following negative examples are offered for further clarification:

- Teach does not match present.
- Explain does not match describe.
- Communicate does not match write.

Another key is to verify that the concepts and contexts match in focus and intended level of complexity. If the performance refers to a concept such as *change,* then the students need to be developing a conceptual understanding of *change* as a concept at the developmentally appropriate level.

One more key is to be certain the context for the performance is appropriate for the standard, indicator, and the developmental level of the students. A small change in context can make a major change in the performance expectations for the students. For example, consider the changes on the level of preparation, conceptual understanding, and performance abilities expected of a student when he/she is asked to explain a concept in the following different contexts:

Explain photosynthesis to …

- your best friend;
- the person sitting behind you;
- your parent or guardian;
- a classmate across the room that you don't know;
- a student two grades below you that you don't know;

- a student two grades above you that you don't know;
- a group of ten classmates while sitting in a circle;
- your class while standing before them;
- a group of ten to twenty parents or guardians of the students in your class; and
- a group of eminent biologists.

A performance ability can not be assumed to have been mastered just because it has been observed in a single context. That is one reason why *multiple validations* are so important. We need to be certain that the context for the teaching and assessing of a given performance ability be carefully established to accomplish the targeted learning. And then, the performance ability needs to be taught and assessed in multiple ways and multiple encompassing contexts before we can with some degree of certainty declare a student proficient.

It is also beneficial to check for alignment with one of the performance frameworks presented in the first section of this chapter and in Appendix D.

Any broad standards, goals, or outcomes (with appropriate indicators) that are being targeted by the performance should also be indicated in this box. Examples: effective communication, problem solving, complex thinking, collaborative achievers, and community contributors.

More specific examples may come from the areas of persuasion, problem solving, decision making, research, and evaluation. A specific example is, "*effectively convey a relevant message* to an audience of your peers through the of use video tape as a medium."

There are also more specific subject matter or content area standards that may be built into the performance unit. These subject matter/content standards will be learned by the students, utilized by them in carrying out the performance, and adequately assessed using the appropriate assessment methodologies. Examples include . . .

- applying decimal arithmetic in varied monetary situations;
- interpreting given pieces of World Literature;

- demonstrating through usage understanding of techniques used in advertising to persuade buyers; and

- designing and conducting a scientific investigation of a given hypothesis.

Box 2: The Performance-Based Assessment Focus

Indicate with a check mark whether the focus of the performance assessment will be the development of a product, the execution of a performance, or the execution of a process. Also, provide a brief but specific description of the performance-based assessment focus. Example brief descriptions include ...

- a motivational video;

- a persuasive presentation to the Board of Education;

- an informative book about spiders;

- a museum showing modern archeological techniques; and

- a note to a fictitious friend explaining one way the law of cosines is applied in surveying.

Box 3: Criteria

The purpose of this box is to identify the major criteria (quality characteristics) that must be met in the students' performance (indicated above in box 2). There should be 3 - 5 statements of criteria. Also, indicate by a check mark whether the focus of the criteria is primarily on the component parts or steps in the students' work or on the impact, effect, or result created because of the students' work. For example, if the students are producing an informational video tape, will the criteria emphasize primarily the component characteristics of the video (e.g., editing, staging, script, framing, sound, etcetera), or will the criteria emphasize primarily the effect of the video – how effective was the video at conveying information to uninformed (but motivated to learn) observers?

Box 4: Universal Concept Connections

If appropriate, identify the universal concepts that will be taught or to which the learning will be connected. Universal concepts are those concepts that are not limited to particular disciplines, subject areas, topics, or time periods. They are the concepts encountered throughout school, work, and numerous other contexts throughout our lives. Examples include ...

- change,
- variation,
- extinction,
- evolution,
- growth,
- conflict, and
- improvement,
- balance.

Each of these concepts exist in areas as diverse as literature and biology. They are as significant and relevant today as they were a thousand years ago. When universal concepts are utilized in a performance, it takes advantage of the power of building on prior learning while also enhancing the base of transferable learning. Refer to Appendix H for additional example universal concepts.

Box 5: Essential Subject Area Concepts and Skills

Good performances are designed so that the students will learn and be assessed on valuable subject area information, concepts, and skills. Identify what those are in this box. Be certain that they are worthy of being taught and assessed through a performance and that they will be taught with appropriate rigor. In this box, indicate the specific subject matter information, topics, skills, or concepts that are to be taught and assessed within the unit. Examples include ...

- major causes of the World War II,
- Shakespearean conventions,
- solving linear, algebraic equations,
- photosynthesis,
- sentence structure,
- propaganda techniques,
- referendums,
- multiplying fractions,
- spread sheet applications,
- determining area,
- food groups, and
- Pierre Renoir's contributions to painting.

Learning & Assessment Focus

Standards & Performance Indicators

The Performance-Based Assessment Focus

Product   Performance   Process

Criteria: Impact   Component

-
-
-
-

Universal Concept Connections

Essential Subject Area Concepts/Skills

-
-
-
-
-

The Management Focus Template

The purpose of this template is to facilitate the determination of the performance management concerns.

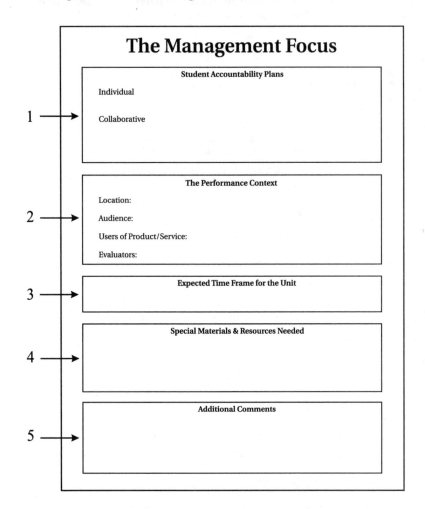

Box 1: Student Accountability Plans

In this box, indicate *for what* and *how* the students will be held accountable as a part of the performance unit. This should be presented from both an individual and a collaborative perspective. (We strongly recommend that serious consideration be given before developing any accountability plans in which a student's grade is impacted by the work of others.)

Box 2: The Performance Context

Location: Indicate the location or setting for the presentation and/or execution of the final performance. The more authentic or outside of school the location, the greater the effort and commitment to quality we tend to see from the students.

Audience: Indicate any individuals or groups that will be invited to witness, observe, and/or celebrate the final performance.

Experience shows that the quality of student's efforts (both in and out of school) tends to be enhanced when there is an actual audience for the final result, or when the product or performance provides a benefit to someone or some group. The more important the audience is to the students, the greater these benefits tend to be. Therefore, when possible and feasible, it is important to get the students' work out of the classroom and before an external audience. If this is not possible, an audience can usually be brought in. Example audiences include ...

- students that are either younger or older,
- parents,
- radio listeners,
- television watchers,
- community members,
- local television news and other personalities,
- local business people,
- administrators,
- board members,
- other teachers,
- judges,
- experts in the area of the performance or product, and
- students in other classes.

Refer to Appendix G for additional potential audiences.

Remember, as an audience is selected, it should be appropriate for the nature of the task and the level of the performance abilities to be assessed. The audience is a major part of the context dimension to a performance – changes in the audience can have a significant impact on the level of complexity and difficulty.

Inviting parents to be part of an audience whenever possible is an excellent way to involve parents, prove the quality of the student's learning, and to earn parental support.

Users of the Product/Service: Planning for a student generated product or service to be actually used to accomplish something or serve some pre-determined purpose enhances the authenticity of the performance and the value that will be placed on it by the students. This is a great opportunity to involve parents and other community members which will also increase credibility and support from them.

Evaluators: Indicate any individuals or groups that will be invited to serve as evaluators and/or outside experts. This also tends to increase credibility, student and parental value, and support from whichever stakeholders you enlist.

Box 3: Expected Time Frame for the Unit or Assessment

Total Unit: Indicate the estimated amount of time the unit/ assessment will take from its introduction to the students until it is totally finished.

Box 4: Special Materials & Resources Needed

Indicate the materials and resources that are necessary for the implementation of the performance. Examples of what might be needed include …

- special chemicals,
- a computer software package,
- yarn,
- masking tape, and
- meter sticks.

Box 5: Additional Comments

Each performance is unique. In this box, record any additional comments or information that you think may be of value to anyone who may utilize the performance.

An example comment is, "During this performance the students are to be engaged in learning by discovering the strengths and weaknesses for scatter, linear, and group testing patterns. They will push you to tell them which methods they should use at different times. Resist the desire to tell them, but support and encourage them as they experiment and discover the consequences of their choices."

Management Focus

Student Accountability Plans

Individual

Collaborative

Performance Context

Location:

Audience:

Users of
Product/Service:

Evaluators:

Expected Time Frame for the Unit

Special Materials & Resources Needed

Additional Comments

Three Performance Scenarios

The second step in designing performances is to craft the performance scenario. (Recall that this is actually where many classroom teachers start – they start with a really neat project and design both ways to build solid alignment.) This brief narrative describes the situation in which the educational purpose of the performance can be observed. The templates presented here are designed to prompt a narrative that represents the way the task (with expansion) can be presented to the students. However, performance tasks tend to produce better results if, after the teacher designs or selects them, they are then re-developed or expanded through a well led dialogue with the students.

Each of the templates provides prompts to be completed by the designer. The focus of the prompts will vary somewhat from template to template, but the following portrays the general nature of what the prompts are designed to bring out:

- the situation or role in which the students are to function;

- the background, perspectives, or points of view from which the students are to operate;

- an open-ended, authenticating, essential question for which an answer is to be found;

- whatever it is that the students are to create, produce, perform, or work through;

- the impact or effect that is to come as a result of the students' efforts;

- challenges and resources that can be expected; and

- an expected completion date.

There are a number of approaches to creating performance scenarios. The following pages describe three varied approaches and the completion of their corresponding templates.

1. **Role Performance Scenarios** in which the students function in a role such as environmental engineer, poet, concerned citizen, oceanographer, flight scheduler, or composer. The role performance approach works best when the task causes the students to use information,

concepts, skills, or abilities in a way that is at least very similar to the way people in "real situations" do. Role performances are excellent vehicles for designing "authentic" tasks. Though role performances can be done in single disciplines, they are excellent for interdisciplinary performances.

2. **Task Performance Scenarios** in which the performance is designed in a more traditional approach – just telling the students the task they are to do. This approach is most appropriate when the task is smaller and/or more narrowly focused. It lends itself nicely to performances that tend not to be interdisciplinary such as when we tell the students to produce an oral or written presentation describing how a subject matter skill may be performed or applied.

An example of a task that might be used with this approach is, "You are expected to prepare and give an oral presentation describing how two current political candidates are using specific persuasion/propaganda techniques."

Another example: "Research a current issue on the Internet in order to determine the 'quality' of the information available with respect to biases, inaccuracies, propaganda techniques, and effectiveness. You are then expect to make well supported, curriculum recommendations regarding the Internet to the School Improvement Team."

3. **Problem-Based Performance Scenarios** in which the performance is presented through the statement of a situation or problem that needs to be resolved. This approach, like the role performance approach, lends itself nicely to bigger and more complex performances, but it is also an easy approach to use when designing smaller performances to teach and assess a single skill or ability.

This approach lends itself to teaching and assessing problem-solving as a process. Problem solving as a process can be as simple as "brainstorming and selecting" when you are faced with deciding which of several equally desirable choices you will pick. It can also be as complex as was represented in the movie *Apollo 13* when the engineers had to develop a system to make the oxygen system function when the constraints and consequences made the task seem almost impossible.

What differentiates complex problem solving from the less complex problem solving is the effect of constraints and consequences. As the constraints (what you have or don't have to work with) become limited and/or conflicting, the problem becomes more complex. In addition, as the consequences of the various alternatives become more extreme and/or conflicting, the problem also becomes more complex. Example constraints that may be a part of a problem include …

- opposing view points to be addressed;

- opposing values on the part of the people involved in the problem;

- insufficient resources;

- insufficient time;

- insufficient funds; and

- unyielding opposing positions.

Complex problems cannot be resolved by a purely algorithmic procedure. They require the use of processes that require a thorough analysis of the situation including the identification of constraints and consequences. The consequences need to be weighted in terms of their relative impact. Possible solutions need to be formulated and evaluated based on the consequences until a solution is identified that fits within predetermined limits with respect to the consequences. (Refer to the problem solving process rubric in the sample rubrics. Also, for an in-depth coverage of problem-based learning, contact the Center for Problem-Based Learning at the Illinois Math and Science Academy in Aurora, Illinois.)

The following is an example of a problem-based task:

> As seniors, you have noticed that the elementary school students in your area do not have sidewalks to use as they walk to and from school. These students are forced to walk in the street when the ground becomes very muddy or buried under too much snow. The street they walk in is the main street that the high school students must drive on to get to and from school at the time the elementary students are also using the street.

The problem that has kept a sidewalk from being built for seventeen years is that the sidewalk would cross between two townships with laws on the books that require different materials for sidewalks. The sidewalk would also be primarily in a planned community with covenants opposing sidewalks because they are not "natural."

Your task is to find a solution that makes it safe for the elementary students to get to school. As far as resources are concerned, the school can provide you with time by providing you with a free period. However, there are no funds. The solution needs to be in place before graduation.

Design Performances to Utilize Authentic Contexts

Regardless of the approach, all three scenario types depend on the establishment of a context. Example contexts in which performances can be designed include the following:

- Meteorology
- Music
- Drama
- Astronomy
- Oceanography
- Social Service
- Art
- Government
- Navigation
- Transportation
- Economics

Refer to Appendix E for more suggestions for performance contexts.

For each of these three approaches, we have included three slight variations for a total of nine templates. We are including guides for completing just one of the templates for each of the three main approaches. The variations for each approach are similar enough that additional guides are not necessary.

Scenario Templates

There are 3 sets of 3 templates each; one set for each scenario type described in the previous section. What follows is a set of templates and guidelines for the completion of each of the 3 scenario types.

Start by choosing either a role performance, task performance or problem-based performance scenario. Your selection will be governed by your style and the focus of the performance. Then choose one of the three templates to use for the type of scenario you selected. Note: For each of the three sets, the variations in prompts are so minor that the directions for completion are given for only one template per set.

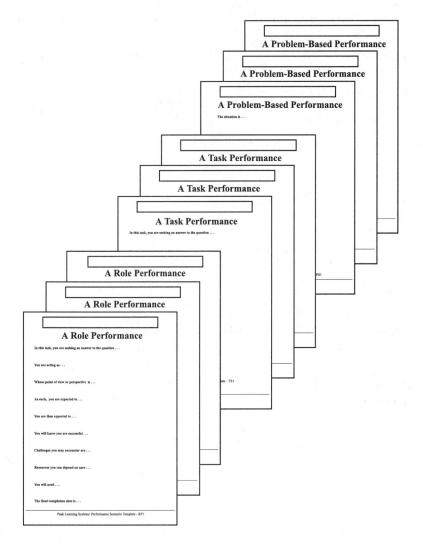

A Guide for Completing the "Role Performance" Scenario Templates

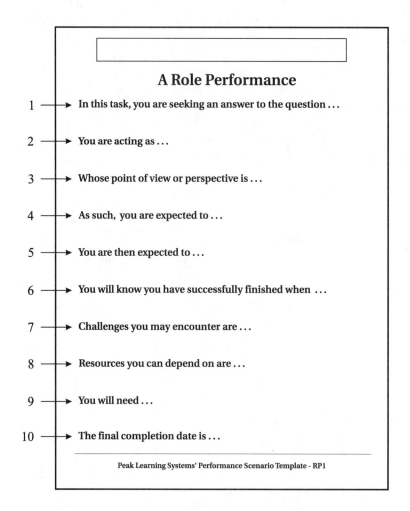

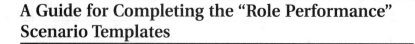

A Role Performance

1 ➝ In this task, you are seeking an answer to the question ...

2 ➝ You are acting as ...

3 ➝ Whose point of view or perspective is ...

4 ➝ As such, you are expected to ...

5 ➝ You are then expected to ...

6 ➝ You will know you have successfully finished when ...

7 ➝ Challenges you may encounter are ...

8 ➝ Resources you can depend on are ...

9 ➝ You will need ...

10 ➝ The final completion date is ...

Peak Learning Systems' Performance Scenario Template - RP1

Prompt 1: In this task, you are seeking an answer to the question ...

Complete this prompt with an *essential question.* An essential question is a question that ...

- is open-ended;
- focuses the performance;
- authenticates the performance by connecting it to "outside of school;"
- provides a basis for discussion to generate interest; and
- is hopefully interesting to the students.

Three example *essential questions* . . .

1. What are the positive and negative economic and ecological consequences of not protecting the Spotted Owl?

2. How do we benefit from animals raised on farms in our area?

3. How can packagers determine the most economical packages?

Finding an answer to the essential question should drive much of what happens during the performance. Since it is nearly impossible to generate just one question that focuses, opens, motivates, and authenticates, this question is not to be the only question – it is to provide the base for the generation of many questions that are parallel and of interest (hopefully) to the students.

(NOTE: Not all variations on this template include the essential question prompt. Essential questions for performances that are narrow in scope can become very contrived and counter productive. If the performance is purely content oriented, the question will tend to focus only on the subject matter, and thus fail to meet the criteria. For example, "How can we use linear equations?" will not provide the benefits intended with an essential question.)

Prompt 2: You are to act as a(n) ...

Complete this prompt with a role that is appropriate and that matches the role of someone who would actually be doing the task in a "real-world" setting. The goal is to develop the task around a role that is as authentic and high level in thinking demands as possible. The following are just a few examples – refer to Appendix F for over 250 usable roles sorted by general classifications:

- aeronautical engineer,
- dietitian,
- museum docent,
- concerned citizen,
- lobbyist,
- contractor,
- political speech writer, and
- colonial period farmer.

Prompt 3: Whose point of view or perspective is ...

Complete this prompt with the point of view or perspective (possibly background) that the students are to assume when performing the task. Six examples:

- ... that you are concerned about endangered species and the possible impact from either protecting them or losing them to extinction.
- ... that you are sincerely interested in helping younger students gain an awareness of and an appreciation for classical literature's relevance to today's adolescents.
- ... that you are troubled by voters being overly influenced by "sound bites" and misleading data.
- ... that you are distressed by the graffiti appearing in your neighborhood.
- ... that you belief the constitution of The United States should not be amended to address what should be done through normal legislation.
- ... that you are opposed to the plan to build a shopping center where neighborhood children have played almost forever.

Prompt 4: As such, you are expected to ...

Complete this prompt with whatever the students are to do that will result in the culminating product, conceptual framework, problem solution, or performance. Several examples:

- ... design, produce, and refine an educational game that is effective in teaching ...
- ... prepare a persuasive presentation to be delivered at a board of education meeting to try to convince them to support ...
- ... build a museum display that is effective at teaching visitors about the ...
- ... create a visual portfolio to show eighth grade students where the math they will be learning in high school is used around their community ...
- ... create a plan for what will be ordered for food and drinks at a pizza party for ...
- ... write a note to an imaginary friend describing how to do what we learned in math today ...

Prompt 5: You are then expected to . . .

Complete this prompt by indicating to the students what they are then expected to do with what they have created or produced (identified with prompt 4). This prompt is particularly important in performances that are designed with "impact" criteria–criteria that stipulate that whatever the students are to produce, do, or create, they are to use it in some way to produce a desired result or effect. More specifically, identify how the students will disseminate, communicate, or utilize what they have created. For example, ". . . use the educational game you have created to teach a group of sixth and seventh graders. Check for the level of their learning, and based on their learning, refine your game as necessary until it is effective as a teaching tool."

Prompt 6: You will know you have successfully finished when ...

Complete this prompt by indicating to the students what needs to occur for them to be done. This can vary from them completing a task that will be scored, to them having to work until an impact has occurred such as museum visitors learn successfully from the displays and presentations. Examples are ...

- your speech meets the criteria we established together in class and are posted on the bulletin board (anchoring video tape is available in the media center).

- four out of five board members indicate that they were convinced because of your speech.

- 80% of the students that play your educational game answer at least 75% of the questions about the topic correctly.

- all the kids that come to the pizza party report that they were satisfied with the food and drink selections.

- after your presentation, the parents can answer at least half the quiz questions about how local farm animals are used.

Prompt 7: Challenges you may encounter are . . .

Complete this prompt by indicating any challenges that you intend the students to address. Examples include ...

- a limited budget,
- apathy on the part of students who will play the game,
- the students who will play the game have a wide range of reading levels, or

- the Board of Education is committed to not spending money on anything that may be seen as frivolous by community members.

Prompt 8: Resources you can depend on are ...

Complete this prompt with all the materials and other items that you intend to make available. Examples include ...

- pencils,

- masking tape,

- blank video tape,

- construction paper, and

- word processing software.

Prompt 9: You will need ...

Complete this prompt with the materials and other resources the students will need to obtain that you wish them to know about at the beginning. Examples include ...

- old newspapers,

- pencils and paper,

- scotch tape, and

- editorial cartoons from a newspaper.

(In complex tasks, it is sometimes important to either not overwhelm the students by including too much detail up-front, or to not circumvent the process they are to be demonstrating by providing information they are to discover as a part of the process.)

Prompt 10: The final completion date is ...

Complete this prompt with the date that the students are to have completed the task. Interim checkpoints and other important timelines will also have to be developed and shared with the students.

Self-Assessing the Role Performance Scenario

The following checklist can be used to self-assess the completed Role Performance Scenario Templates.

Self-Assessing
A Role Performance Scenario

CHECKLIST

Reflections	✔	Needed Modifications
1. The role in which the students are to function is an authentic, thinking role narrow enough in scope for the given task.		
2. The perspective or point-of-view represented is clear and appropriate for the task, students, parents, and community.		
3. What the students are to create or produce addresses the essential question, requires complex thinking skills, and has a purpose the students, parents, and other stakeholders consider worthwhile.		
4. What the students are to create or produce will be disseminated, communicated, or used to achieve the pre-intended impact, effect, or result in measurable ways.		
5. The intended impact, effect, or result is effectively articulated and will be expected and checked for.		
6. The challenges and available resources are such that the performance task is reasonable.		
7. The completion date is reasonable and flexible.		

A Role Performance

In this task, you are seeking an answer to the question . . .

You are to act as a(n) . . .

Whose point or view or perspective is . . .

As such, you are expected to . . .

You are then expected to . . .

You will know you have successfully finished when . . .

Challenges you may encounter are . . .

Resources you can depend on are . . .

You will need . . .

The final completion date is . . .

A Role Performance

You are to act as a(n) . . .

Whose point or view or perspective is . . .

In this task, you are seeking an answer to the question . . .

As such, you are expected to . . .

You are then expected to . . .

You will know you have successfully finished when . . .

Challenges you may encounter are . . .

Resources you can depend on are . . .

You will need . . .

The final completion date is . . .


```
┌─────────────────────────────────────────────────────────────┐
│                                                               │
│                                                               │
└─────────────────────────────────────────────────────────────┘
```

A Role Performance

You are to act as a(n) . . .

Whose point or view or perspective is . . .

As such, you are expected to . . .

You are then expected to . . .

You will know you have successfully finished when . . .

Challenges you may encounter are . . .

Resources you can depend on are . . .

You will need . . .

The final completion date is . . .

A Guide for Completing the "Task Performance" Scenario Templates

These templates are very similar to the "Role Performance" templates. In fact, the prompts on the templates are actually the same. The only difference is that there is *not* a prompt for a role. Therefore, please refer to the guide for completing the "Role Performance" scenario.

A Task Performance

In this task, you are seeking an answer to the question . . .

The point of view or perspective you are to assume is . . .

As such, you are expected to . . .

You are then expected to . . .

You will know you have successfully finished when . . .

Challenges you may encounter are . . .

Resources you can depend on are . . .

You will need . . .

The final completion date is . . .

Peak Learning Systems' Performance Scenario Template - TS1

A Task Performance

In this task, you are seeking an answer to the question . . .

You are to represent the point of view or perspective that . . .

As such, you are expected to . . .

You are then expected to . . .

You will know you have successfully finished when . . .

Challenges you may encounter are . . .

Resources you can depend on are . . .

You will need . . .

The final completion date is . . .

A Task Performance

You are expected to . . .

You are then expected to . . .

You will know you have successfully finished when . . .

Challenges you may encounter are . . .

Resources you can depend on are . . .

You will need . . .

The final completion date is . . .

A Task Performance

In this task, you are seeking an answer to the question . . .

As such, you are expected to . . .

You are then expected to . . .

You will know you have successfully finished when . . .

Challenges you may encounter are . . .

Resources you can depend on are . . .

You will need . . .

The final completion date is . . .

A Guide for Completing the "Problem-Based Performance" Scenario Templates

These templates are very similar to the "Role Performance" templates and the "Task Performance" templates. There is, however, a major difference in that the scenario to be developed with a Problem-Based Performance template is built around a posed problem or situation that needs resolving. The prompt numbers indicated below are for this template only and do not correspond to those on the "Role Performance" template.

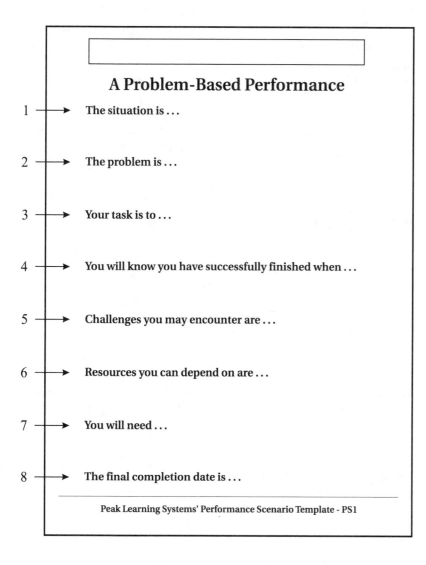

A Problem-Based Performance

1 ➔ **The situation is . . .**

2 ➔ **The problem is . . .**

3 ➔ **Your task is to . . .**

4 ➔ **You will know you have successfully finished when . . .**

5 ➔ **Challenges you may encounter are . . .**

6 ➔ **Resources you can depend on are . . .**

7 ➔ **You will need . . .**

8 ➔ **The final completion date is . . .**

Peak Learning Systems' Performance Scenario Template - PS1

Prompt 1: The situation is …

Provide a brief, clear description of a situation that has a complex problem embedded in it. Here we establish the background context that is necessary for putting the problem into perspective while providing a base for many possible constraints controlling solutions to the problem. For example, in a performance dealing with resolving conflicts like the Spotted Owl issue, this is where we would explain the background and the current situation as it exists in the area.

Prompt 2: The problem is …

Complete this prompt with a concise statement of the problem to be solved. In order to assess problem solving, the problem needs to be ill-structured. The problem should not have a single approach or response – in fact, the route taken and the determined solution should be almost unpredictable.

For example, "A developer and a large faction of the community wish to have a large shopping center built in an area that has been available for children to use to play ball. An equally large faction of the community is opposed to the idea. The city council is forced to determine what should be done."

Prompt 3: Your task is …

Indicate precisely what it is that you wish the students to do to complete the task description. For example, "Prepare and present a recommendation to the city council."

Prompt 4: You will know you have successfully finished when …

Complete this prompt by indicating to the students what needs to occur for them to be done. This can vary from them completing a task that will be scored, to them having to work until an impact has occurred such as museum visitors learn successfully from the displays and presentations.

An example: "… at least four out of five council members indicate that they were convinced because of your presentation."

Prompt 5: Challenges you may encounter are ...

Complete this prompt by indicating any challenges that you intend the students to address. Examples include ...

- a limited budget, and
- apathy on the part of many community members.

Prompt 6: Resources you can depend on are ...

Complete this prompt with all the materials and other items that you intend to make available. Examples include ...

- audio visual equipment and supplies, and
- a budget of fifty dollars.

Prompt 7: You will need ...

Complete this prompt with materials and other resources the students will need to obtain and that you wish them to know about at the beginning. Examples include ...

- legal advice, and
- office supplies.

(In complex tasks, it is sometimes important to either not overwhelm the students by including too much detail up-front, or to not circumvent the process they are to be demon-strating by providing information they are to discover as a part of the process.)

Prompt 8: The final completion date is ...

Complete this prompt with the date that the students are to have completed the task. Interim checkpoints and other important timelines will also have to be developed and shared with the students.

A Problem-Based Performance

The situation is . . .

The problem is . . .

Your task is . . .

You will know you have successfully finished when . . .

Challenges you may encounter are . . .

Resources you can depend on are . . .

You will need . . .

The final completion date is . . .

```
┌──────────────────────────────────────────────────────────────────────┐
│                                                                        │
└──────────────────────────────────────────────────────────────────────┘
```

A Problem-Based Performance

The situation is . . .

As such, you are expected to . . .

You will know you have been successful when . . .

Challenges you may encounter are . . .

Resources you can depend on are . . .

You will need . . .

The final completion date is . . .

```
┌─────────────────────────────────────────────────────────────┐
│                                                               │
└─────────────────────────────────────────────────────────────┘
```

A Problem-Based Performance

The problem is . . .

As such, you are expected to . . .

You will know you have successfully finished when . . .

Challenges you may encounter are . . .

Resources you can depend on are . . .

You will need . . .

The final completion date is . . .

The Performance Action Plan—The Performance Structure

The third step in designing performances is to determine the specific, observable, overlapping phases that the students are to complete as a part of working through the performance.

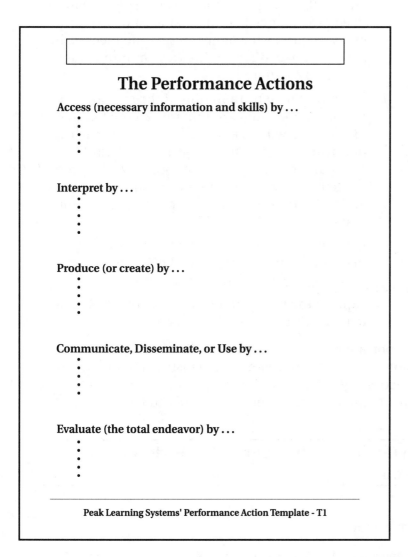

The Performance Actions

Access (necessary information and skills) by . . .
-
-
-

Interpret by . . .
-
-
-

Produce (or create) by . . .
-
-
-

Communicate, Disseminate, or Use by . . .
-
-
-

Evaluate (the total endeavor) by . . .
-
-
-

Peak Learning Systems' Performance Action Template - T1

This template facilitates the determination of the specific *performance actions* within each phase of the performance. The purpose of the template is to . . .

- facilitate alignment with the task's intended long-term, transferable learning focus through an analysis of the performance actions that will be expected;

- ensure that the performance at least simulates the five performance actions that exist in virtually every major performance in real-life (access, interpret, produce, disseminate (or communicate or use), and evaluate);

- facilitate the determination of the specific performance actions that are inherent in the task, will be taught, and will be assessed as a part of the overall performance (the specific ways in which the students are to access information, mentally process it to create meaning, create or produce something, and use it to achieve the purpose of the performance);

- help ensure a tight alignment between the performance and its targeted broad goals, long-term learning focus, and standards; and

- capture the performance task actions in a logical teaching progression for the performance.

Important Note: Each action identified will require a decision as to the appropriate level of instruction that will be needed to support it and the appropriate method of assessment based on the targeted standards and indicators.

A Guide for Completing "The Performance Actions" Template

Overview

For each performance action phase, identify the specific essential actions that **will be needed, expected, taught, and**

assessed. In Appendix B, there is an extensive list of action verbs that are sorted into the five performance action categories. This list is very helpful in clarifying language and maintaining focus on the major educational purpose(s) for the performance. The performance actions that are identified for each phase should meet the following criteria:

- they are essential for a high quality effort and result;

- they are limited to those that will be actually taught and assessed;

- they are determined to be crucial whether or not they will be evaluated/scored;

- they contain a verb that precisely, according to dictionaries and experts, directs the intended actions for the desired results. For example, present, explain, describe, and teach all have very different meanings in a similar context. Great care should be taken to identify the actual action that will be taught and assessed; and

- they ensure that the broad educational goal, the specific long-term learning focus, and the targeted standards and indicators are being targeted in specific ways.

Self-Reflection and Self-Assessment as Crucial Components within each Performance Action

Just as any successful person reflects over, assesses, and evaluates his/her efforts almost continuously, so should students as they work through and complete a performance task or assessment. As a part of each performance action phase, the students need to evaluate what they've done, learned, and achieved. To facilitate this in planning, the template includes a prompt for evaluation in each phase.

Refer to Appendix I for numerous reflection, assessment, and evaluation prompts.

Completing the Template

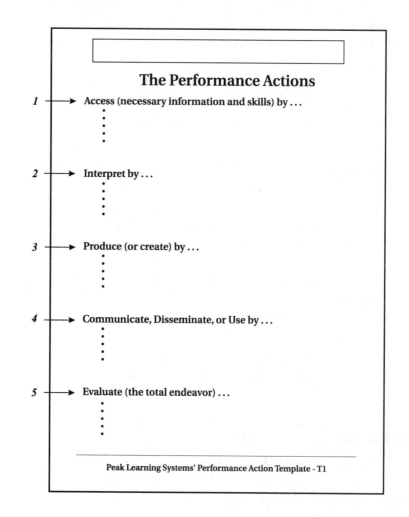

Peak Learning Systems' Performance Action Template - T1

Prompt 1: Access (necessary information and skills) by ...

Indicate the specific *accessing* actions that the students are to do in order to access whatever information, skills, and concepts they will need to perform the task. Each action should be stated in the form of a verb followed by a phrase. Verbs that are typically used include read, listen, research, survey, investigate, dialogue (with others to obtain a perspective), question, brainstorm, interview, and observe. (See Appendix B for an extensive list of appropriate verbs.) The following are examples of *access actions*:

- interviewing personnel representing the various roles in "Such 'n Such" company to obtain their perspectives regarding the ...

- brainstorming with your team to generate ideas regarding ...

- reading _____ in order to determine his/her perspectives.

- listening to the teacher's lecture on the reasons for ...

- surveying your neighbors to determine their preferences regarding ...

Prompt 2: Interpret by ...

Indicate the specific actions that the students are to perform in order to evaluate and put into usable form the information, skills, and concepts they access to complete the task. Again, each action should be stated in the form of a verb followed by a phrase. Verbs commonly used include prioritize, organize, evaluate, determine, analyze, compare, contrast, decide, solve, and integrate. (See Appendix B for an extensive list of appropriate verbs.) The following are examples of *interpret actions*:

- comparing and contrasting your findings in order to select those that are in common across all sources.

- determining the nature and extent of documentation that is necessary to persuade the city counsel to support your position.

- organizing the samples you collect in no more than five categories that are supported by three experts in the field.

- determining those uses for local farm animals that are most important to both the economic well-being of the farm and of the community.

- evaluating the accuracy and usability of all information, concepts, and skills accessed for use in this performance.

Produce (or create) by ...

Indicate the specific actions that the students are to perform in order to produce (or create) a model, product, conceptual framework, performance, plan, or solution *that will achieve the desired impact, effect, or result.* The following are examples of what the students can create or produce:

- advertisements
- graphs
- tables
- charts
- journal articles
- educational games
- museum displays
- nutritional plans
- documentaries
- books
- editorials
- software with documentation

Refer to Appendix A for numerous ways that information, concepts, and skills can be disseminated or used.

Each action should be stated in the form of a verb followed by a phrase. Verbs typically used include make, build, depict, develop, construct, fabricate, create, and produce. (See Appendix B for an extensive list of appropriate verbs.) The following are examples of *produce actions*:

- developing a plan of action for persuading …
- building a model that will clarify the concept for the people with whom you will be working.
- designing an addition to the hospital that will meet the needs of the board and fit within the constraints they establish.
- making a museum display that your parents study to learn which farm animals in our area are most valuable and why.
- preparing a persuasive presentation including written, oral, and visual components that …
- composing a song that best conveys what you and your classmates value from your years together at "Any Town" High School.

- designing and making an outfit that would be appropriate for a holiday, family get-together and that you and your parent(s)/guardian(s) like.

- writing a note that effectively describes at least one application of what you've learned in this last unit.

Prompt 3: Communicate, Disseminate or Use by ...

Indicate the specific actions that the students are to perform in order to achieve the intended impact, effect, or result for the performance. This is the action phase in which the students are expected to actually give information, concepts, and skills to others or to use them to accomplish something. Each action should be stated in the form of a verb followed by a phrase. Verbs typically used include explain, teach, describe, present, convince, display, distribute, make (aware), move, portray, convey, and perform. (See Appendix B for an extensive list of appropriate verbs.) The following are examples of *communicate, disseminate, or use actions*:

- teaching your parents the five most important uses for farm animals (using your museum display).

- presenting your proposal to the Board of Education.

- distributing your voters guide to all the registered voters in your precinct.

- presenting your artwork depicting local issues at an art fair in the mall.

- using your game to teach the benefits of protecting endangered species to a group of sixth graders.

Prompt 4: Evaluate (the total endeavor) by ...

Indicate the specific actions the students are to perform in order to evaluate the effectiveness of their total effort and to develop a realistic but appropriate improvement plan. Be certain to include actions that will have the students evaluating the overall endeavor and developing do-able and observable improvement plans for one or more of the major performance task actions. These plans are to be implemented in the next performance.

Performance task actions in this phase will utilize verbs such as evaluate, assess, judge, critique, appraise, improve, grow, amend, and refine. Each action should be stated in the form of a verb followed by a phrase. (See Appendix B for an extensive list of appropriate verbs.) The following are example *evaluate actions:*

- assessing the effectiveness of your cooperative learning procedures in order to identify at least one specific way to do even better next time.

- assessing the quality of your presentation by surveying your audience as to what they learned and how they felt about it. Identify one thing you will do to make your next presentation more effective.

- evaluating the effectiveness of your consensus building processes in order to identify steps for improvement.

┌───┐
│   │
└───┘

The Performance Actions

Access (necessary information and skills) by . . .

-
-
-
-

Interpret by . . .

-
-
-
-

Produce (or create) by . . .

-
-
-

Communicate, Disseminate, or Use by . . .

-
-
-
-

Evaluate (the total endeavor) by . . .

-
-
-
-
-

Example Performance Based Unit – Expanded Version

THE PERFORMANCE FOCUS (THE OVERVIEW)

PAGE 1 OF 7

Romeo & Juliet – The Looking Glass

Clip art courtesy of CorelDraw 7.0

In this performance, the students are to write an original script conveying a universal concept and message from *Romeo and Juliet*, and to video tape the production of their script.

The Essential Question To be Answered

What universal concepts and issues dealt with in classical literature continue to be relevant today, and how might these be used to enhance our lives now?

Grade Level

High School (9th Grade)

Subject Area

Language Arts

Authored By

Shari Graham of Peak Learning Systems

Example Performance Based Unit – Expanded Version

THE LEARNING & ASSESSMENT FOCUS

PAGE 2 OF 7

Standards & Performance Indicators

The students will use themes and topics from texts to make connections, see patterns, and demonstrate a deep and rich understanding of enduring issues and recurring problems studied over time.

By ...

creating and performing a script that effectively conveys a universal message from a classical literature selection to an audience.

The Performance-Based Assessment Focus

☑ Product   ☐ Performance   ☐ Process

The Product, Performance, or Process Focus:

A video tape of a performance of an original script

Criteria: ☑ Impact   ☑ Component

- content, language, and visuals are appropriate for audience
- script, production and acting performed to class developed levels
- message presented to adequate depth for message and audience
- major points effectively supported with clear and relevant examples
- organization is effective for message and audience

Universal Concept Connections

Conflict

Essential Subject Area Concepts/Skills

- Shakespearean conventions
- Interpretation of Shakespearean passages
- Dramatic elements in *Romeo and Juliet*
- Compare and Contrast procedures
- One Act Script Development
- Historical information concerning the Elizabethan Age and the Shakespearean theater

Example Performance Based Unit – Expanded Version

THE MANAGEMENT FOCUS

PAGE 3 OF 7

Student Accountability Plans

Individual	Each student is accountable for showing knowledge and skills through quizzes, tests, essays, observation, and written or oral explanation of the final tape's messages and the processes that were a part of the development of the script, performance, and video production.
Collaborative	Each student is responsible for completing his/her role responsibilities within the unit. Roles are developed such that each person must play a part and the team cannot be successful without the contributions of each member.

Performance Context

Location:	school and home
Audience:	classmates, eighth grade language arts students, and parents
Users of Product/Service:	not applicable
Evaluators:	peers and teacher

Expected Time Frame for the Unit

Four weeks

Special Materials & Resources Needed

Video tape and associated equipment

Additional Comments

(enter comments here)

Example Performance Based Unit – Expanded Version

THE ROLE PERFORMANCE

PAGE 4 OF 7

Romeo and Juliet – The Looking Glass

In this task we will be seeking answer(s) to the question . . .

What universal concepts and issues dealt with in classical literature continue to be relevant, and how might these be used to enhance our lives?

You're acting as a(n) . . .

Members of production teams for educational materials.

As such, your point or view or perspective is . . .

That you believe adolescents should see classical literature not only as a selection in their curriculum, but also as a source of valuable information and ideas concerning situations and relationships in which they may find themselves.

You are expected to . . .

Design and produce a video (twelve to fifteen minutes in length) that depicts and communicates a universal concept and message found in *Romeo and Juliet* that is still very relevant to modern young people. Your video needs to be interesting and entertaining enough to captivate a mostly adolescent audience. It also must be considered appropriate for your audience by the editorial review board.

And then . . .

Present your finished video for screening to a selected audience of adolescents, parents, and teachers.

Example Performance Based Unit – Expanded Version

THE ROLE PERFORMANCE (CONTINUED)

PAGE 5 OF 7

You will know you have successfully finished when . . .

Your script and tape meet the class developed standards, most of your screening audience can site specific evidence to support their statements that your video was sufficiently entertaining, and they can identify the message your tape was created to convey.

Challenges you may encounter are . . .

- creating a tape that is effective and entertaining for an audience that most likely will have little interest at first,

- working effectively with a group that must meet pre-established standards, and

- producing an effective product without a budget or large amounts of time.

Resources you can depend on are . . .

- video equipment available through the media center,

- school supplied video tape, and

- a local television news anchor who will visit to serve as our "expert" with technical production issues.

The final completion date is . . .   Four weeks from today

Example Performance Based Unit – Expanded Version

The Performance Actions

Page 6 of 7

Romeo and Juliet – The Looking Glass

Access (necessary information and skills) by . . .

- reading *Romeo and Juliet* and assorted associated references
- researching through references and interviews to determine significant messages others have attributed to *Romeo and Juliet*
- interviewing adolescents to gather their thoughts as to what makes videos entertaining
- interviewing a variety of people to determine significant universal concepts and messages others have attributed to *Romeo and Juliet*
- as a team, brainstorming concepts and issues that are considered appropriate and meaningful

Interpret by . . .

- determining significant concepts and messages still relevant today
- comparing and contrasting concepts and messages identified by the production team
- evaluating identified concepts and messages in order to select most appropriate
- identifying, evaluating, and selecting ideas for communicating the team's selected concept and message

Produce (or create) by . . .

- developing a project plan
- developing a script
- using the team's script to produce a video

Example Performance Based Unit – Expanded Version

THE PERFORMANCE ACTIONS (CONTINUED)

PAGE 7 OF 7

Communicate, Disseminate, or Use by . . .

- presenting the finished video to the designated audience
- answering questions from the audience

Evaluate the overall processes by . . .

- evaluating and continually accessing until information is adequate for the task
- evaluating and refining the team's script until it is effective
- evaluating and refining what has been produced and making appropriate revisions until standards are met
- evaluating through surveying the audience to determine effectiveness, refine if necessary
- determining as a team those collaborative skills the team did best, supporting conclusions with actual data, and determining refinements that the team and individuals can make to be able to function more effectively and efficiently together in the future

Abbreviated Performance Designers

On the following pages are the abbreviated Performance Designers. Just like the previous designers, these designers also address the 3 facets of the performance design process: 1) The Overview and Major Focus of the Performance, 2) The Performance Scenario, and 3) The Performance Structure.

The abbreviated designers follow a similar format and flow to the full designers and may be easier to use in completing performance designs for classroom use. Please refer to the directions for the full designer for guidance in completing the abbreviated designers.

Abbreviated Performance Designer – Cover Page

Created By

Peer Reviewed By

Date:

Intended Use:

Grade Level:

Subject Area:

Time Required:

Resources Needed:

Abbreviated Performance Designer – The Overview

Educational Purpose			
Standard			
Declarative Knowledge	Assessment	Procedural Knowledge	Assessment

The Essential Question/Issue

The Performance Overview
What are the students to create/produce/do?
The primary criteria are?
What are the students to do with it?
What is its purpose?
Who will be the audience?
What will be the setting?
How will it be judged/scored?

Abbreviated Performance Designer – The Student Page

You are to …

You will be successful when …

In addition, you will be assessed for …

Additional information you will need is …

The amount of time you will have to complete this task is …

Abbreviated Performance Designer – The Action Plan

The students are to *access* information and/or skills by ...			
Access Skills?	With What?	Checked	Scored
• • • •			

The students are to *interpret* by ... (Thinking Behaviors)			
Interpretive Skills?	With What?	Checked	Scored
• • • •			

The students are to *produce/create* by ...			
Creation/Production Skills?	With What?	Checked	Scored
• •			

The students are to *disseminate or apply* by ...			
Dissemination/Application Skills?	With What?	Checked	Scored
• •			

The students are to *evaluate/adjust* (throughout and at the end) by ...			
Evaluative Skills?	With What?	Checked	Scored
• • • •			

Abbreviated Performance Designer – Cover Page

"The Looking Glass" - Romeo & Juliet

Created By
Shari Graham East Grand Rapids School District East Grand Rapids, Mich. 49506

Peer Reviewed By
Spence Rogers

Date:

Intended Use:	Classroom instruction/assessment
Grade Level:	9 th
Subject Area:	Language Arts
Time Required:	Four weeks
Resources Needed:	Video tape and associated equipment

Abbreviated Performance Designer I – The Overview

Educational Purpose			
Standard			
Use themes and topics from texts to make connections, see patterns, and demonstrate a deep and rich understanding of enduring issues and recurring problems studied over time.			
Declarative Knowledge	**Assessment**	**Procedural Knowledge**	**Assessment**
• Shakespearean poetic conventions • Dramatic elements in **Romeo and Juliet** • Historical information concerning the Elizabethan Age and the Shakespearean theater	quizzes & test quizzes, tests, & essays quizzes, tests, & essays	• Interpret Shakespearean passages • Compare and Contrast procedures • One Act Script Development • Collaborative Work	essays essays product observations

The Essential Question/Issue
What universal concepts and issues dealt with in classical literature continue to be relevant, and how might their messages be used to enhance our lives in the twentieth century?

The Performance Overview

What are the students to create/produce/do?

Students are to write an original script conveying a universal concept and message found in **Romeo & Juliet**. They are also to video tape the production of their script.

The primary criteria are?

- content, language, and visuals are appropriate for audience
- script, production, and acting are performed to class developed levels
- universal concept presented to adequate depth
- major points effectively supported with clear and relevant examples
- organization is effective for message and audience

What are the students to do with it?	Present video to classmates and invited guests
What is its purpose?	To communicate connections found between literature and real life
Who will be the audience?	Classmates, eighth grade language arts students, and parents
What will be the setting?	Classroom
How will it be judged/scored?	Teacher/rubric

Abbreviated Performance Designer II – The Student Page

You are to …

act as a member of a production team for educational materials. Your company believes that adolescents should see classical literature not only as a selection in their curriculum, but also as a source of valuable information and ideas concerning situations and relationships in which they may find themselves. Your team is to work with **Romeo and Juliet,** and your task is to design and produce a video (12 to 15 minutes in length.) In this video you are to depict and communicate a universal concept and message that your team feels is appropriate and meaningful to today's adolescents. Your team's video needs to be interesting and entertaining enough to captivate a mostly adolescent audience. It also must be considered appropriate for your audience by the editorial review board.

You will be successful when …

- your script and tape meet the class developed standards,
- when most of your screening audience can site specific evidence supporting their statements that your team's video was sufficiently entertaining, and
- the majority of the audience can identify the universal concept and message your tape was created to convey.

In addition, you will be assessed for …

- various poetic conventions used by Shakespeare, (Quizzes and Tests)
- dramatic elements found in **Romeo and Juliet**, (Quizzes, Tests, and Essays)
- historical information concerning the Elizabethan Age and the Shakespearean Theater, (Quizzes, Tests, and Essays)
- interpreting Shakespearean passages, (Essays)
- compare and contrast procedures, (Essays)
- collaborative work. (Observation)

Additional information you will need is …

- several video cameras and vcr's are available through the school media center,
- the school will provide the tape for your team's final video, and
- a local television news anchor will visit and serve as our "expert" with technical production issues.

The amount of time you will have to complete this task is …   4 weeks from today

Abbreviated Performance Designer III – The Action Plan

The students are to access **information and/or skills by …**			
Access Skills? **With What?**		**Checked**	**Scored**
• reading *Romeo and Juliet* and assorted associated references,			X
• researching to determine significant universal concepts and messages others have attributed to *Romeo and Juliet*,		X	
• interviewing to determine significant universal concepts and messages others have attributed to *Romeo and Juliet*,		X	
• interviewing adolescents to gather their thoughts as to what makes videos entertaining, and		X	
• as a team member, brainstorming concepts and issues that are considered appropriate and meaningful.		X	

The students are to interpret **by … (Thinking Behaviors)**			
Interpretive Skills? **With What?**		**Checked**	**Scored**
• determining significant concepts and messages still relevant today,		X	
• comparing and contrasting concepts and messages identified by production team,			
• evaluating identified concepts and messages in order to select most appropriate, and		X	
• identifying, evaluating, and selecting ideas for communicating team's selected concept and message.		X	

The students are to produce/create **by …**			
Creation/Production Skills? **With What?**		**Checked**	**Scored**
• developing a project plan,		X	
• developing a script, and		X	
• using the team's script to produce a video.			X

The students are to disseminate or apply by ...			
Dissemination/Application Skills? **With What?**		**Checked**	**Scored**
• presenting the finished video to the designated audience, and		X	
• answering questions from the audience.		X	

The students are to evaluate/adjust (**throughout and at the end**) by ...			
Evaluative Skills? **With What?**		**Checked**	**Scored**
• evaluating and continually assessing until information is adequate for the task,		X	
• evaluating and refining the team's script until it is effective,		X	
• evaluating what has been produced and making appropriate revisions until the standards are met,		X	
• evaluating by surveying the audience to determine effectiveness, refining if necessary, and		X	
• determining as a team those collaborative skills the team did best, supporting conclusions with actual data, and determining refinements that the team and individuals can make to be able to function more effectively and efficiently together in the future.		X	

Abbreviated Performance Designers – Cover Page

Note to a Friend

Created By
Jim Ludington Gananda Central School District Walworth, New York 14568

Peer Reviewed By
Spence Rogers

Date:

Intended Use:	Classroom instruction/assessment
Grade Level:	12
Subject Area:	Math - 12
Time Required:	Take home - 4 days
Resources Needed:	None

Abbreviated Performance Designer I – The Overview

Educational Purpose			
Standard			
Express mathematical ideas, concepts, and skills orally and in writing.			
Declarative Knowledge	**Assessment**	**Procedural Knowledge**	**Assessment**
Amplitude, period, phase shift, applications	test	• graph trig functions of the form y = a ***function*** (bx + c) • write descriptions of procedures • creating effective visuals	• test • product • product

The Essential Question/Issue
Not Applicable

The Performance Overview

What are the students to create/produce/do?

A written note with supporting visuals describing how to graph sine, cosine, tangent, secant, cosecant, and cotangent functions including checks for understanding.

The primary criteria are?

The "note" is …

- neat/legible – Criteria for Credit,
- correct,
- thorough,
- supported with effective visuals, and
- understandable.

What are the students to do with it?	Have it tested for understandability by other students
What is its purpose?	Teach others (simulated)
Who will be the audience?	Course III (younger) students
What will be the setting?	Classroom
How will it be judged/scored?	Teacher / rubric

Abbreviated Performance Designer II – The Student Page

You are to …

write a note to an "imaginary friend" in Course III describing the procedures for graphing the six trigonometric functions. The trig functions are to be of the form y = a **function** (bx + c). Support your written procedures with original examples and visuals. Your procedures, examples, and visuals need to be effective enough that Course III students can follow what your note says and do the process correctly. Be certain to include checking activities (created by you) so that the readers can check their understanding.

You will be successful when …

your note meets the "Criteria for Credit" and the standards that will be clarified in the rubric we will develop together in class.

(NOTE: Please refer to the attached rubric.)

In addition, you will be assessed for …

- an understanding of amplitude, phase shift, and period.

- a knowledge of naturally occurring applications of sine curves.

Additional information you will need is …

The amount of time you will have to complete this task is …   4 days

Abbreviated Performance Designer III – The Action Plan

The students are to access **information and/or skills by ...**			
Access Skills?	**With What?**	**Checked**	**Scored**
• participating in class in order to acquire graphing knowledge and skills,		X	
• brainstorming ideas for examples and note format, and		X	
• referring to math and science texts for examples and applications.		X	

The students are to interpret **by ... (Thinking Behaviors)**			
Interpretive Skills?	**With What?**	**Checked**	**Scored**
• organizing concepts into a logical order for teaching,		X	
• determining aligned examples, and		X	
• determining appropriate checking activities.		X	

The students are to produce/create **by ...**			
Creation/Production Skills?	**With What?**	**Checked**	**Scored**
• writing a complete and effective note incorporating supporting visuals and checking activities.			X

The students are to disseminate or apply **by ...**			
Dissemination/Application Skills?	**With What?**	**Checked**	**Scored**
• turning in your note to be tested by a Course III student.		X	

The students are to evaluate/adjust **(throughout and at the end) by ...**			
Evaluative Skills?	**With What?**	**Checked**	**Scored**
• checking the correctness of procedures and examples with peers,		X	
• checking a "draft" with peers/parents for clarity - refine as needed,		X	
• refining your note based on errors made by the Course III student, and		X	
• determining specific ways to improve on similar efforts in the future.		X	

Chapter 5

QUICK DESIGNERS:
PERFORMANCE TASK DESIGN TEMPLATES
FOR PEOPLE IN A HURRY

A Cautionary Note to Shortcuts

When time is short, it's helpful to have quick and easy procedures to complete our essential tasks. This is as true for designing performance tasks as for anything else.

The purpose of this chapter is to provide a "down and dirty"
performance designer. It is very useful when time is of the
essence or when providing staff-development for new
comers to performance design. However, as with all short-
cuts, there are inherent dangers.

Care needs to be taken to ensure that performance designs are
valid, reliable, and address worthwhile content. Ultimately,
how this is achieved is not as important as it being achieved.
When these shortcut designers are used, take care to ensure
that essential quality levels are met.

Guidelines for Completing The Quick Performance Task Designer

There are only two pages to the Quick Designers, and the
second page is optional. Page one is to prompt the task and
its essential criteria. The second page is to prompt the
specific performance actions and is most important if the
performance task is to take an extended period of time.

Page one of the Quick Designer calls for:

1. **The Title for the Performance Task.**

    As with almost anything, it's helpful to have names or
    titles. Provide a catchy, brief, and descriptive title for your
    performance task.

2. **The Learning Target(s) for the Task.**

    These may be referred to as the standards, indicators,
    outcomes, or objectives, depending on the terminology
    being used in your community or area. Where appropri-
    ate, be sure to include both content and process targets.
    For example, a content target might be that the students
    are expected to demonstrate a knowledge of the major
    events that led up to the American Civil War, and a corre-
    sponding process target might be that the students are

expected to demonstrate their ability to gather, evaluate, organize and integrate information in order to produce an accurate and meaningful factual report.

3. **The Performance Task.**

Provide a performance task being certain to address each of the following:

Format – specify what the students are to produce (generate/do) as a part of the performance task – the form in which the students are to show the targeted learning. Examples include letters, reports, speeches, oral presentations, educational games, video games, solutions to problems, debates, and lessons taught. Refer to Appendix A for additional format ideas.

Purpose – specify what the purpose is for what the students are to produce. For example, is it to entertain, inform, persuade, generate interest, resolve, or teach.

Audience – specify the intended audience, or simulated audience, for the students' work. In other words provide the answer to the question, "Who is to observe, receive, benefit from, or use what the students are producing as a part of the performance task?"

Content – specify the specific content that the performance is to include/demonstrate. Examples include: causes of the American Civil War, Applications of Trigonometric Functions, Extinct Species, Japan, Supply-Side Economics, and *King Lear.*

Expectation – specify the expectation or standard that the students' work is to meet.

The following is an example of a performance task that addresses format, audience, purpose, content, and expectation ...

> Imagine you are planning a pizza and wings party menu for five of your friends and you have a twenty-five dollar gift certificate to pay for all the food. Your task is to prepare a *menu and a written justification for it (format)* to share with *your friends (audience)* for *their approval (purpose)*. Attached is a list of your friends' likes, dislikes, and dietary needs. Also attached is a price list from the local pizzeria. Since the pizzeria will not give change when gift certificates

are used, your challenge is to design a menu that not only satisfies your friends' taste preferences and dietary needs, but also comes within $.50 cents of the $25.00. *Be certain your menu includes costs for each item and a total (including 5% sales tax) (content). Also, be certain your justification for your menu meets both the needs of your friends and your financial limitations (expectations).*

Note: This is a commonly used performance task for upper elementary grades. This particular example was developed by Gary Wilson and Teresa Tracy of the Lockport City School District in Lockport, NY. It is used as a part of the L.C.S.D. Benchmark Performance Assessment Initiative.

4. **The Criteria for the Task.**

    Specify all relevant criteria for the performance task. With each task there should be content criteria and at least one of either product, performance, or process criteria. For the above example, we would include content criteria stipulating that the arithmetic usage is to be appropriate and accurate. We would also include product criteria stipulating that the menu and the justification are to be well organized, consistent with the tastes and dietary needs of the friends, and consistent with the financial limitations presented in the task.

Page 2 of the Quick Designer is intended to be used as appropriate to plan for the specific performance actions that are to be a part of the performance task. Its use is most appropriate for extended tasks in which the students will be assessed for their ability to perform acquisition, integration, production, dissemination, and evaluation behaviors. Please refer to Chapter 4, Section "Using Templates to Develop the Performance Action Plan" for further explanation and examples.

The Quick Task Designer

Title

The Learning Target(s)

The Performance Task				
Format	Purpose	Audience	Content	Expectation

Criteria			
Content	Product	Performance	Process

The Quick Task Designer

CONTINUED

The students are to *access* information and/or skills by …	Checked	Scored

The students are to *interpret* by …	Checked	Scored

The students are to *produce/create* by …	Checked	Scored

The students are to *disseminate or apply* by …	Checked	Scored

The students are to *evaluate/adjust* by …	Checked	Scored

The Quick Task Designer
Math/Probability Example

Title
Three Doors

The Learning Target(s)
The students will demonstrate the ability to use experimentation and probability concepts to draw conclusions and make recommendations.

The Performance Task

Format	Purpose	Audience	Content	Expectation

Imagine you are a good friend of someone who is going to be a contestant on the show "Let's Make a Deal." Your friend knows he will be asked to pick one door out of three in hopes of picking the door with a good prize behind it. He also knows he will be shown what's behind one of the doors after he makes his original pick. The problem he will face is what he should do after that when the host offers to let him keep his original door or switch. Your task is to theorize through experimentation what choice he should make, and develop and present a written recommended action to him that is supported by a sound and convincing argument.

Criteria

Content	Product	Performance	Process
• Mathematical concepts and computations are accurate and correctly used. • Argument is logical and shows sound reasoning.	• Paper is easily understood. • Well organized. • Convincingly written. • Mechanically sound.	• not applicable	• Experiment & data collection is done with accuracy and precision.

Due to the brevity of this task, the "optional" second page is not included. Please refer to the section, "Guidelines for Completing The Quick Performance Task Designer" earlier in this chapter for an explanation of how and when to use page 2.

Reflection Questions

1. What are the important points in this chapter?

2. How do I feel about what I've read?

3. What questions do I have?

4. How can I use what's here?

Chapter 6

ALIGNING CURRICULUM, INSTRUCTION, & ASSESSMENT

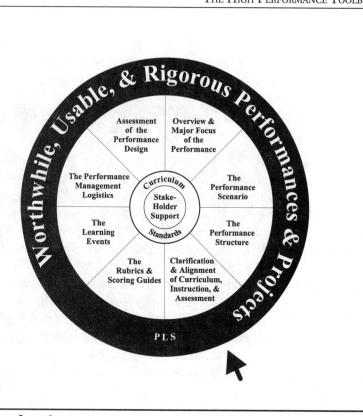

Introduction

The work of Dr. Alan Cohen and Dr. Joan Hyman-Cohen has shown us the power of instructional alignment. "Alignment explains 60% of the variance in academic test scores." ("An Interview with Doctors Joan Hyman-Cohen and S. Alan Cohen." *The Journal of Quality Learning*. April, 1996, Volume 5, Number 4, 29-32.)

One of the great dangers with performance-learning is becoming so focused on the activity that that's what you get – lots of activity and very little intended learning. It is essential when planning performances to ...

1. deliberately determine what specific knowledge, concepts, skills, and abilities the students are to learn as a result of engaging in the performance;

2. determine precisely what the students need to do (what behaviors) to show each of the learnings targeted in number 1;

3. select or develop assessment strategies that are effective and efficient as procedures through which the students will demonstrate those behaviors identified in number 2; and

4. develop or select instructional strategies (including backup strategies for those students requiring additional time, support, or modalities) that effectively and efficiently facilitate and support the students' learning of the information, concepts, skills, and abilities targeted.

When determining the targeted curriculum for the performance, we are interested in determining precisely what the students are to know (declarative knowledge) or be able to do (procedural knowledge) as a result of engagement in the performance. According to Dr. Robert J. Marzano in his book *A Different Kind of Classroom: Teaching with Dimensions of Learning* (ASCD, 1992), it is important to differentiate between *Declarative Knowledge* and *Procedural Knowledge*. The following explanations of these two types of learning are offered to add some clarity, but since they are not the main focus of this book, we strongly recommend a careful study of Dr. Marzano's work regarding this topic. (Rather than only make reference to Dr. Marzano's work, we strongly recommend that you buy a copy of his book, *A Different Kind of Classroom – Teaching With Dimensions of Learning*. The book is available through ASCD. You won't regret adding it to your library.)

Identify the Targeted Declarative Knowledge

Declarative knowledge "involves what the students need to know and understand." It includes facts, concepts, principles, and generalizations. It is that knowledge that people have with respect to concepts and information such as:

- freedom,
- change,
- denominator,
- resistance,
- conflict,
- grammar rules,
- roses, and
- elephants.

⋆Declarative knowledge does not involve processes or steps. It is the type of knowledge that is typically assessed on paper-pencil tests.

According to Dr. Marzano, the process of learning declarative knowledge has three phases …

1. "constructing meaning" - in the simplest sense, interpreting new learning based on what we already know (prior knowledge). During this phase, we utilize strategies that help the students make sense of new learning by finding connections with a prior concept. Analogies and metaphors can help during this phase.

2. "organizing" - in the simplest sense, determining essential and non-essential characteristics of the learning and then putting the essential characteristics of the new learning into some symbolic or subjective representation – creating the "big picture." Graphic organizers and concept maps are two common approaches to facilitating this phase.

3. "storing" - in the simplest sense, doing something that will facilitate memory and recall. Creating elaborate mental images is a powerful approach for moving the learning into long-term memory.

When planning instruction for the identified declarative knowledge curriculum components, it is important to address these three phases of declarative knowledge acquisition.

Distinguish Between Knowledge and Understanding

As curriculum is developed, it is not uncommon to use the word "understand." The question then becomes, what does someone have to do to prove they do have an understanding of something and not just knowledge about it. An example to help clarify the difference – many or us have knowledge of the Holocaust, but most of us don't truly understand it. Another example is that most of us can describe "television" for quite some time and to a great deal of detail, but most of us cannot explain television. This second example helps to clarify the difference between knowing a lot and understanding.

As we develop performance learning units or performance assessments, it is important to clarify what types of student behavior can demonstrate understanding. Grant Wiggins has done extensive work in clarifying what distinguishes understanding. In order to offer a quick perspective as to his findings, the following are ten questions that help determine what someone who has understanding of something should be able to do. We offer them as a base for answering the question, "If we are assessing understanding of something, for what should we be looking?"

1. What misunderstandings or misconceptions should we check to see if they can detect?

2. What subtleties should we look to see that they can discern?

3. What connections should we be able to see them make?

4. What small distinctions should we be able to see them make?

5. What different viewpoints regarding it should they be able to explain?

6. What aspects of it should we be able to see them defend convincingly?

7. What aspects of it or its use should they be able to evaluate and provide meaningful feedback?

8. In what contexts and to what extent should we be able to see them apply it?

9. What types of examples should we be able to see them generate?

10. What obstacles or barriers should we be able to see them overcome?

For in-depth coverage in this area, we recommend you contact Grant Wiggins at The Center on Learning, Assessment, and School Structure in Princeton, New Jersey.

Identify the Targeted Procedural Knowledge

Procedural Knowledge, according to Dr. Marzano, involves what the students need to be able to do – a skill, process, or procedure that "may or may not be linear." Procedural knowledge is usually assessed by engaging students in a demonstration or performance that requires the students actually do the procedure being assessed.

"Learning procedural knowledge also involves three phases," according to Dr. Marzano. The three phases that he identifies are …

1. "constructing models" – a set of steps for an algorithmic procedure (they are absolute and lead to the correct result), a set of rules for a tactic procedure (they provide general guidance as to how to accomplish something like "interpreting a bar graph"), and a set of very general rules for a strategy (they are not specific to any particular situation as in a strategy for decision making). Common strategies for this phase include:

   - the teacher explaining her procedures and thinking as she works through procedures (commonly referred to as "think aloud") while also writing the steps on the board or on butcher paper; and

   - having the students develop flowcharts for the procedure.

2. "shaping" – developing conceptual understanding. A common strategy for this phase is to provide guided practice (with only a few examples) during which the teacher monitors the process carefully and provides "just-in-time" feedback.

3. "internalizing" – practicing until the procedure can be done with relative ease. As we have heard before, practice doesn't necessarily make perfect, but it certainly makes permanent.

An Overview of the Templates

The following templates are to facilitate the identification and alignment of the targeted declarative and procedural curricu-

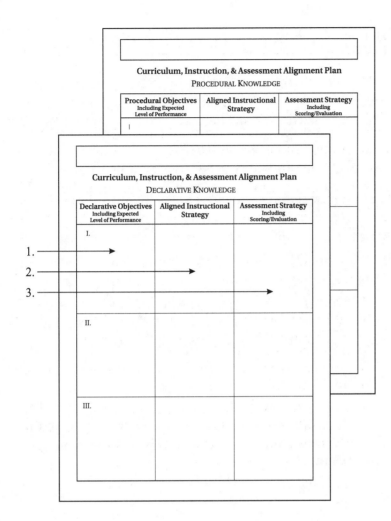

lum components, effective instructional strategies, and valid assessment strategies.

There are two curriculum, instruction, and assessment templates – one for declarative knowledge and the other for procedural knowledge. Though the process for determining what is to be taught in each area is basically the same, the instruction and assessment strategies are considerably different.

Prompt 1:

In these boxes on both templates, indicate the targeted declarative or procedural knowledge objectives – be specific enough so that it is clear precisely what it is the students are to know or be able to do. Also, include clarification of the level of difficulty that is expected. Examples …

Declarative: the students will understand the concept of a sine curve. This will be shown by their ability to explain how sine curves are used to describe periodic behaviors and to generate supporting examples.

Procedural: the students will construct graphs of sine functions. The sine functions to be graphed will be of the form y = a sin (bx + c) where a, b, and c are any real numbers.

Declarative: the students will know the five major causes of the civil war (as developed in class).

Procedural: the students will write a summary of a nonfiction article. The article is to be from any of five different areas based on individual student interest (news, sports, music, literature, computers) and at a 7.0 reading level.

Prompt 2:

In these boxes on both templates, indicate the intended instructional strategies that are appropriate for the identified declarative or procedural knowledge. Refer to the example templates that follow.

Prompt 3:

In these boxes on both templates, indicate the assessment strategies that are appropriate for the targeted declarative and procedural knowledge. Options here can range from "observation" to "paper-pencil test" to a "performance-based assessment" with appropriate rubrics for validating or evaluating. (See Chapter Two.) For further clarification, refer to the partially completed example templates on the following four pages.

Curriculum, Instruction, & Assessment Alignment Plan

DECLARATIVE KNOWLEDGE

Secondary Mathematics Example

Declarative Knowledge Including Expected Level of Performance	Aligned Instructional Strategy	Assessment Strategy Including Scoring/Evaluating
I. the students will understand the concept of a sine curve with respect to its shape and its representation of periodic behaviors.	Students will be given examples of "things" in life that behave consistently with a sine curve. They will also be given examples of "things" whose behaviors are distinctly not consistent with sine curves. They will be asked to determine the characteristics that distinguish sine curve behaviors from others. Student teams will be asked to construct a "generalization map" for sine curves. Students will be asked to draw scenes that replicate sine curves.	Students will be asked to identify occurrences in nature that approximate sine curves – they will be asked to defend their conclusions. A rubric will be used to evaluate their responses.
II.		

Curriculum, Instruction, & Assessment Alignment Plan

DECLARATIVE KNOWLEDGE

A Language Arts (Short Story) Example

Declarative Knowledge Including Expected Level of Performance	Aligned Instructional Strategy	Assessment Strategy Including Scoring/Evaluating
I. Students will understand the following basic literary elements in a short story: • protagonist • antagonist • plot • climax • conflict • setting	Concept maps, short story examples, and comparisons to life will be used to develop understanding.	Students will be asked to take a situation from their own lives and provide examples with supporting evidence for each of the elements. They will also be asked to read a short story, clearly articulate each of the elements, and provide supporting evidence for their conclusions.
II.		
III.		

Curriculum, Instruction, & Assessment Alignment Plan

PROCEDURAL KNOWLEDGE

An Example from Secondary Mathematics

Procedural Objectives Including Expected Level of Performance	Aligned Instructional Strategy	Assessment Strategy Including Scoring/Evaluating
I. the students will acquire the ability to construct the graph of a sine function of the form $y = a \sin (bx + c)$.	The teacher will model the procedure with several examples while "thinking aloud" and recording the "rules" on butcher paper. Teams of students will construct flowcharts for graphing sine functions. Teams of students and then students as individuals will be asked to graph several sine functions until proficient.	As individuals, students will be asked to accurately graph sine functions (as noted) and write correct descriptions of the processes followed.
II.		

Curriculum, Instruction, & Assessment Alignment Plan

PROCEDURAL KNOWLEDGE

An Example from Language Arts

Procedural Objectives Including Expected Level of Performance	Aligned Instructional Strategy	Assessment Strategy Including Scoring/Evaluating
I. the students will be able to develop a plot line for an original short story regarding issues relevant to adolescents.	The teacher will present a graphic organizer used for identifying and developing plot lines. The teacher will model the use of the organizer with several examples while "thinking aloud" and recording the "rules" for using the organizer to identify and develop plot lines on butcher paper. Teams of students and then students as individuals will be asked to develop several plot lines for common "events."	As individuals, students will be asked to develop (and defend) a plot line that will be used for his/her original short story addressing an issue relevant to adolescents.
II.		

Curriculum, Instruction, & Assessment Alignment Plan

DECLARATIVE KNOWLEDGE

Declarative Knowledge Including Expected Level of Performance	Aligned Instructional Strategy	Assessment Strategy Including Scoring/Evaluating
I.		
II.		
III.		

Curriculum, Instruction, & Assessment Alignment Plan

PROCEDURAL KNOWLEDGE

Procedural Objectives Including Expected Level of Performance	Aligned Instructional Strategy	Assessment Strategy Including Scoring/Evaluating
I.		
II.		
III.		

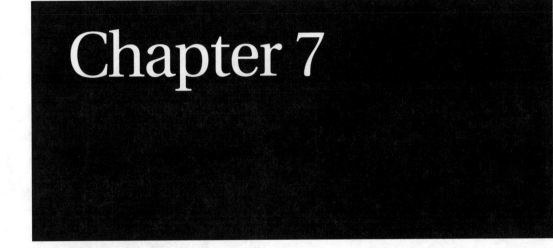

Chapter 7

RUBRICS

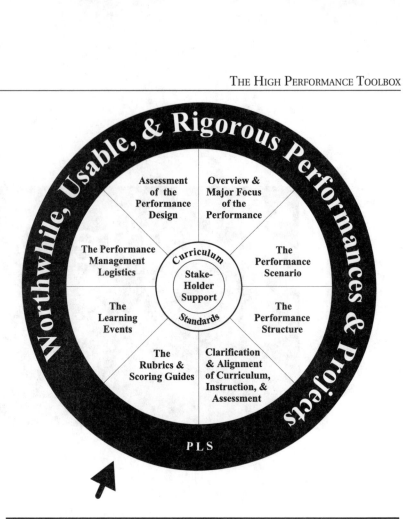

The Word Rubric has a Long History

The word rubric has its origins in the Latin word rubrica which means red chalk. Gradually the word rubric evolved to mean reddish in color, and the word rubricate evolved to mean to print in red ink. About nine hundred years ago, red ink was used for printing important directions in prayer books. It also evolved as the ink commonly used to denote the Word of God in many Bibles. As a result of these uses, the word rubric gradually came to mean the criteria used to either evaluate the level of quality in an endeavor or to provide guidance to people seeking to reach high quality levels as a result of their efforts.

Rubrics are Used Extensively in Everyday Life

Most people use, or at least encounter rubrics on a daily basis, but they typically don't label them as such. Whenever people give descriptions of what they think makes a good restaurant, pizza, symphony, baseball game, ski run, or action movie, they're giving their rubrics, but they probably don't call them that. When someone is asked to recommend a restaurant, that person usually doesn't respond, "Okay, but first tell me what your rubric is for restaurants." The person is much more likely to ask, "What are you looking for in a restaurant?" The person is asking for a rubric, and will use the response she gets to evaluate the restaurants she knows in order to recommend the one that best meets the criteria given. Another example occurs whenever friends ask us how we would rate a movie we've seen and why. In essence, they're asking us for our evaluation and our rubric. Additional examples of simple rubrics surface whenever we ask questions like …

- How do you like your swordfish prepared?
- What do you like in a vacation spot?
- How do you want my book cover to look?
- What will you be looking for when you evaluate my teaching?
- What will the recital be like if it's excellent? What if it's just okay?
- What makes a résumé great?

Because rubrics are so common in everyday life, and also because there are so many myths and complicating perspectives about using rubrics in education, the following pages will be devoted to demystifying rubrics through real-life examples. The important rubric related concepts we will be focusing on are …

- quality levels,
- focus,
- exemplars, and
- anchors.

Our real-life examples begin with a friend's pizza rubric. "I think a great pizza is an old fashioned, hand-tossed pizza with a thick, golden brown crust, lots of spicy, Italian tomato sauce, three or four kinds of cheeses, thick and spicy pepperoni slices, fresh mushrooms and onions, and flavorful green peppers."

In this situation, our friend's pizza rubric is a pretty good, *one level* rubric. By one level we mean that the only description of a pizza provided is the one she considers to be a great pizza. It is assumed with a one level rubric that the single level of quality provided is sufficient for clarity. When asked about pizza preferences, most people don't see a need to expound on world class pizza, great pizza, good pizza, poor pizza, and unacceptable pizza. However, if our friend were going to become the newspaper's pizza critic and publish her evaluations of pizzas from restaurants throughout the area, she would need to develop descriptions of numerous quality levels in order to accurately and fairly label each restaurant's pizza. In this scenario, she would also be expected to publish her criteria along with her evaluations. The consumers could then form their own judgments about where to go for pizza based on the published evaluations and criteria, and the restaurant's personnel could determine what changes need to be made in order to get higher evaluations.

Another important point that can be made with our pizza example concerns the importance of clarifying the rubric's focus. In the example, the rubric is for what our friend thinks is a great pizza. Others may not agree with her. It is for this reason that the precise focus for a rubric must be clearly identified. "Carol thinks a great pizza is one that ..."

If it is important to have a rubric with a focus that represents a broader opinion base and less of a single person's subjectivity, then it is essential to utilize more than one person's judgment. To do this, we have several "pizza experts" provide us with samples of what they consider to be exemplary pizzas (we call these examples *exemplars*). Because of the wide variety of pizza types, our experts will soon find themselves in trouble. They will have to tighten their focus to a particular type of pizza such as "deep dish meat pizzas." Then experts will have to select several exemplars of whatever type of pizza they will address first. Next they will determine the characteristics their exemplars have in common – these common characteristics become the criteria that determines whether or not that type of pizza is to be certified as great.

As our panel of experts develops the rubric for a great particular type of pizza, they will identify through actual pizza samples what differentiates great, good, acceptable, and poor pizzas from one another. For each of these four levels, they will provide us with clear, written descriptions (criteria) and actual pizza samples representing each level. These samples are called "anchors" because they anchor the words to concrete examples for added clarity.

How do we know if the rubric is good? It's good if whenever a pizza is tested against it, the quality level of the pizza can be determined with reasonable ease and certainty. It is also good if someone can use the rubric to determine what differentiates a pizza at one quality level from the levels above and below it.

A Rubric is a Set of Criteria Used to Judge Quality

A rubric is any established set of statements (criteria) that clearly, precisely, accurately, and thoroughly describe the varying, distinguishable, quality (or developmental) levels that may exist in something (a product, organization, creation, system, etcetera) or in an action (performance, process, skill, ability, etcetera). The most common uses for rubrics in education at this point in time is evaluating, scoring, and assessing "student work" in order to accurately determine its level of quality. This is no different from how rubrics are used outside of school. Several examples of this are ...

- the movie is "two thumbs up;"
- the restaurant is a five star; and
- the figure skating compulsories' exhibition is a 5.9.

There is another very valuable use for rubrics – guiding/ coaching students to desired levels of performance. (e.g., an excellent novel has these characteristics, your new restaurant will be excellent if ..., a good "jigsaw" in the classroom looks like ..., your high-jumping will be excellent when ..., your lab report, handwriting, drawing, or homework will be excellent when ...) Unfortunately this is an incredibly powerful and valuable use for rubrics that is more common outside education than inside education.

Rubrics are Needed Whenever Quality Needs to be Consistently Judged or Attained

We need rubrics whenever the quality of someone's efforts is important to us. We also need rubrics whenever someone else's quality expectations with respect to our efforts is important. Whether we are trying to describe the quality we desire in something, or we are trying to evaluate the quality of something that already exists, it is important to have a rubric. In school, we need to develop rubrics whenever it is important that all students do well and the criteria for doing well is not known.

Once everyone involved knows the rubric for a given endeavor, the rubric is no longer needed as a formal document. This is not to say the criteria does not need to be met, it is only saying we don't need to continuously repeat the obvious. An example from outside of school can help to clarify this point. While we were having dinner at a friend's house, the friend found it necessary to remind his daughters of the family "dining etiquette rubric." By saying, "I hope we haven't forgotten how we're supposed to behave at dinner," our friend was simply reminding his daughters of their well established, though probably forgotten in the excitement, rubric for dinner time behavior.

The Ideal Number of Quality Levels in a Rubric Varies from Context to Context

The number of quality levels that need to be defined in a rubric is dependent on ...

- the rubric's focus;
- its intended purpose;
- the developer's ability to clearly and precisely determine the nuances that differentiate the possible quality levels; and
- the specific context for its use.

Consequently, there is not a magic number of quality levels that we can say there should always be. The number will vary from rubric to rubric. For example, how many of us want to take the time to clarify the distinctions between outstanding, excellent, very good, good, acceptable, mediocre, poor, and unacceptable family restaurants just so we can recommend a restaurant to a friend? Not even restaurant critics try for eight levels. However, at the Vail Ski School, in Vail, Colorado, they have clearly identified with text and video clips ten levels of skiing ability.

There are two very important lessons regarding the number of quality levels to be defined in a rubric that we can gain from the Vail Ski School example.

1.   **The statements of the various levels of a rubric need to differentiate from one another in discernible and important ways.** The ski instructors have produced for public consumption an outstanding ten level rubric using qualitative criteria. The rubric clearly describes through the use of easy to follow text and outstanding supportive video clips the observable nuances that distinguish the various levels of skiing in terms of timing, control, weight shifts, positions, and other specific techniques and observable distinguishing characteristics.

2.   **The ability to observe and describe qualitative as opposed to only quantitative characteristics is developmental.** Vail's most experienced ski instructors can go even further then the video does to clearly describe and model numerous levels within each of the ten levels. The ability to develop rubrics that do this well is dependent on the developer's depth and breadth of knowledge regarding the rubric's focus and his/her experience in putting into words what differentiates those levels. For example, most beginning skiers can only describe a few levels of skiing ability, and typically, they describe those levels in mostly quantitative terms. Beginners will talk about the number of falls, the length of time without falling, the number of turns made, the distance between the skis, and so on. When the beginner does refer to how smooth and effortless an expert's skiing appears, he/she usually can't put into words what they are seeing that allows them to say that. If asked, he/she would find it very difficult to explain the true differences between what Vail's rubric refers to as level eight, nine, or ten skiers. Even an expert skier without experience in articulating nuances in skiing can typically see the differences,

but struggles to put them into words. Typically one will hear them say, "I know it when I see it." The point to be made is that the more experienced we become in observing, developing, and using qualitative criteria in real situations, the better we become at doing it.

In general, the number of quality levels developed in a rubric should be …

- limited to the number that is most beneficial to the evaluators and those whose efforts are being evaluated for the given context. Creating too many levels for a situation is a waste of energy and tends to alienate people because of micro-management. Creating too few levels can result in confusion, failure, and anger.

- limited to the number in which the developer can truly describe both the qualitative and the quantitative nuances with respect to each level.

- an even number (2, 4, 6, 8, …) to force careful and more accurate differentiation between levels. When rubrics have an odd number of quality levels defined, the evaluators tend to gravitate quickly to the levels in the middle rather than carefully distinguishing between levels.

- adequate for both the evaluators and the performers to be able to accurately identify the level of performance and what needs to be done to reach a higher level.

There is one last but very important point regarding the number of quality levels that are most appropriate for a rubric. It is very possible, that some criteria will have fewer levels than others. For an example, the evaluation form at McDonalds restaurants provides only two choices for *accuracy of order* – accurate or not accurate. However, they do have 4 quality options from which customers can choose for other items. An example from school is in a writing rubric – there might be only two options regarding the appropriateness of language for school use.

In summary, there is no magic number of levels that should be developed for a rubric, but there can be an inappropriate number of levels. Movie critics tend to use four levels. So do restaurant critics. Classroom teachers often use two, four or six, depending on the situation. The Vail Ski School uses ten, and we've seen writing rubrics with twelve. *The correct number of quality levels is the number that will produce quality results in the context in which the rubric is used.*

Rubrics are an Essential Key to Quality Work from Students

Though most of us in education have utilized the basic thought behind rubrics, in many cases we have not tapped their full power as tools to support and evaluate performances and learning. In the school environment, it becomes extremely important that the rubric be very well defined. We've all heard students sincerely say to us, "I thought I did what you wanted. What did I do wrong, or what didn't I do?" What they've actually been saying is that either our rubric wasn't understandable to them or it wasn't specific or complete enough in terms of what was truly expected.

When rubrics are not clear, both teachers and students become frustrated and/or disappointed. People don't enjoy working hard on something, thinking they're getting it right, and then finding out that it isn't. When an unclear rubric is being used to evaluate a student's efforts, everyone becomes caught in traps of uncertainty and subjectivity. We also end up with scores, grades, and evaluations that are or can be inconsistent from moment to moment, year to year, and event to event.

Many of the problems associated with rubrics in school can be resolved by ...

- clearly and precisely determining up-front the intended use for the rubric (e.g., guide/coach/evaluate), the target for the rubric (e.g. persuasive presentation), and a statement (with examples as necessary for clarification) of what the highest quality expectation is (e.g., the intended audience is persuaded through your rationale that your position is appropriate and reasonable).

- obtaining and providing solid examples (anchors) for each quality level identified in the rubric.

- when the students cannot be engaged in the development of the rubrics, involving them in instructional activities that create a conceptual understanding of the levels within the rubrics.

- engaging students in the process of developing the rubrics using three or more exemplars (examples of the most outstanding quality levels expected) and examples to become the anchors for the definitions of quality levels below exemplary.

- only developing the number of quality levels within the rubrics that can be justified by the intended use, and the ability of the developers to describe in *qualitative* terms the nuances that distinguish the levels. (When quality is defined in quantitative terms it is usually a signal, but not always, that the true nuances of the various levels have not been identified and clarified.)

Excellent Rubrics Adhere to Specific Criteria

Experience has shown us that no one seems to like anyone else's rubrics. Quite often, experts don't like other experts' rubrics. This fact does not mean that experts are developing rubrics incorrectly. What it does say to us is that rubrics require clear and precise statements of their quality targets *and excellent anchors to support the various levels* – all of which tend to either not exist or not accompany the rubric.

However, if you are asking, "What is an excellent rubric?" what you are asking for is a *rubric for rubrics*. The following is a two level *rubric for rubrics*. Two levels in the sense that only one is presented, and anything less than that is considered less than an excellent rubric. More extensive *rubrics for rubrics* will be presented later in this chapter along with examples of rubrics to serve as anchors. Note: this rubric starts with the quality definition for a rubric – the rubric is not solely a list of essential characteristics of quality rubrics.

A Rubric for Rubrics

An excellent rubric is one that can be used to accurately determine the level of quality of the rubric's focus and that can be used to provide accurate guidance as to what improvements need to be made for the rubric's focus to be at a higher level of quality.

A Rubric for Rubrics

A Quality rubric is one for which those associated with its use can show that it …

- evaluates its target accurately and consistently with a minimum level of unexpected subjectivity;
- is clear to everyone associated with its use;
- focuses on the characteristics that truly determine and distinguish between quality levels;
- is based on actual examples for each level and is accompanied by examples (anchors*) for clarity; and
- has the number of levels that are appropriate for its use and the developmental levels of its developers and users.

---

* What follows is an example rubric that is to serve as an *anchor* for the above *rubric for rubrics*. It is a rubric for a performance task in mathematics (though it can be easily adapted to any skill area) in which the students have to show their ability to perform a skill and describe the process they are using. The rubric is designed to be generic and calls for specific details to be determined before scoring. Note that in the rubric there is reference to the quality expectations in terms of accuracy, thoroughness, and understandability of both the math work and the description of it. This rubric is generic in that it can be used with any math problem at any level. To be used effectively in a given context it too must be accompanied by anchors and clarifying conditions based on the specific math problems.

An Example Rubric

Doing & Describing Mathematical Procedures		
This generic rubric requires the specifics for the targeted procedure to be provided.		
	Content	**Description of Procedures**
Exemplary **5 points**	Solution is correct. The work/process shown is logically and accurately presented with enough detail to be followed easily and to show the essential concepts. Essential steps to be shown are:	The description of the process is precise (detailed), accurate throughout, complete, and easy to follow. It matches the actual work shown and works effectively to find a solution to the given problem.
Competent **4 Points**	Solution is correct. The work/process shown is logically and accurately presented (*with the exception of minor errors in notation*) with enough detail to be followed by an expert and to show the essential concepts. Essential steps to be shown are:	The description of the process is precise (detailed), accurate throughout with only 1 or 2 minor errors in notation (that don't hide the essential concepts), complete, and follow-able. It matches the actual work shown and works effectively to find a solution to the given problem.
Developing **(Not Yet)**	Solution is incorrect due to errors that do not reflect an error with the targeted concept(s). The work/process shown is sketchy and/or contains errors in notation, but there is enough accuracy & detail shown that an expert can observe the basic concepts and direction. Essential steps to be shown are:	The description of the process matches the student's work, but there are enough errors in notation, omissions, and language usage that it is difficult, but possible to follow by an expert.
Emerging **(Not Yet)**	Solution is incorrect and there are major errors in the work, though one can see an awareness of the basic concepts by:	The description of the process is difficult to understand, contains numerous errors or omissions. It cannot be followed to a workable solution without a great deal of correction and or insertion of essential procedure – however, the reader can locate at least one logical and clear action to take that is appropriate and important to the concept.
Not Score-able – no attempt, unacceptable errors, or unrelated ramblings		

Analytic, Holistic, and Primary Trait Rubrics and Performance Checklists

1. **Analytic Rubrics** are rubrics that address the component parts or characteristics of a product, performance, or process separately. Within analytic rubrics, there is typically one criteria statement for each essential component part or characteristic; they tend to be given in list form, and each one is evaluated separately. For example an *excellent* Halloween treat in some neighborhoods is one that is ...

   - completely sealed,
   - liked by most kids,
   - bite size,
   - a standard, well recognized name brand, and
   - fresh.

   Examples would be bite-size, individually wrapped Snickers or Butterfingers.

   The "list format" used with most analytic rubrics facilitates making individual judgments. Analytic rubrics are best utilized when either it is important to evaluate or provide guidance with the individual criteria separately, or when detailed evaluative information is important and there is adequate time for detailed evaluation. Analytic rubrics, therefore, tend to be the approach of choice when in a teaching context.

2. **Holistic Rubrics** are rubrics that address the product, performance, or process as a whole, rather than addressing each component separately. Holistic rubrics include the essential criteria for a product, performance, or process, but they tend to be written in paragraph form. The paragraph format facilitates evaluating through overall judgments as to which "paragraph" (exemplary, proficient, developing, emerging, or not score-able) best describes the effort. For example, in many neighborhoods, excellent Halloween treats are treats that ...

   > are fresh, individually and completely sealed, small, well recognized national brands that kids tend to like. Examples include candies similar to the individually wrapped, bite-size Milky Way bars.

Holistic rubrics are best utilized when addressing major endeavors to avoid micro-management, or when quick scoring or impressions are necessary. Holistic rubrics tend to be the method of choice at the system level or for final, end of the term projects.

3. **Primary Trait Rubrics** can be either holistic or analytic – what distinguishes them is that they focus on a particular trait. For example, if one were to adjust a writing rubric so that it focused primarily on the characteristics of persuasive writing, then it would be referred to as a *primary trait rubric*. In order to reduce a great deal of duplication of efforts, many teachers, schools, and districts develop general rubrics, and then modify them to create a series of primary trait rubrics.

4. **Performance Checklists** Currently, there is a great deal of confusion regarding checklists. Often very powerful analytic rubrics are referred to as "only checklists." This is a reference that makes us uncomfortable, because to us, the format of a rubric does not determine whether it is a good rubric or not. A checklist is precisely what the word implies – a list of items to be checked-off as they are completed or observed during evaluation.

> We would like to reserve the word "rubric" to refer to those sets of statements that literally define quality – whether they are in a table, checklist, or paragraph form. Another way of looking at it is, "a checklist can be a rubric, and a rubric can be a checklist, but just because something is a checklist does not mean it is or is not a rubric." Many times for expediency's sake, we create a checklist of items that tend not to have quality levels attached to them. The following is an example of a performance checklist very similar to one developed in a pre-kindergarten classroom in the District of Columbia Public Schools. It is for a performance in which the students were to produce a book.

Our book needs to have …

____ a cover

____ a title page

____ an index

____ a table of contents

____ an introduction

_____ illustrations

_____ words

_____ page numbers

_____ a back cover

Though many refer to a performance checklist such as this as a rubric, we prefer to think of it as "Basic Requirements." The reason is that though everything on the list is an important component of a book, and it would be difficult to call a book a quality book if any of the listed items were missing, there is no specification of expected quality for each of the items. In our opinion, each of the items on the list is deserving of a rubric.

Another example of a checklist comes from a first grade classroom in Minnesota.

My letter has ...

_____ periods

_____ capitals

_____ five facts about bears

_____ signature

One last example of a checklist comes from the math classrooms of Spence Rogers and John Booth in the Glendale Union High School District in Glendale, Arizona. The checklist was referred to as the *Criteria for Credit* for homework assignments.

_____ name, date, period number, and assignment number in upper right-hand corner;

_____ stapled in upper left;

_____ all problems completed, or a space left for them;

_____ work shown; and

_____ work done in pencil.

Note that in the *Criteria for Credit* example, the performance checklist was treated as basic requirements to be met. When the conditions established in the list were met, then the quality of the mathematics in the assignment would be assessed.

With checklists, one must decide if the items listed are to be basic requirements to be checked off as they are completed to specified levels of quality that are established elsewhere, or if the items are to be scored based on some percentage, point, or weighting system with the understanding that all items do not need to be completed.

An example from outside of school for checklists is …

In order for cars to leave the factory, they must have, amongst other things, …

- four wheels,

- a brake system,

- a steering system,

- a frame,

- a body,

- seats,

- doors,

- instruments, and

- a means of propulsion.

This is not the rubric – this is the list of major automobile components that must be included in order for the car to be shipped from the factory. In actuality, each of these components must be built and installed according to a specific set of "standards" (which we call rubrics).

Another name for a performance checklist is *assessment list*. A benefit that can come from using the phrase *assessment list* is that the phrase clearly implies that whatever is in the list is important. However, a disadvantage is that the term assessment can either appear unnecessarily demanding or become overused and loose its strength. The phrase *assessment list* is also being used to refer to what we call a rubric frame (addressed later in this chapter).

In summary, performance checklists are valuable tools forlisting the basic requirements with respect to a product, performance, or process. In many cases, the checklist is all that is needed because the criteria for each item on this list are clearly understood by all. However, if the criteria for the items on the list are not well known, and if it is important that each item be done well, then it is necessary to create the needed rubrics.

5. **Rated Checklists** are the simplest rubrics to develop, most appropriate in many cases, and potential trouble when used for scoring student work that carries a lot of weight. A *rated checklist* is a list of important characteristics (much like a performance checklist), but with the addition of an undefined rating scale. An example for an oral presentation might look something like this …

Example Rated Checklist for an Oral Presentation

Criteria	Great 5 points	Good 4 points	Fair 3 points	Poor 2 points	Not Yet Inc.	Score
Content						
Organization						
Eye Contact						
Interest						
Visuals						
Delivery						
Total Score						
Percentage (Total Score divided by Total Possible (30))						

A corresponding grading scale may look something like this …

Total Points	Grade
27 - 30	A
24 - 26	B
21 - 23	C
18 - 20	D
0 - 18	I – Improve for a score and grade.

The rated checklist above (which many people use as a rubric) is relatively easy to understand and use on the surface. However, because there is no criteria to clarify what is meant by each level, scores produced on it are highly subjective and not defensible.

6. **Weighted Checklists** are a little more complicated to use than rated checklists, but still quite simple. Weighted checklists solve the problem that some components of a performance are more important than others, and therefore, do deserve more credit (weight) in a grade.

In a weighted checklist, each characteristic is assigned a number of points based on its relative worth. For example, if our previous example were weighted, it might look something like this ...

Example Weighted Checklist for an Oral Presentation

(Weighting is based on the desire to weight content as the most important. This might be the case in a subject-matter class. In a speech class, organization, delivery, and visuals would probably be weighted higher.)

Criteria	Great 100%	Good 80%	Fair 70%	Poor 60%	Not Yet Inc.	Score
Content	50	40	35	30	Inc.	
Organization	10	8	7	6	Inc.	
Interest	5	4	3	1	Inc.	
Visuals	10	8	7	6	Inc.	
Delivery	25	23	18	15	Inc.	
Total Score						
Percentage (Total Score divided by Total Possible (100)). (This example was developed so the numbers would be relatively easy.)						

3 NOTES OF CAUTION:

1. Sometimes in our efforts to be fair or to keep things simple, we have created situations that are hard to defend. For example, some teachers will assign points between those indicated in the scale – the problem is there is no criteria to defend this practice if the score is challenged. If you have the need to assign a score somewhere in-between two in your scale, consider going exactly midway – it's a little easier to defend than splitting hairs.

2. Because developing descriptions of what each level of a performance is like can be very difficult and time consuming, we sometimes use weighted/rated checklists. The more important the score is to a student's grade, the more likely our score will be challenged and not defensible if we

do not have clearly and precisely identified descriptors of each quality/score level (criteria).

3. We strongly recommend providing examples and descriptive phrases to support each identified criteria and level in any rubric or rated checklist.

Impact Criteria Focuses on the Results Achieved by the Performance

Traditionally, much of what we have asked of students has been evaluated or scored based on the quality of the components or steps and not on the *impact* or *effect* caused by their work. For example, persuasive essays tend to be evaluated on their technical qualities (which are certainly important) and not on their effectiveness at persuading a specified audience. Another way of saying this is that they tend to be evaluated on their technical strengths and not on their persuasiveness. We would like to suggest that in school the emphasis should be on varying levels of both – not just one or the other. It is important to note, however, that in the workplace, community, or home, effect or impact from one's efforts tend to be more important than the technical strengths of the component parts.

When rubrics take on an *impact* focus, they have criteria in them such as ...

- a majority of the audience was convinced by the supporting evidence;

- most of the students playing the educational game learned at least 80% of the facts being taught;

- most of the readers of the poem indicated in a survey that they were moved by it; and

- the parents and visitors to our horse, rock, snake, and ocean museums were able to answer most of the quiz questions.

We believe that it is the lack of impact criteria in expectations for students that has lead to so many business leaders making statements like, "Today's graduates sure know a lot – but they don't know how to use it, communicate it, or work with others to solve complex problems." As we talk about authentic assessment, it's not just important that the students learn real world information and skills, *it's also essential that they can use the information, skills, and concepts effectively.*

Static and Dynamic Criteria Address Fixed and Flexible Criteria

The word static implies fixed or not movable. Therefore, static criteria are those criteria that define fixed standards to be met or measured against. Examples of static criteria are ...

- The description is clear, precise, and accurate.
- The chart is accurate and easy to read.
- The painting clearly shows the conditions on the battle field during the revolutionary war.
- The height jumped exceeds five feet.
- The mile is run in less that 6 minutes.
- The sentences are punctuated correctly.

Static criteria are most appropriate when the level of one's ability to do something is that which is to be documented. For example, if we're looking for a student that can keyboard at a rate of eighty words per minute, then we will be looking for static criteria. However, if I'm more interested in someone who is continuously striving to improve in keyboarding, then static criteria will not provide me with the information I need.

Static criteria is essential in today's world, but it is certainly not sufficient. Typically, as students enter the world, the expectations put on them will be both static and dynamic. For example, if one were looking for a keyboarder, one would probably be interested in both the applicant's current keyboarding proficiency level and his/her proven growth potential.

Dynamic criteria define growth or improvement standards that are to be met or measured against. Examples of dynamic criteria are ...

- Keyboarding speed and accuracy are improving at a rate of 10% monthly.

- The height jumped is increasing at a consistent rate.

- The eye contact with the audience is becoming more natural with each presentation.

- The handwriting is consistently improving in legibility.

- The supporting arguments are becoming increasingly more convincing and relevant to the audience.

Static and dynamic criteria can be combined. For example, "The punctuation does not detract from the reader's ability to understand the message, and it shows steady improvement from previous writings."

It is our opinion that in the process of teaching and assessing learning, both static and dynamic criteria are essential. We believe there should be clear expectations as to what is a quality level of performance. We also believe it is equally important to establish and monitor clear expectations for improvement.

Reflection Questions

1. Why are impact criteria so important for student performances?

2. What's one way you can enhance student learning and performance by using impact criteria?

3. What is one way you can expand your use of dynamic criteria to improve the quality of performance from all students?

4. How are both static and dynamic criteria a part of everyday out-of-school, expectations?

A Four Level Rubric for Rubrics

What follows is a four level rubric for rubrics that is based on the desired impact from a rubric — referred to as The Quality Definition.

A "Quality" Definition for a Rubric: We will know that our rubric is quality when it is easily understood and used effectively as either …

- a guidance tool to consistently produce products, performances, and processes at desired levels of quality/standards while encouraging and allowing continuous improvement and creativity; or
- an evaluation tool to produce consistent evaluations of products, performances, and processes across events and evaluators.

Reflection Question

1. How can you use the following Rubric's Rubric to help you use rubrics more effectively?

A Rubric's Rubric

Exemplary Rubrics *are consistently effective for accurate and thorough evaluations and/or guidance.*	The rubric is … ■ based on diverse, exemplary models of a clearly identified product, performance, or process, its intended purpose or impact, and the embedded targeted learning. ■ accompanied by 3 or more diverse, aligned examples for each level. ■ composed of clear, precise, thorough & accurate criteria to define each quality level. ■ each identified criteria for the exemplary level is accurately addressed for each level. ■ totally understood and easily used by all involved. ■ promoting and not stifling or penalizing of creative approaches.
Acceptable Rubrics *are mostly effective for accurate and thorough evaluations and/or guidance.*	The rubric is … ■ based on at least one exemplary model of a clearly identified product, performance, or process, its intended purpose or impact, and the embedded targeted learning. ■ accompanied by at least one aligned example for each level. ■ composed of clear, thorough & accurate criteria to define each quality level. ■ the most defining identified criteria for the exemplary level is addressed for each level. ■ understood by all involved. ■ not stifling or penalizing of creative approaches.
Developing Rubrics *are marginally and inconsistently effective for evaluations and/or guidance.*	The rubric is … ■ based on an example of a clearly identified product, performance, or process, its intended purpose or impact, and the embedded targeted learning. ■ accompanied by an example aligned with the highest level. ■ composed of components for criteria with insufficient quality definition for the presented quality levels. ■ the defining criteria for the exemplary level is not addressed for each level. ■ understood by most involved. ■ penalizing of creative approaches.
Emerging Rubrics *are consistently ineffective for evaluations and/or guidance.*	The rubric is … ■ based on a vaguely identified product, performance, or process. ■ not accompanied by clarifying examples. ■ based on hopes and beliefs. ■ there is very little consistency with criteria from level to level. ■ understood by some students at best. ■ stifling or penalizing of creative approaches.

Rubrics Distinguish Between Identifiable Quality Levels Within Performances

The highest quality levels within a rubric should at least promote and/or accept creative approaches to achieving the results expected of an exemplary performance. In fact, paraphrasing what we once heard Iris Mcginnis, formerly from the Anoka-Hennepin District and the Minnesota Department of Education, say in a workshop, "Define the heck out of the second level from the top as excellent quality, and let the top level be all of that and more." For another perspective, John Booth of the Glendale Union High School District in Arizona has said, "The top level of a district assessment rubric should be more than an 'A,' and the second level should be about what one would normally expect an 'A' to be." With such high expectations, an issue that needs to be resolved is how to label the levels of a rubric.

There is no magic set of perfect labels for quality levels. However, it is important to select labels that show a logical sequence and appropriate differentiation between levels. Also, it is our belief that the labels should denote positive, validating perspectives toward the work and the students at the different levels, while at the same time, clearly denoting the quality differences accurately.

The following lists of possible labels for the different quality levels of a rubric are offered to facilitate efforts in designing and using rubrics.

Common Labels for the Top Quality Level of a Rubric

We recommend that the top level of a rubric define superior work that is what one might traditionally say is at the very minimum "A" work. Where points are being used, efforts fitting this level need to be receiving points that equate to an "A."

> Advanced
>
> Distinguished
>
> Exceeds Expectations
>
> Exceeds Standards
>
> Excellent

Exceptional

Exemplary

Expert

Exquisite

Fantastic

Grand

Great

Highly Successful

Impressive

Magnificent

Outstanding

Professional

Remarkable

Star Performance

Super

Superb

Superior

Topnotch

Wonderful

World Class

Common Labels Second Highest Quality Level

We recommend that the second level of a rubric define high quality, but not superior, work – what one might traditionally say is at the level of a high "B." Where points are being used, efforts fitting this level need to be receiving points that equate to the bottom level of an "A" or the top to mid level of a "B."

Accomplished

Competent

Credible

Creditable

Effective

Efficient

Excellent

Masterful

Meets Expectations

Meets Standards

Polished

Proficient

Professional

Skilled

Successful

Talented

Common Labels for the Third Highest Quality Level

The third level of a rubric needs to define mediocre quality work that is at what one might traditionally say is at the level of a "C" or a high "D." Where points are being used, efforts fitting this level need to be receiving points that equate to the mid level of a "C" at best or the top to mid level of a "D." Work at this level would tend not to be acceptable in the world outside of school. Therefore, when not scoring and documenting initial efforts but coaching to and expecting quality work, this level of a rubric will tend not to have points associated with it. In these circumstances, the work is considered incomplete.

Acceptable

Adequate

Admissible

Amateur

Apprentice

Approaching Expectations

Approaching Standards

Developing

Passable

Presentable

Respectable

Satisfactory

Common Labels for the Fourth Highest Quality Level

We recommend that the fourth level of a rubric define weak work – what one might traditionally say is at the level of a "D" or a "F," but that definitely shows evidence of effort and some beginning levels of understanding. Where points are being used because of scoring and documenting, efforts fitting this level need to be receiving points that equate to the mid level of a "D" at best or the top to mid level of an "F." Work at this level would not to be acceptable in the world outside of school. Therefore, when not scoring and documenting initial efforts but coaching to and expecting quality work, this level of a rubric will not have points associated with it. In these circumstances, the work is considered incomplete.

> Awareness
>
> Beneath Expectations
>
> Beneath Standards
>
> Developing
>
> Discovering
>
> Emerging
>
> Incomplete
>
> Intermediate
>
> Needs Improvement
>
> Needs Work
>
> Neophyte
>
> Not-Yet
>
> Novice
>
> Rookie
>
> Tenderfoot

Common Labels for the Lowest Quality Level

We recommend that the lowest level of a rubric define weak work – what one might traditionally say shows no attempt, total misunderstanding of the task, major misconceptions, or acts of insubordination. Where points are being used because of scoring and documenting, efforts fitting this level need to not receive points. Besides the fact that work at this level would be totally unacceptable in the world outside of school, it does not show anything to which points could be assigned as fair measure of the targeted knowledge or skills. It is therefore, considered to be "not score-able."

Incomplete

Needs Improvement

Needs Work

No Attempt

Not Score-able

Not Started

Not Yet

An 8 Step Process for Developing Rubrics

What follows is an 8 step process that is effective for developing rubrics.

Step 1:

Determine precisely the product, process, or performance for which the rubric is to be written. Be certain that the primary learning target is included in this determination. Examples include …

- summary of a technical article regarding …;
- maps of …;
- video tape of …;
- persuasive presentation about …;
- oral presentation about …;
- debate regarding …;
- teaching of …;

Step 2:

Determine the intended audience/users for/of the rubric and whether the rubric will be used primarily for coaching or scoring. Examples include …

- students - coaching;
- expert evaluators - scoring;

- parents - (validating/celebrating);

- teacher - scoring; or

- all of the above - coaching and scoring.

Step 3:

Determine the intended purpose, impact, effect, and/or result that is expected to be apparent as a result of the product, performance, or process. This can be done by answering the following question, "If this ___ were done excellently, what would we observe (hear, see, feel, …) Examples include …

- specific presentation skills … (component emphasis);

- visitors to the museum actually learning the information … (impact emphasis);

- the members of the panel being persuaded as a result of … (impact emphasis);

- the members of the community reporting they have adequate and fair information because of the voters' guide and that they believe it was very professionally done (impact and component emphasis); and

- the students showing sound mathematical reasoning … (component emphasis).

Step 4:

Obtain three exemplars (models of the highest expected quality level) and several examples that demonstrate unacceptable characteristics.

Step 5:

Determine what the product, performance, or process should look, sound, or feel like when it is really good by determining the three to five major characteristics (criteria) that the exemplars have in common. Study the unacceptable examples to help refine the exemplary criteria. Strive to identify the qualitative characteristics that determine the exemplary quality levels for each criteria. When completed, include anchors to support the rubric. For example, excellent eye contact might be described as "natural and supportive eye contact throughout the presentation."

Step 6:

Develop the unacceptable quality description for each criteria by modifying/negating each exemplary criteria appropriately.

Step 7:

Develop and label appropriately any desired intermediate quality levels for each criteria. Make modifications throughout the levels as clarity develops. (Be certain to include anchors for each level developed.)

Step 8:

Determine common errors to avoid and other characteristics that would render the rubric target not-score-able.

A Process for Developing Rubrics from Samples of Student Work

Another approach to developing a rubric for a given product, performance, or process is to identify the characteristics that distinguish varying quality levels of existing examples of student work.

It is very difficult to develop an effective rubric before you have examples of student work on which to base your decisions. That doesn't mean that a rubric shouldn't be developed until after the fact. It simply means, that before student work is available, an effective rubric will be a "best professional guess" to be fine tuned as examples become available. (Quite often excellent examples to support rubric development can be obtained from the work produced by students that are one grade level above.) What follows is an 8 step process based on developing rubrics based on examples of student work.

Step 1:

In advance, do the best job you can in clarifying the quality expectations for the targeted product, performance, or process.

Step 2:

Using the criteria you have previously identified (perhaps through the eight step process presented in the previous section), sort the examples of student work into the number of different quality levels you can discern and describe in clear and precise language.

Step 3:

For the exemplary examples, determine the three to five quality characteristics (criteria) they have in common. Develop the clearest statements you can for each one. (Example: natural and supportive eye contact equally distributed for each member of the audience.)

Step 4:

For each characteristic identified in step 3, determine (by comparison to the poorest, but score-able, student work), the statements that describe the lowest score-able, quality levels. (Example: only made occasional eye contact with a very small part of the audience.)

Step 5:

Using clear and precise language, describe each identified criteria quality level remaining for each characteristic. For example, excellent eye contact might be described as "natural and supportive eye contact throughout the presentation."

Step 6:

Double check to be certain that each characteristic identified at the top level is addressed for each level of the rubric.

Also, Check to be certain that your criteria statements are not so "compound" that it is difficult to score. For example, when a criteria statement says, "visuals are clear, easy to see from the back, well organized, colorful, and neat," what do you do if one adjective isn't accurate. In other words, avoid strings of qualifying traits; they create scoring nightmares.

Step 7:

Double check your completed rubric against the samples of student work, and refine as necessary.

Step 8:

Preserve and display examples (anchors) for each quality level of the rubric.

Essential Targets for Rubric Criteria

Rubrics that are to be used with student work should address in some way the following criteria areas. Following this section is an extensive set of qualitative and quantitative terms that can be used with the *criteria* terms listed below to develop the statements for the various quality levels included in a rubric.

When developing criteria, the first consideration is what is the noun (for products and parts of performances) or verb (for processes, skills, and parts of performances) that distinguishes the criteria area. For example, is it the …

argument	staging
computations	example
appearance	defense
vocabulary	conclusion
support	process shown
sketching	eye contact
diagram	chart
graph	voice
evidence	

The developed criteria statement will then be the appropriate combination of the noun (or verb) with adjectives (or adverbs). For example …

- an excellent defense for a position is one that is accurate, detailed, relevant, and convincing;

- an acceptable defense for a position is one that is accurate, somewhat relevant, and convincing;

- a "work in development" defense for a position is one that is accurate, but too superficial or irrelevant to be convincing; and

- a "bare beginning" defense for a position is one that is inaccurate and/or irrelevant, and certainly not convincing.

Content - The subject matter included as part of the student work should be expected to be of high quality. The following terms are useful in clarifying content expectations ...

- accurate
- valid
- precise
- deep
- broad
- relevant
- insightful
- supported/justified
- logical
- clear/understandable
- apt
- focused
- thorough

Form - What the students produce should be done in such a way that it has quality form. The following terms are useful in clarifying form expectations ...

- organized
- effective style for audience and purpose
- focused
- correct mechanics/usage
- logical/appropriate sequence

Impact - When the students' work is expected to have an impact (be used to cause some effect or result), the performance is closer to authentic in terms of accountability. An impact expectation also helps to maintain interest or motivation on the part of the students. The following terms are useful in clarifying impact expectations ...

- problem solved
- persuasive/convincing

- moving
- others learned
- message conveyed
- successful/effective/efficient application
- informing
- engaging
- winning
- interesting

Process - Employers and universities are both stressing the importance of students learning process in addition to subject matter alone. The following items are useful in clarifying process expectations ...

- effective
- efficient
- logical
- fluent
- supported/justified
- correct procedures
- correct use of skills
- purposeful
- thoughtful
- correct
- responsive

Appearance and Presentation - As students advance in school and also advance in their outside of school endeavors, it becomes increasingly important that their work have a quality, "professional" look. The following items are useful in clarifying appearance and presentation expectations ...

- adheres to professional standards
- demonstrates craftsmanship
- aligns with "outside-of-school" role expectations
- utilizes highest quality materials
- polished, elegant, smooth, genuine, authentic, and fluent

Reflection Question

1. How can you be certain your rubric addresses what's really important?

Qualitative and Quantitative Terms—A Mini Thesaurus for Rubrics

The following is offered to facilitate the selection of appropriate qualitative terms. These terms are *grouped by general category, and they are not necessarily synonymous*. It is important to remember that without anchors, these terms can convey very different messages to different people. (For a more extensive thesaurus of rubric terms, refer to *The Rubric Thesaurus* (Peak Learning Systems, 1997).

Accurate

exact, correct, precise, close, faithful, conforms, in accordance, unerring, right, true, truthful, authentic, sound, valid, flawless, faultless

Adequate

suitable, fit, fitting, commensurate, appropriate, sufficient, enough, ample, satisfactory, competent, presentable, admissible, passable, tolerable, acceptable, all right, allowable, fair, mediocre, average

Appropriate

suitable, fitting, proper, fit, congruous, apt, pertinent, applicable, relevant, germane, to the point

Apt

appropriate, proper, becoming, felicitous, suitable, congruent, fitting, well-adapted, relevant, pertinent

Articulate

clear, lucid, intelligible, understandable, comprehensible, eloquent, well-spoken, fluent, graceful, congruous

Attractive

pleasing, nice looking, pretty, beautiful, appealing, enchanting, enticing, alluring, delightful, pleasant, lovely, stunning, striking, handsome, tasteful, elegant, picturesque, exquisite

Big

colossal, gigantic, monstrous, enormous, huge, large, jumbo, gargantuan, giant, mountainous, towering, vast, immense, massive

Bold

courageous, daring, unafraid, fearless, presumptuous

Bright

shining, light, radiant, shiny, glossy, luminous, clever, intelligent, smart, resourceful, inventive

Broad

comprehensive, inclusive, all-inclusive, composite, exhaustive, extensive, all-embracing, general, universal, vast, far reaching

Clear/Understandable

defined, distinct, discernible, recognizable, well-defined, well-marked, visible, vivid, graphic, unhidden, undis-guised, unconcealed, perceptible, distinguishable, audible, hearable, articulate, enunciated, comprehensible, ascertainable, intelligible, legible, coherent, unconfused, evident, plain, obvious, apparent, unmistakable, unques-tionable, indisputable, conclusive, transparent

Colorful

multi-colored, variegated, kaleidoscopic

Considerate

kind, caring, sensitive, thoughtful, compassionate, concerned, mindful, benevolent, beneficent, friendly, gracious, obliging, patient, sympathetic, tender, accom-modating, welcoming, valuing, loving

Convincing/Persuasive

incontestable, indisputable, conclusive, unmistakable, compelling, plausible, credible, believable, logical, sound, valid, authoritative, well supported

Correct

accurate, exact, precise, close, unerring, on target, on the mark, on the money, on the button, factual, actual, literal, true, true to life, flawless, perfect, errorless, proper, suitable, fitting, appropriate

Effective

results getting, efficacious, capable, competent, efficient, adequate, sufficient, fit, functioning, useful, operative, practical

Efficient

efficacious, effectual, operative, causative, productive, generative

Eloquent

articulate, well spoken, poetic, graceful, oratorical, smooth

Excellent

impressive, distinguished, exceptional, exemplary, exquisite, fantastic, first rate, great, magnificent, marvelous, meritorious, outstanding, professional, remarkable, super, superb, superior, wonderful, accomplished, admirable, competent, credible, effective, efficient, laudable, masterful, meets or exceeds expectations or standards, polished, proficient

Exciting

lively, moving, impressive, stimulating, invigorating, spirited, enthusiastic, provocative, agitating, moving, inspiring, riveting, interesting, thrilling, delighting, exhilarating

Expressive

cogent, telling, forceful, dynamic, compelling, interesting, exciting, succinct, emphatic, vivid, impassioned, revealing

Fluent

eloquent, articulate, well-spoken, smooth, graceful, fluid, smooth-sounding, uninterrupted, graceful, effortless

Focused

on the mark, centered, converged, on target, pertinent, to the point, directly applicable, well suited

Frequently

often, almost always, repeatedly, consistently, customarily, ordinarily, usually, regularly, commonly, usually, generally

Good

satisfactory, okay, acceptable, tolerable, presentable, admissible, all right, virtuous, moral, honorable, wholesome

Important

consequential, significant, noteworthy, substantial, valuable, imperative, influential, eminent, distinguished

Infrequently

seldom, rarely, almost never, very rarely, scarcely, occasionally, rare, infrequent, almost never

Insightful

intuitive, perceptive, intelligent, astute, profound

Interesting

engaging, engrossing, absorbing, riveting, provocative, stimulating, amusing, entertaining, exciting, inviting, fascinating, captivating

Justified/Supported/documented

defended, supported, evidenced, sustained, bolstered, backed, proved, substantiated

Logical

deductive, inductive, inferential, reasonable, rationale, sound, sensible

Moving

convincing, persuasive, impressive, inspiring, inspirational, touching

Organized

systematized, arranged, ordered, coordinated, categorized, planned, well formatted, well framed, connected

Persuasive/Convincing

incontestable, indisputable, compelling, believable, logical, sound, irresistible

Plain

ordinary, simple, commonplace, monotonous, uninteresting

Powerful

potent, vigorous, dynamic, strong, aggressive, assertive, forceful

Precise

explicit, detailed, distinct, clear, exact, accurate, meticulous

Relevant

pertinent, to the point, applicable, congruous, apt, appropriate

Reliable

dependable, trustworthy, unfailing, infallible, well founded

Simple

easy, effortless, basic, rudimentary

Small

tiny, little, petite, microscopic, teeny, mini, midget, miniature, minuscule

Superficial

shallow, superfluous, meaningless, insignificant, unimportant

Valid

sound, logical, well-grounded, well-founded, reasonable

Valuable

important, useful, beneficial, helpful, advantageous, memorable, cherished, favorite, valued, precious

Frame Rubrics to Avoid Recreating Wheels

A rubric frame is a set of generic criteria for a particular type of product, performance, or process that needs to be present no matter what the context for the expectation or the developmental level of the students. These generic criteria can then be easily "contextualized" by adding the specifics for the given situation.

The concept of framing a rubric is very similar to what the automobile and construction industries have been doing for years. In order to reduce the expenditure of excess time, money, energy, and other resources, they design, develop, and refine a frame until it is "solid" for its intended purpose. Then they use that frame over and over again in vehicles or homes that really appear quite different because of how they are "finished" or "contextualized."

As educators, we can take advantage of this "frame" approach to improve the efficiency and effectiveness of our efforts. For example, students are being expected to provided explanations virtually across all of education. The process and criteria for a good explanation are virtually the same everywhere; what varies is the content being explained, the difficulty of the content with respect to the assumed background of the audience, and the context in which the explanation is to occur. A good explanation, no matter what it is an explanation of, isn't done until it has effectively conveyed or created understanding in others. This implies that clarifying what a good explanation is requires identifying the typical, identifiable characteristics of a good explanation. The content and context specifics can be identified as they are needed in specific situations.

Once the essential common characteristics of good explanations have been identified, they can be used over and over again as the "backbone or frame" when developing rubrics involving the explanation of anything in any context. The details will vary, the frame remains constant. This content and context customizing takes place from teacher to teacher, grade level to grade level, or discipline to discipline depending on the intended use for the rubric.

For example, when students are expected to teach one another "things," what they teach and in what context are different in almost every situation. How difficult what they're teaching is to the learners with their backgrounds and learning needs varies every time. But, barring technique and style differences, there are basic essential characteristics of "effective teaching" that are easily identified, taught, and enhanced to meet each situation. To determine these essential characteristics, we need to first determine what the experts say "to teach" means. "According to many dictionaries, to teach is to convey to others knowledge or skills that you have and the learners do not have."

Note that the expert definition makes no reference as to how it is to occur, but it does imply the teacher isn't done teaching until the learner has learned. Therefore, a simplified generic rubric frame might look something like the example rubric frame on page 235.

This example shows a recurring pattern in a rubric frame in that it:

- starts by identifying the desired quality result/definition as supported by experts;

- includes the essential components and excludes reference to particular situations or approaches;

- articulates in a generic way very high standards through the use of definitive language tied to desired effect of each component; and

- comes full circle to be certain that the beginning determination of what constitutes quality is checked for and met.

The example rubric frame for "teaching" can be expanded to include varying quality levels based on expected variations in effectiveness and/or efficiency for each main component.

Framing a rubric is very advantageous in that it

- ultimately will save a tremendous amount of development time;

- provides consistency across the disciplines and grade levels; and

- reduces instructional time as students become expert in process and essential components of products, performances, and processes.

However, the process does surface a very difficult question. "Where is it desirable to put the greatest emphasis? Do we focus on the means to the end, or on an effort effectively achieving the desired or intended result?" The answer is dependent on "the what" the performance is designed to be teaching and/or assessing.

Reflection Question

1. What could be the benefit(s) of developing Rubric Frames? To you? To students? To a school? To a district?

Rubric Frame

EXAMPLE RUBRIC FRAME FOR THE PROCESS OF TEACHING

Assessment Focus

Teaching

Quality Definition

Quality Teaching results (by expert definition) in knowledge or skills being conveyed to others.

Essential Quality Criteria

To *Teach* with quality it is necessary to ...

- determine what it is that the learners are expected to know or be able to do with clarity, precision, and accuracy (know what they have to learn);

- determine what the learners will need to do to provide adequate evidence that they have learned what they were to learn;

- develop an instruction plan with appropriate materials and strategies that are aligned with the desired learning and matched with the teacher's instructional skills and the learners' background, learning needs, and levels;

- provide the planned instruction while checking for effectiveness and making modifications as necessary to maintain learning progress; and

- request and gather the evidence that the learner does know or can do what has been taught.

Rubric Framing - The Process

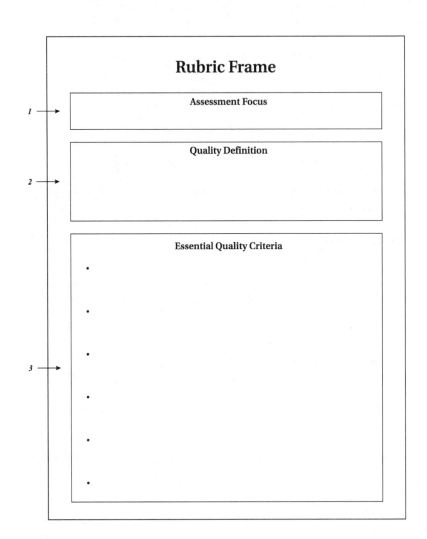

The following is an explanation of how to complete the rubric framing template. It is important to recognize that framing a rubric does only that. The process is designed to produce the essential criteria that are then developed into any desired number of quality levels for the rubric.

Step 1:

Clearly identify the targeted generic product, performance, or process.

See Appendix A for numerous format ideas for performance tasks including mostly products and performances, along with a few processes. These ideas are often referred to as "dissemination vehicles."

Example products: short stories, feature stories, concept maps, editorials, and scientific investigation reports.

Example performances: persuasive presentation, informative presentation, role play, and dramatic reading.

Example processes: teaching, debating, problem solving, and consensus building.

Step 2:

Clearly identify an agreed upon quality definition for the targeted product, performance, or process. This will typically be tied to its intended use/effect/impact. It will also be used as the base for the criteria frame.

Example: Present – to bring to the notice of, or into the presence of someone.

Example: Teach – to convey to others knowledge or skills that you possess.

Step 3:

Through careful analysis, determine those components/ criteria (typically 3 - 5) that are necessary and sufficient for the targeted product, performance, or process to be considered quality.

Note: The last component brings the rubric frame full circle – expecting the defining quality definition to be met.

The 8 step rubric development process explained earlier in this chapter can greatly help with this step.

Step 4:

Evaluate and refine the frame with respect to:

- clarity (Is it easily understood?);

- precision (Does it have adequate detail and examples?);

- accuracy (Are the statements accurate?);

- breadth (Does it cover the bases?);

- depth (Does it address the real issues deeply enough to be effective?); and

- results orientation. (Does it come full circle and expect the quality definition?)

Step 5:

Develop the completed rubric as needed.

- Use the rubric frame as the base to add the specific content and contextual demands determined by a particular targeted product, performance, or process.

- Use examples of actual, exemplary student work to be certain of expectations.

- Develop varying quality levels as appropriate for each component.

- Check for use of student language.

- Use your finished rubric as your map to guide the students through a process of co-developing the final rubric with you.

Rubric Frame

Assessment Focus

Quality Definition

Essential Quality Criteria
 ■ ■   ■   ■   ■

14 Common Rubric Errors

The following represents the common errors that are made when developing rubrics.

1. Vague terms *without clarifying examples.*

   Examples: Adjectives like nice, good, many, more, and appropriate without actual examples to clarify.

2. Negatively stated criteria.

   Example: Inadequate eye contact.

3. Not observable criteria – including criteria that are attitudinal, perspectives, beliefs, values, or states of mind.

   Examples: appreciate, value, believe, and enjoy.

4. Criteria that are not relevant or more appropriately addressed elsewhere – see "Basic Requirements."

   Example: professional attire in a rubric for a classroom oral presentation (If this type of expectation is to be stated, separate it from the rubric for the presentation.)

5. Criteria that are not, or can not be required/expected.

   Example: A criteria that states persuasion will occur from a persuasive essay if, in fact, it won't or isn't truly required.

   A standard that states a value, belief, state of mind, or perspective that is not enforceable or truly assessable.

6. Missing performance components that are essential for high quality.

   Example: excluding criteria such as "checking for understanding" in a rubric addressing teaching

7. Too many and/or insignificant components addressed by the rubric.

   Example: Your paper must have between 300 and 500 words; be word processed; be double spaced; provide three or more relevant examples; be free of spelling errors; etcetera.

   More than five standards for any particular effort, or major phase of one, diminish the value of each. Include these expectations on a list of basic requirements so the rubric can focus on the true qualitative criteria.

8. Lack of supporting examples or models.

    Example: The old adage "A picture is worth a thousand words" continues to provide valuable guidance. In most cases, text within a rubric will not consistently deliver the message intended. If a rubric requires organization of possible causes of a given situation, provide at least one example (three are preferable) of a good organizational system in a similar but different context.

9. Criteria NOT based on actual examples of the targeted effort.

    Examples: When we develop a rubric without basing it on actual examples we are studying or have observed, we tend to exclude essential criteria or develop criteria that are not appropriate for the task or the students.

10. Not matched to the developmental level of students.

    Example: Expecting young children to perform a function they are not developmentally capable of doing.

    Limiting criteria and expected quality levels to a level that is not challenging to the students.

11. Not co-developed by students.

    Example: A teacher developing a rubric by him/herself for a classroom project and then just giving it to the students expecting high levels of commitment and understanding. People tend to hit the targets they set for themselves because they are more committed to them and they understand them better.

12. More quality levels than can be supported by the intended use, nature of the standard, or beyond what the developers can articulate effectively.

    Examples: If one were developing electrical wall outlets, it would be ludicrous to define more quality levels for safety than one.

    In early developmental stages in rubric development we tend to focus more on numerical criteria distinctions as opposed to qualitative distinctions which are often more accurate or appropriate as distinctions (e.g. In real life situations, is support for an argument evaluated more by the number of supporting statements or by how convincing the supporting statements are?)

13. Fewer quality levels than necessary or appropriate for the intended use or nature of the standard.

Example: Complex skills like singing and drawing need to be supported by definitions of quality levels and examples of typical stages people will go through in the development of those skills.

14. Criteria not consistent with expert opinion.

Example: The criteria for explain and describe should be considerably different based on how most dictionaries define both terms, however, many of us use them interchangeably in the classroom because of expediency. Relevance for the learners, reduced bias from the developers, rigor of the content, and accuracy of language and instruction are all enhanced by checking with the "experts."

Scoring and Grading with Rubrics

Once the rubric is developed, it is important to determine how the criteria are to be weighted. Seldom are all the criteria considered to be of equal value.

It is also important to determine whether or not all quality levels are eligible for earning points. If one is scoring a district, school, or system level assessment, scores are almost always given for each identified quality level. However, many classroom teachers will insist the work within all or some criteria must at least be at the level of the second or third highest level to be considered score-able. Efforts below the score-able levels are considered to be "not yet," and the students are expected to refine the effort until it reaches a score-able level.

There are a number of options for addressing the weighting issue, but they can all be facilitated by creating a micro rubric form to be duplicated so that each student's scores can be recorded. Refer to the example below in which the scores shown reflect the amount available and the blank cells are for recording the student's score. An option is to circle or hi-lite the student's scores for each criteria. Scores can be reported separately for each criteria or can be totaled.

The example shown shows arbitrarily selected point values. It is important to be certain the point distribution reflects the appropriate weighting and potential "report card" grading situation. For example, if 4 equates to 100% (or an "A"), then 3 equates to 75% which is a "C" in most systems. This range is probably too broad for most classroom situations.

Below is a sample of a scoring form that can easily be used when employing rubrics for evaluation. With this form the scorer can either circle the *one score* for each criteria or record it in the empty space to the right. The scores for each criteria can either be added for a total score, or recorded separately.

Student's Name:	Gayle Dalton	Date:
Assessment/Unit:	Romeo & Juliet	
Student Total Score:	13 out of 24	

Weight Factor →	Criteria 1 1x		Criteria 2 2x		Criteria 3x	
Exemplary	4	**4**	8		12	
Competent	3		6	**6**	9	
Developing	2		4		6	
Emerging	1		2		3	**3**
Not Score-able	no points or score earned					

A slight variation that is based on a commitment to high expectations for all students considers the bottom two quality levels for each criteria to be "Not Yet" or "Incomplete"

For additional information on scoring, refer to the sections titled *Rated Checklists* and *Weighted Checklists* earlier in this chapter.

Student's Name:	Fred Jones	Date:
Assessment/Unit:	Romeo & Juliet	
Student Total Score:	Incomplete	

Weight Factor →	Criteria 1 1x		Criteria 2 2x		Criteria 3x	
Exemplary	4		8		12	**12**
Competent	3	**3**	6		9	
Developing	IC		IC	**IC**	IC	
Emerging	IC		IC		IC	
Not Score-able	no points or score earned					

Example Rubrics, Checklists, and Rubric Frames

The example rubrics that follow are shared as just that. Without the artifacts, or opportunities to observe the level of understanding, commitment, or effects, the rubrics cannot be adequately judged, nor should they be. We can all be purists, and say things in ways that work better for us, but, in our opinion, that is not the measure of quality. The measure of quality in any endeavor is the level of commitment to continuous improvement.

We believe in, and continuously strive to model, continuous improvement. Therefore, the issue is, do the rubrics result in better work, engagement, involvement, and learning by all associated with them, and are they seen as steps along a pathway to even higher performance by everyone?

Waiting to develop and share only perfect rubrics is like waiting to build the perfect computer. Computers just keep getting better, and so do the rubrics people are developing. Examine the numerous real-life examples shared here and ask yourself, "What or how can I learn from them?"

We would like to thank all those teachers who have shared their efforts.

A NOTE OF CAUTION: In classroom situations, anchors are essential to support the rubrics—even though they are not included in this section.

Reflection Question

1. What ideas can you use from the following examples?

5 Primary Classroom Rubrics about Quality

The following five rubrics are from the primary classroom of Jan Hicks, in Lockport, New York. They were developed by the students. In order to provide parallel language, they have been slightly modified from the form in which they appeared on the classroom wall.

In all these first grade examples, notice the students' last criteria makes the rubric an impact rubric. Without their last criteria, the rubrics would be lists of good behaviors but not necessarily effective at addressing the real issues.

Quality Readers

- Read loudly
- Sound out words
- Skip words and read other words in the sentence
- Ask a friend in a quiet voice
- Look in a dictionary or a word book for a word
- Understand what they read

Quality Listeners

- Look at the speaker
- Stay quiet
- Try to sit still
- Listen
- Don't fool around
- Don't talk
- Show understanding

Quality Speakers

- Speak in loud voices so everyone can hear
- Look at the audience
- Are understood

Quality Writers

- Make neat letters
- Make letters sit on the line
- Make words sit on the line
- Make spaces between words
- Do capitals and periods right
- Write so others understand

Quality Workers

- Are helpful
- Take turns
- Work together
- Solve problems in a nice way
- Do quality work

More Sample Rubrics, Checklists, and Rubric Frames

The following sample rubrics, checklists, and rubric frames are from various classrooms and various grade levels. Some were developed by teachers and some by students and teachers working together.

Rubric for *A Note to a Friend* (Specific Content and Anchors Need to be Provided)

	Content Accuracy	Description Thoroughness & Clarity	Example Complexity	Visual Display	Mechanics
Exemplary 5 points	The content is free of any math errors.	Description is logical, accurate, well organized, & very thorough - easy to understand.	The complexity & depth of the examples exceeds the standards established for the assignment.	It is very easily read & interpreted due to lay out, neatness and use of color and shading. Graphics are accurate.	Criteria for credit met.
Competent 4 points	The content contains only one or two inconsequential errors - all essential skills and concepts are apparent.	Description is mostly logical, accurate, organized - it is complete but not thorough - understandable to a pro.	The complexity & depth of the examples meets the standards established for the assignment.	It is interpretable due to lay out, neatness and use of color and shading. Graphics are mostly accurate (only inconsequential errors.)	
Developing Incomplete	A major math conceptual error is present, but much is correct and shows "essential" understanding.	Description is incomplete, illogical, inaccurate, and/or unorganized enough to show limited understanding - clarified with discussion.	The complexity & depth of the examples meets the most common and essential standards established for the assignment.	It is difficult but possible to interpret. Graphics are mostly accurate (only inconsequential errors.)	
Emerging Incomplete	Major math conceptual errors exist. Awareness only is apparent.	Description is very flawed and not truly follow-able.	Standards not met.	Nearly impossible to locate and interpret essential concepts.	Criteria for credit not met.
Not Score-able		No attempt or totally incomprehensible			

This rubric was developed by Jim Ludington and Spence Rogers for use in Jim's classroom at Gananda High School.

Problem Solving Rubric – (Content & Context Specifics Need Identification With Anchors)

PAGE 1 OF 2

	Problem Clarification	Constraint Identification	Solution	Evaluation	Recommendation
Great	The problem is clarified to adequate depth and breadth. All relevant known information is gathered and organized in a logical fashion. Information needed for solution is completely determined with accuracy, depth, and breadth.	All relevant obstacles and constraints are accurately and thoroughly determined and weighted as to their relative importance in the situation to a level that shows an in-depth understanding of the problem.	Plausible & appealing alternative solutions to the problem are determined that address the constraints and obstacles as completely as possible.	The solutions are exhaustively tried/tested and evaluated against all the obstacles and constraints as they are weighted to determine the solutions utility and attractiveness.	Presents a recommended solution and provides thorough rationale for it. The recommendation is based on the problem and all the obstacles and constraints - shows a thorough understanding of the situation and the problem solving process.
Good	The problem is clarified to adequate depth and breadth. The important relevant known information is gathered and organized in a workable fashion. The most important information needed for solution is determined with accuracy, depth, and breadth.	Important, relevant obstacles and constraints are accurately and thoroughly determined and weighted as to their relative importance in the situation. Weighting shows some lack of thorough understanding of the situation and constraints.	Plausible alternative solutions to the problem are determined that address the important constraints and obstacles in the problem as completely as possible.	The solutions are tried/tested and evaluated against all the obstacles and constraints as they are weighted to determine the solutions usability.	Presents a recommended solution but provides incomplete, but fairly convincing rationale for it – addresses accurately most of the obstacles and constraints. Shows a functioning understanding of the situation and the problem solving process.

Problem Solving Rubric – (Content & Context Specifics Need Identification With Anchors)

PAGE 2 OF 2

Developing	The problem is only superficially clarified. Some important relevant known information is gathered. Information is poorly organized for task. Some important Information needed for solution is determined with accuracy, depth, and breadth.	Most important, relevant obstacles and constraints are accurately determined. Some irrelevant obstacles and/or constraints may be determined. Weighting as to relative importance in the situation shows lack of understanding of the total situation, but understanding of weighting process.	At least one solution to the problem is determined, but it fails to address one or more of the important constraints and obstacles in the problem.	The solutions are tried/tested ineffectively and or incompletely evaluated against all the obstacles and constraints.	Presents a recommended solution and provides minimal or some irrelevant, or some inaccurate rationale for it – excludes some important obstacles and/or constraints and/or evidence necessary for support - shows a minimal understanding of the situation and the problem solving process.
Emerging	"A" problem is identified – but it is not the central issue/problem and/or the information collected or identified has numerous errors.	Fails to accurately identify the important obstacles, and constraints and weighting is off enough to imply a lack of understanding of the problem and/or the process.	The solution fails to address the important constraints or obstacles in the problem and therefore does not appear reasonable or plausible.	The evaluation of the solution(s) is at best superficial – shows no true understanding of how to evaluate the solution or the meaning of the constraints and obstacles in the problem.	Presents a recommended solution. The support shows a lack of understanding of the problem, obstacles and constraints, and the nature of evidence necessary to support a position. Some awareness of process is shown.
Not Scorable	No relevant problem identified.	No relevant obstacles & constraints identified.	No attempt to solve the problem.	No evaluation or only personal opinion is presented.	No support provided.

Rubric for Rubricators

Rubricators are people who develop and use rubrics. Determine which of the columns representing different levels of rubricators best describes you as a developer and user of rubrics.

Level / Criteria	Professional Rubricator:	Hobbyist Rubricator:	Developing Rubricator:	Emerging Rubricator:	Not Yet Rubricated:	Scores
Core Rubric Knowledge	I can teach an advanced workshop about rubrics that includes adherence to standards, use of exemplars & anchors, scoring analytically & holistically, & appropriate uses of both scoring and coaching rubrics.	I can coach others about a lot of the topics in the workshop about rubrics mentioned to the left, but I'll be looking for more knowledge & ideas.	I feel fairly confident about rubrics, but I wouldn't feel comfortable volunteering for too much coaching of others.	I know some basic definitions and procedures, but not enough to help anyone else in a significant way.	I don't really know what rubrics are, but I've heard or believe they may be useful.	
Rubric Development Skills	I develop both coaching & scoring rubrics that are consistently effective.	I develop rubrics that work fairly well – but some glitches arise.	My rubrics help improve student work, but they don't consistently define quality, differentiate levels well, and/or promote top quality.	My rubrics are not reliable.	I don't know how to develop a rubric.	
Involvement of Students	I consistently involve the students in the development of both the scoring & coaching rubrics.	With most rubrics, I involve the students in the development.	I seldom involve the students in the development of the rubrics.	I develop rubrics on my own, &/or I obtain them from others myself.	I don't even involve myself in the development or acquisition of rubrics.	
Criteria-Based Thinking	I read, eat, sleep, dream, and think rubrically, feel good about it, and it works!	I think rubrically a lot – but limit it to working hours.	For me, rubricated thinking is typically an afterthought.	I think rubrically so seldom that it surprises me when it happens.	I don't know if I'm a rubricated thinker, but if I am, can it be cured with penicillin?	
					Total Score	

©1997-1998 Peak Learning Systems (303) 679-9780; Adapted from *The High Performance* Toolbox by Rogers & Graham (Peak Learning Systems, 1997)

Rubric for: Addressing an Audience

ANCHORS REQUIRED FOR EACH LEVEL

	Position	Development	Organization	Audience	Language
4	Position is clearly and tightly identified.	Position fully and convincingly supported.	Logically and effectively organized for the task and situation.	Audience needs are effectively identified and met.	Language used eloquently and effectively.
3	Position stated clearly, but not tightly defined.	Position fully supported but not convincingly.	Logically organized for the task and situation.	Audience needs are mostly identified and met.	Language used effectively.
2	Position stated but not clearly nor tightly defined.	Position mostly supported (some gaps in logic).	A logical organizational plan, but not consistently followed.	Audience needs are minimally identified and met.	Most of the time language is used effectively.
1	Stated position is very unclear but there.	Minimal support offered.	Some organization apparent, but not appropriate or logical for the task.	Only basic audience needs are minimally identified and met.	Seldom is language used effectively.
Not Scorable	Task not attempted or completely missed the mark.				

Checklist for: *Our Museum Display*

Our museum display is quality because …

	Requirements	Yes	No
1.	Our animal is shown in its natural habitat.		
2.	Newborns and interesting information about them are shown.		
3.	Correct information about our animal is shown.		
4.	Information about our animal's predators is shown.		
5.	Our museum clearly shows two important ways our animal helps people.		
6.	Everything in our display is the right size.		
7.	Our display is three dimensional.		
8.	Our display uses all the right colors.		
9.	Everything is labeled neatly and correctly.		

Shared by Roz Rogers from her inservice teaching with Joan Armon in
Golden, Colorado. (First Grade)

Rubric Frame

Assessment Focus

Compare/Contrast (the process)

Quality Definition

Comparing and Contrasting have been done with quality when the significant similarities and differences have been identified for a given purpose.

Essential Quality Criteria

Clearly and precisely with sufficient depth and breadth ...

- determine specifically the intended purpose for the results of comparing and contrasting.

- determine all similarities relevant to the given purpose.

- determine all differences relevant to the given purpose.

Rubric Frame

Assessment Focus

Determine (the process)

Quality Definition

The conclusion needed for a specific purpose is drawn.

Essential Quality Criteria

- The intended use for the resulting conclusion is identified clearly, precisely, and with adequate depth and breadth.

- Optional conclusions and their associated consequences with respect to the ultimate purpose are identified based on solid research.

- The most advantageous conclusion is decided upon based on appropriate criteria and weighting.

Rubric Frame

Assessment Focus

Teach (the process)

Quality Definition

The learners learn the intended information, skills, or concepts.

Essential Quality Criteria

- What is to be learned is clearly and precisely determined.

- Efficient and aligned assessment methods to verify the learning are developed.

- Aligned instruction, organization, and supporting materials that are consistent with the learners needs are developed and used.

- The effectiveness of the instruction is assessed and appropriate modifications are made until the learning has occurred.

Rubric for

A Math/Science/Language Arts project in which the students determined how a concept from either their math or science curriculum is used by a professional outside of school. This rubric is used to guide and evaluate the math or science within the students presentations of their findings.

	Accuracy	Thoroughness	Complexity
5	The written, visual, and oral presentations are free of any math and/or science errors.	The description of how the math or science concepts are applied is logical throughout and thorough.	The complexity of the concepts and applications described exceed the level to which they have been taught in school.
4	The mathematical and/or scientific errors are inconsequential.	The descriptions are mostly logical and/or at least thorough enough to be understood by an expert capable of filling in the gaps.	The complexity of the concepts and applications are no more than one year below grade level.
3	One or more major errors are present, but they are corrected upon questioning.	The descriptions are incomplete enough and/or illogical enough to confuse even experts, but they are corrected by the students when questioned.	The complexity of the concepts and applications are not challenging as shown by being 2 or more years below grade level.
Needs refining before it can be scored	Major errors exist and cannot be corrected.	The descriptions are incomplete or illogical and cannot be corrected.	Concepts and applications do not go beyond common knowledge.

Contributed by Jim Ludington and Mark Pellegrino
of Gananda High School in Walworth, New York.

Rubric for

Writing (Generic – Secondary Level)

	Purpose	Support	Organization	Impact	Usage/ Mechanics
Excellent 5	■ Establishes & maintains a clear purpose consistent with the task. ■ Demonstrates a confident, clear & strong understanding of audience & task. ■ Clear & tight focus.	■ Ideas are developed insightfully & in depth. ■ Ideas presented go beyond statements of the obvious. ■ Supporting details are explicit, effective, & vivid.	■ Consistently & effectively organized. ■ Transitions are cohesive & smooth.	■ Effectively & eloquently achieves intended impact.	■ At most, only a few inconsequential errors that do not interfere with the understanding of the piece or distract from its overall impact.
Proficient 4	■ Establishes a discernible purpose consistent with the task. ■ Demonstrates a strong awareness of audience & task. ■ Clear focus.	■ Ideas are stated but not developed to their necessary depth. ■ Ideas are acceptable, but tend to be "safe" and predictable. ■ Supporting details are colorful, appropriate, and mostly effective.	■ Effectively organized. ■ Transitions are cohesive.	■ Effectively achieves intended impact.	■ More than a few errors, but they do not cause significant interference with the understanding of the piece or distract from its overall impact – careful proofing is still apparent.
Novice 3	■ Attempts to establish a purpose consistent with the task, but it remains too loose. ■ Demonstrates a limited awareness of audience & task. ■ Focus is confusing at times.	■ Ideas are stated but not developed. ■ Ideas are skimpy & superficial. ■ Supporting details are colorless, & somewhat appropriate & effective.	■ The organization of the piece introduces some confusion and/or weakens the piece's impact. ■ Transitions are weak and mechanical at best.	■ Marginally achieves intended impact.	■ Multiple errors &/or error patterns are present. They are extensive &/or significant enough to hinder understanding &/or detract from the intended impact.
Emerging Inc.	■ A purpose is not established. ■ Demonstrates a minimal awareness of audience & task. ■ No clear focus.	■ There aren't any truly discernible ideas. ■ Ideas show no original thinking. (clichés, etc.). ■ Supporting details are non-existent or ineffective.	■ The organization makes the piece difficult to follow and understand. ■ Transitions are not evident or introduce some confusion.	■ Impact attempted but not achieved.	■ Errors &/or error patterns are significant enough to almost block understanding.
Not Scorable	No understanding of the task is apparent.				

Rubric for

An Outline Integrating Information from 2 Related Articles

	Content Integration	Order/Sequencing	Mechanics/Format
Exemplary 4	Headings and supporting detail are complete, clearly stated, and accurate. All relevant information is used – clearly shows the ability to integrate the information from the two articles.	Shows logical and accurate sequencing with supporting details placed with proper headings and subheadings.	Standard outline form is neatly and correctly used with proper use of capitals, indentations, numbering, lettering, titles, headings, subheadings, and support detail.
Proficient 3	Headings and supporting detail are mostly complete, clear, and accurate. A majority of relevant information is used – shows the ability to integrate information from the two articles.	Shows a logical and accurate sequencing. Only one or two supporting details are misplaced.	Standard outline form is used correctly with only minor errors in use of capitals, indentations, numbering, lettering, titles, headings, subheadings, and support detail.
Developing 2	Headings and supporting detail are lacking in completeness and accuracy. Some relevant information is used from one or both articles – several important supporting details are missing or incorrectly connected.	An attempt to order is apparent, but it is not logical based on the articles and/or there are numerous errors in placement of supporting details.	Standard outline form is used with numerous errors in use of capitals, indentations, numbering, lettering, titles, headings, subheadings, and support detail.– some lack of knowledge of outline format/mechanics is apparent.
Emerging 1	Headings and supporting detail are lacking considerably in completeness and accuracy – supporting details are missing, irrelevant, and/or significantly misconnected or inaccurate.	Little sequencing is apparent and/or supporting details are mostly misplaced.	Only basic awareness of outline format is apparent.
Not Scorable	Blank paper or assignment totally misunderstood.		

Shared by Cathy Tocco and Kay McKernan of the Lockport City School District in Lockport, NY. This rubric is used, with slight variations, for the 5th grade Language Arts Benchmark Performance Assessment.

Criteria for Credit*

When work meets the Criteria for Credit, then it is eligible for grading and credit.

The work is . . .

- neat,
- organized down (not across),
- free of "cross-outs,"
- stapled, labeled, and arranged properly,
- done in a timely way, and
- signed as evidence of "best effort."

With

- The directions are followed.
- Important steps are shown.
- Answers are indicated and well labeled.

For qualifier status, . . .

- errors are corrected,
- the assignment is complete, and
- it is signed as evidence of "zero defects."

*Developed and used in secondary mathematics.

Template Duplicating Masters

The next pages are blank templates for you to use in developing rubrics. Several variations are provided for flexibility.

Scoring Sheet

#	Item to be Scored	Avail. Points	Self Pnts/Date		Other Pnts/Date		Other Pnts/Date		Tchr. Pnts/Date	
Student:										
Other Evaluators:										
1.										
2.										
3.										
4.										
5.										
6.										
7.										
8.										
9.										
10.										
11.										
12.										
	Totals									

Comments

Scoring Sheet

#	Item to be Scored	Avail. Points	Self Pnts/Date		Other Pnts/Date		Tchr. Pnts/Date	
Student:								
Other Evaluators:								
1.								
2.								
3.								
4.								
5.								
6.								
7.								
8.								
9.								
10.								
	Totals							

Comments

Evaluators' Signatures

_____   _____

_____   _____

Scoring Sheet

Student _____

Basic Requirements: The following are to be completed as qualifiers for final evaluation.

		In Progress		Done
1.	☐	☐	☐	☐
2.	☐	☐	☐	☐
3.	☐	☐	☐	☐
4.	☐	☐	☐	☐
5.	☐	☐	☐	☐

Essential Criteria: The following criteria are weighted as indicated. Progress dates and/or levels and final evaluations are also indicated.

	Criteria	Points Available	Progress			Final Score
1.		_____	____	____	____	_____
2.		_____	____	____	____	_____
3.		_____	____	____	____	_____
4.		_____	____	____	____	_____
5.		_____	____	____	____	_____
6.		_____	____	____	____	_____
7.		_____	____	____	____	_____
Totals		_____	____	____	____	_____

Comments/Scales/Evaluator

Rubric For:

	Criteria

Rubric For:

Weighted Rubric For:

Weight Factor & Score	_____ x Score = _____	_____ x Score = _____

Rubric For:

Weighted Rubric For:

Weight Factor & Score	____ x Score = ____	____ x Score = ____	____ x Score = ____

Rubric For:

Weighted Rubric For:

	__ x Score = ___	__ x Score = ___	__ x Score = ___	__ x Score = ___
Weight Factor & Score	__ x Score = ___	__ x Score = ___	__ x Score = ___	__ x Score = ___

Rubric For:

Weighted Rubric For:

Weight Factor & Score	_ x Score = __	_ x Score = __	_ x Score = __	_ x Score = __	_ x Score = __

Rubric For:

Criteria/Standards					

Rubric For:

Rubric For:

Rubric For:

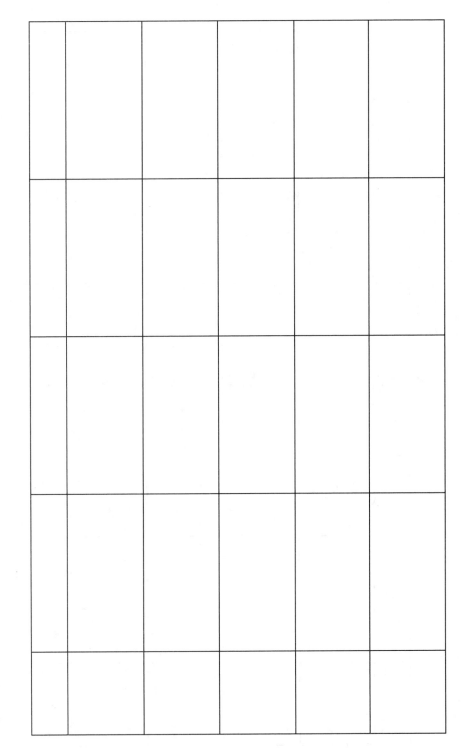

Rubric For:

Rubric For:

Rubric For:

```

```

To Be Considered Exemplary ...

To Be Considered Competent ...

To Be Considered Developing ...

To Be Considered Emerging ...

To be Considered Not-Score-able ...

Checklist for

	Requirements			
1.				
2.				
3.				
4.				
5.				
6.				
7.				
8.				
9.				
10.				

Comments

Chapter 8

LEARNING EVENTS, CHECKPOINTS, & LOGISTICS: GETTING DETAILS UNDER CONTROL

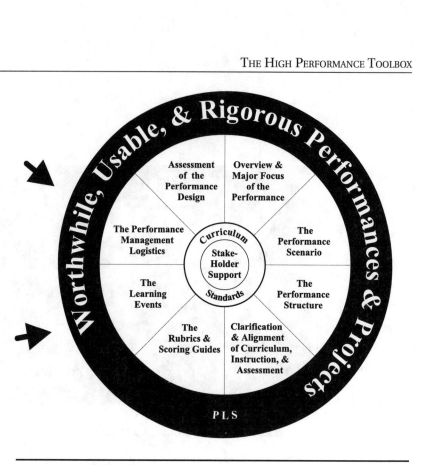

Learning Events

Planning the learning events is determining and sequencing the step-by-step series of instructional activities, assessments, and other events that are to occur throughout the performance learning unit. Learning events include …

- assignments,
- discussions,
- guest speakers,
- journal entries,
- interviews,
- library research,
- quizzes,
- videos,
- computer lab usage,
- field trips,
- instructional activities,
- assessments,
- introductory activities,
- presentations,
- tests, and
- writings.

The purpose of this section is to provide a graphic planner with an example to facilitate the planning of learning events within a performance or project. On the next page is an example learning events planner for the *Romeo and Juliet* Unit that was first introduced as an example in Chapter 4.

Learning Events Plan

AN EXAMPLE

Romeo and Juliet – The Looking Glass

Anticipated Date	Event	Purpose	Scored
Jan 28	Lead discussion around *the essential question.* Assign interviewing relatives and researching expert opinions.	Generate interest and focus the unit.	
Jan 29	Overview Role Performance Expectations.	Clarify task and establish framework.	
Jan 30 - Feb 14	Read and discuss *Romeo and Juliet* from the perspective of the established curriculum and the essential question.	Students learning the essential elements from the curriculum guide and developing insights for their performance task.	
Feb 8	Test	Check for understanding of above.	✗
	Etcetera		

Comments

```
┌─────────────────────────────────────────────────────────────┐
│                                                               │
│                                                               │
└─────────────────────────────────────────────────────────────┘
```

Learning Events Plan

Anticipated Date	Event	Purpose	Scored

Comments

Learning Events Plan

CONTINUED

Anticipated Date	Event	Purpose	Scored

Comments

Performance Checkpoints

Successfully implementing student performances that are extensive and spread over time requires clearly identifying specific checkpoints. Some people compare the "checkpoints" in a performance to the mile markers along a highway. Both indicate where we have been, where we are, and how much further we have to go. In a student performance, checkpoints are used to identify and check significant component tasks or phases of the overall performance. These checkpoints should not be just any points along the way. They should be those significant points along the way for which a successful and quality completion is important to the success of the total performance.

Example checkpoints that have been used in a variety of performances are …

- brainstormed, selected, and refined a topic;
- completed a cover design;
- obtained adequate and appropriate references;
- completed appropriate visuals or graphics;
- completed costume designs;
- illustrated the booklet;
- completed the table of contents;
- completed first draft; and
- submitted the proposal to the board.

Checkpoints can be quite similar to, if not the same as, the "basic requirements" that were discussed in Chapter 7. A set of checkpoints for a performance is not truly a rubric. In fact, we strongly recommend developing clear criteria (a rubric) for each checkpoint in order to guide the students to a quality completion.

The following graphic represents just one box from the *Performance Checkpoint Templates* on the following two pages.

Checkpoint #1		
(1. Briefly describe the checkpoint in this section of the box.)		
(2. In the spaces below, indicate whether the checkpoint is to be scored, the score when it is earned, and any appropriate dates and initials.)		
Scored? Yes /		No ☐
Dates:		
Initials:		

Indicate in the box if the checkpoint is to be scored by indicating the total possible points for the checkpoint after the slash (/) – otherwise use the "no" box to indicate it is not to be scored. There are three spaces for initials and dates to facilitate the monitoring of the checkpoints' completion.

Reflection Question

1. Why are checkpoints essential for top quality performances from all students?

Checkpoint #1

Scored?	Yes	/	No ☐
Dates:			
Initials:			

Checkpoint #2

Scored?	Yes	/	No ☐
Dates:			
Initials:			

Checkpoint #3

Scored?	Yes	/	No ☐
Dates:			
Initials:			

Checkpoint #4

Scored?	Yes	/	No ☐
Dates:			
Initials:			

Checkpoint #5

Scored?	Yes	/	No ☐
Dates:			
Initials:			

Checkpoint #6

Scored?	Yes	/	No ☐
Dates:			
Initials:			

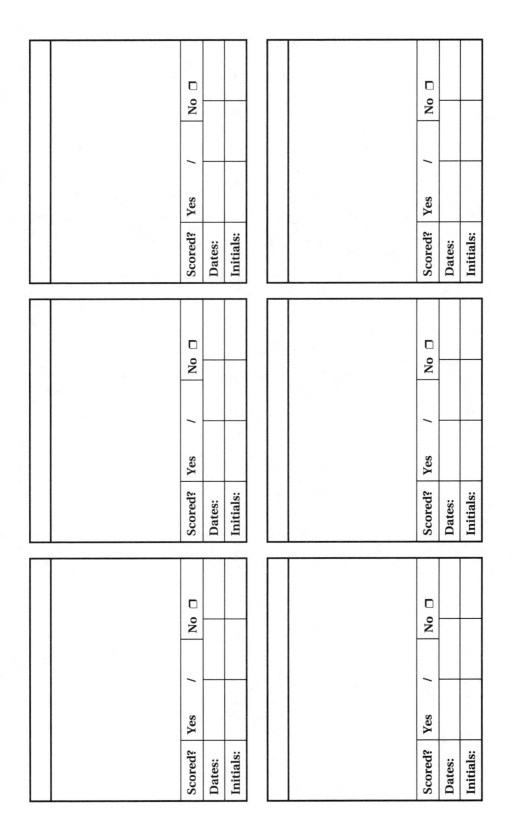

Planning the Logistics

The success of any complex project, such as implementing a performance task, is dependent on the effective attention paid to detail. For that reason, the following template has been developed. Its purpose is to facilitate the identification of the major details that need to be addressed.

When planning for the performance, take the time up-front to identify the details that will need to be taken care of throughout the performance. It is particularly important to determine as soon as possible all of the details that will depend on or affect others.

The Performance Logistics Planner is primarily for the use of the teacher. However, we believe that the students can absolutely be involved at this level.

Reflection Questions

1. What are the advantages of planning for the logistics up-front?

2. What could be the consequences from inadequate planning?

Performance Logistics Planner

1. The unit's beginning date/time:

2. Expected ending date for the unit:

3. Expected beginning date &/or time for final performance:

4. Time required for each final performance:

5. Anticipated time required for all final performances:

6. Checkpoints and dates:	Expected Date	Scored	Points
1.		yes/no	
2.		yes/no	
3.		yes/no	
4.		yes/no	
5.		yes/no	
6.		yes/no	
7.		yes/no	

7. Permissions needed	Person responsible	Date needed	Completed
1.			
2.			
3.			

8. People to be informed	Person responsible	Date needed	Completed
1.			
2.			
3.			

9. Audience(s) to be invited	Person Responsible	Date Needed	Completed
1.			
2.			
3.			

10. Evaluators to be invited	Person Responsible	Date Needed	Completed
1.			
2.			
3.			

11. Outside assistance requested	Person Responsible	Date Needed	Completed
1.			
2.			
3.			

12. Outside experts to be invited	Person Responsible	Date Needed	Completed
1.			
2.			
3.			

13. Resources to be requested	Person Responsible	Date Needed	Completed
1.			
2.			
3.			
4.			
5.			

14. In school assistance to be requested	Person Responsible	Date Needed	Completed
1.			
2.			
3.			

15. Plans for gaining parental support:

16. Other logistical plans, special instructions, or comments:

Project Planner Template

Once again, complex projects involving numerous people require careful planning. On the following pages is a Project Planner Template to facilitate …

- sequencing project responsibilities that need to be completed;
- identifying responsible parties;
- establishing time frames; and
- tracking responsibilities as they are completed.

This template is designed to be used by both the teacher and the students.

Project Planner Template

PAGE _____ OF _____

Project:

Team Leader:

Team Members	Roles
1.	
2.	
3.	
4.	
5.	
6.	
7.	
8.	
9.	

Project Purpose

Completion Date:

Essential Responsibility	Person Responsible	Begin Date	End Date	Completed
1.				
2.				
3.				
4.				
5.				

Project Planner Template Continued

PAGE _____ OF _____

Essential Responsibility	Person Responsible	Begin Date	End Date	Completed
6.				
7.				
8.				
9.				
10.				
11.				
12.				
13.				
14.				
15.				
16.				
17.				
18.				
19.				
20.				
21.				
22.				
23.				
24.				
25.				

Project Planner Template Continued

PAGE _____ OF _____

Essential Responsibility	Person Responsible	Begin Date	End Date	Completed
26.				
27.				
28.				
29.				
30.				
31.				
32.				
33.				
34.				
35.				
36.				
37.				
38.				
39.				
40.				
41.				
42.				
43.				
44.				
45.				

Project Planner

TIMELINE

PAGE _____ OF _____

Enter essential tasks, indicate beginning and ending dates, and show the time duration by drawing an arrow from the beginning date to the ending date. At the top of the date columns, enter the dates that are appropriate for the unit.

Item	Task	Dates																		

Planning Calendars

Planning calendars are provided on the following pages to support performance task implementation. The calendars are for periods of ...

- one week,
- two weeks,
- three weeks,
- four weeks,
- five weeks, and
- six weeks.

One Week Planning Calendar

Sun	Mon	Tues	Wed	Thurs	Fri	Sat
Date	Date	Date	Date	Date	Date	Date

Notes

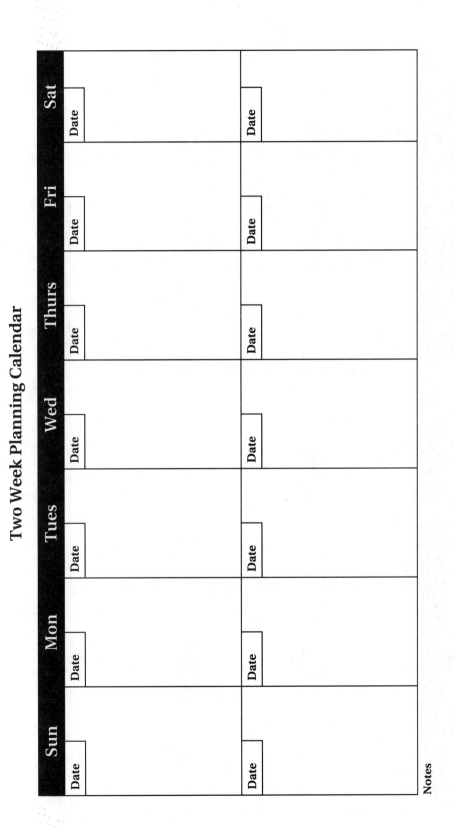

Two Week Planning Calendar

Three Week Planning Calendar

Sun	Mon	Tues	Wed	Thurs	Fri	Sat
Date	Date	Date	Date	Date	Date	Date
Date	Date	Date	Date	Date	Date	Date
Date	Date	Date	Date	Date	Date	Date

Notes

Four Week Planning Calendar

Sun	Mon	Tues	Wed	Thurs	Fri	Sat
Date	Date	Date	Date	Date	Date	Date
Date	Date	Date	Date	Date	Date	Date
Date	Date	Date	Date	Date	Date	Date
Date	Date	Date	Date	Date	Date	Date

Six Week Planning Calendar

Sun	Mon	Tues	Wed	Thurs	Fri	Sat
Date	Date	Date	Date	Date	Date	Date
Date	Date	Date	Date	Date	Date	Date
Date	Date	Date	Date	Date	Date	Date
Date	Date	Date	Date	Date	Date	Date
Date	Date	Date	Date	Date	Date	Date
Date	Date	Date	Date	Date	Date	Date

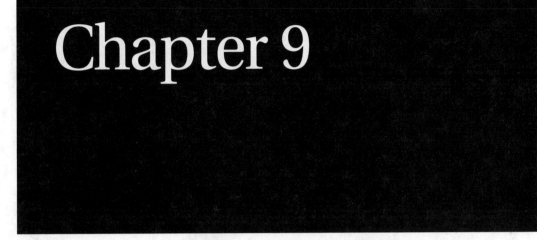

Chapter 9

ASSESSING PERFORMANCE DESIGNS

Introduction

It is important to assess any effort that will effect others. Therefore, we have included in this chapter three performance assessment design tools.

In order to be relatively confident in the assessment results, the performance design needs to be …

- self-assessed by the designers;

- assessed by others at the same level and in the same subject area(s); and

- assessed by other educators (and non educators also) that are not at the same level or in the same area(s).

Assessing Performance Designs I

To assess a performance design, determine how convinced you are as to whether or not each statement is accurate with respect to your performance.

Academic value of the performance

The performance task, project, or performance assessment ...	Yes!	Not Sure	No!
1. is tightly aligned with specific local, regional, or national standards.	☐	☐	☐
2. is targeted on specific content learning targeted by local, regional, or national assessment efforts.	☐	☐	☐
3. is targeted on learning worthy of the time and energy required by it.	☐	☐	☐
4. replicates or simulates outside of school challenges, applications, and constraints.	☐	☐	☐
5. requires students show an in-depth understanding.	☐	☐	☐
6. requires students demonstrate needed and transferable concepts, knowledge, skills, and abilities.	☐	☐	☐
7. actually shows what it is intended to show.	☐	☐	☐

Scorability of the assessment components and/or usability of the rubrics

The rubrics/scoring guidelines ...	Yes!	Not Sure	No!
1. distinguish clearly between levels of performance.	☐	☐	☐
2. require credible, distinguishable evidence of the targeted knowledge, skills, and abilities.	☐	☐	☐
3. are matched to the intended impact of the performance type.	☐	☐	☐
4. are developed from real world exemplary examples and from actual student work. (Anchors are available for scoring.)	☐	☐	☐
5. are such that they require adequate depth and breadth of specific learning so as to replicate real world expectations.	☐	☐	☐
6. provide useful information to the students for achieving quality levels within the performance.	☐	☐	☐
7. provide useful feedback to the students for improving future performance levels.	☐	☐	☐
8. provide useful information to teachers, evaluators, and other interested parties.	☐	☐	☐

Assessing Performance Designs I

PAGE 2 OF 2

Usability of the performance

The performance task, project, or performance assessment ...	Yes!	Not Sure	No!
1. provides teachers with useful and desired information for making instructional decisions.	☐	☐	☐
2. clearly defines the roles of the teachers and students.	☐	☐	☐
3. has directions throughout that are clear and concise for all involved.	☐	☐	☐
4. is do-able based on availability of time and other resources.	☐	☐	☐
5. is developmentally do-able and challenging for students and teachers.	☐	☐	☐
6. has necessary instructional systems and other support systems planned to ensure success.	☐	☐	☐

Value Seen By Stakeholders

The performance task, project, or performance assessment ...	Yes!	Not Sure	No!
1. is seen as valuable by students.	☐	☐	☐
2. is seen as valuable by parents.	☐	☐	☐
3. is seen as valuable by colleagues.	☐	☐	☐
4. is seen as valuable by the district.	☐	☐	☐
5. is seen as valuable by members of the community.	☐	☐	☐
6. is *engaging* (active, challenging, and interesting) for students.	☐	☐	☐
7. allows/encourages the appropriate amount of latitude to the students with respect to style and approach.	☐	☐	☐
8. is such that students are involved in the development of the rubrics/scoring guidelines or has procedures planned for developing understanding of the scoring expectations by the students.	☐	☐	☐
9. has an identified audience and/or use that the students value.	☐	☐	☐
10. is such that students feel safe from personal embarrassment.	☐	☐	☐

Assessing Performance Designs II

MICRO VERSION

The performance task, project, or performance assessment …	Yes!	Not Sure	No!
1. is tightly focused on subject matter, information, skills, and/or concepts targeted by local, regional, and/or national standards and assessments.	☐	☐	☐
2. truly assesses (and provides credible evidence) what it is claimed to as verified by outside experts.	☐	☐	☐
3. provides desired and usable data to students, teachers, parents, and other appropriate stakeholders.	☐	☐	☐
4. is score-able.	☐	☐	☐
5. provides consistent results over time and across groups.	☐	☐	☐
6. is seen as worthwhile by the students, parents, teachers, and other stakeholders.	☐	☐	☐
7. focuses on desired effects of student actions in addition to the specific actions. (e.g. persuasiveness in addition to the use of specific persuasion techniques and writing or speaking skills.)	☐	☐	☐
8. is do-able with available resources and time-frames.	☐	☐	☐
9. expects accuracy, sound reasoning, depth, breadth, and convincing support from the students.	☐	☐	☐
10. is well understood by all involved.	☐	☐	☐
11. has expectations based on both actual student work and experts in the field.	☐	☐	☐
12. has expectations clarified through actual examples (anchors).	☐	☐	☐
13. provides for appropriate flexibility and creativity.	☐	☐	☐
14. is seen as safe, valuable, challenging, do-able, and interesting to the students.	☐	☐	☐
15. is consistent with research regarding the brain & learning.	☐	☐	☐
16. is engaging to the students.	☐	☐	☐

Assessing Performance Designs III

Assess your performance design using the criteria given in the table below. For each criteria, assess the performance with respect to the four point scale provided: (4.) "Yes, absolutely and getting better!"   (3.) "Yes, but it's not as much at it could or should be – feels shaky."   (2.) "It's starting to develop."   (1.) "No, not at all. I don't know how to do it."

Performance Focus	Quality Expectations	Importance to Stakeholders	Roles	Management & Feasibility
__ A. The content is challenging, rigorous, accurate, and consistent with curriculum standards and standardized testing. __ B. The content is connected to universal concepts. __ C. Transferable process skills are taught and assessed. __ D. The learning is connected to prior learning and real-world applications. __ E. The students are expected to construct meaning and depth. __ F. The students can articulate the benefits of the learning.	__ A. The design is at the developmentally appropriate level for the students. __ B. Both static and dynamic criteria are appropriately used. __ C. Students are involved in the research and development of the criteria and rubrics. __ D. Criteria and timelines are consistent with real-world expectations. __ E. Criteria are understood by all involved. __ F. Valid and reliable assessment are designed and used.	__ A. The students believe the performance is worthwhile and challenging. __ B. Parents, community members, colleagues, and administrators believe the performance is worthwhile. __ C. An audience important to the students is utilized.	__ A. The students are actively involved in planning and development. __ B. The students are actually performing the complex processes like problem solving. __ C. The teacher plays the role of facilitator. __ D. Parents and other members of the community play resource roles.	__ A. Necessary resources are reasonably obtainable. __ B. The performance is seen as do-able by the teachers, the students, the parents, and the administrators. __ C. The design lends itself to multiple learning styles and intelligences. __ D. Appropriate scaffolding is designed to support the learners. __ E. The performance can be accomplished with available resources - including time. __ F. The performance implementation is developmentally appropriate for the teacher. __ G. The performance is brain-compatible

Assessing Performance Designs IV – Performance Task "Equalizer"

The concept of an Equalizer for a music system makes a wonderful metaphor to help us look at performance tasks realistically. At different times in our lives and with different types of music, we set our equalizers at different levels of bass, mid-range, and treble in order to meet our tastes and

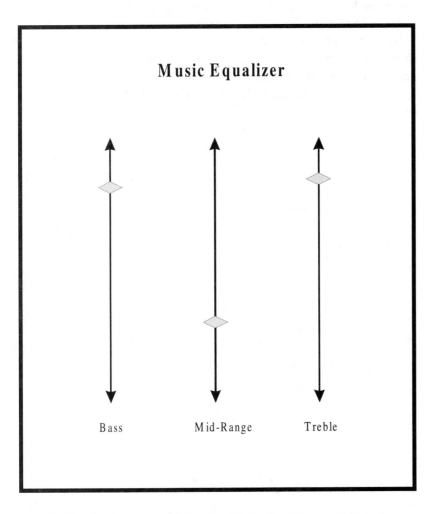

Music Equalizer

Bass   Mid-Range   Treble

needs. Similarly, we can take a quick look at the equalizer to see the tonal levels at which the music is going to be played.

Like with music, performance tasks can (and probably should) vary considerably in terms of the levels of the major educational attributes. We call these major attributes content, performance actions, and context. By content we are referring to the subject matter or major concepts being taught or utilized. Performance actions is a term to refer to the actions the students are taking with the content. And the context refers to the setting, challenges, and conditions of the task that greatly impact the required depth and breadth of performance action displayed.

The Performance Task Equalizer shows the levels of long-term significance of the content, performance actions, and contexts being addressed. It is important not to try to build real-life, authentic, out-in-the-world performances out of important subject matter that doesn't fit in that context. Similarly, if we don't ever involve students in rich, engaging, real-world, authentic tasks, they will have to wait until they are outside of school for anyone to know if they can learn and apply learning on their own.

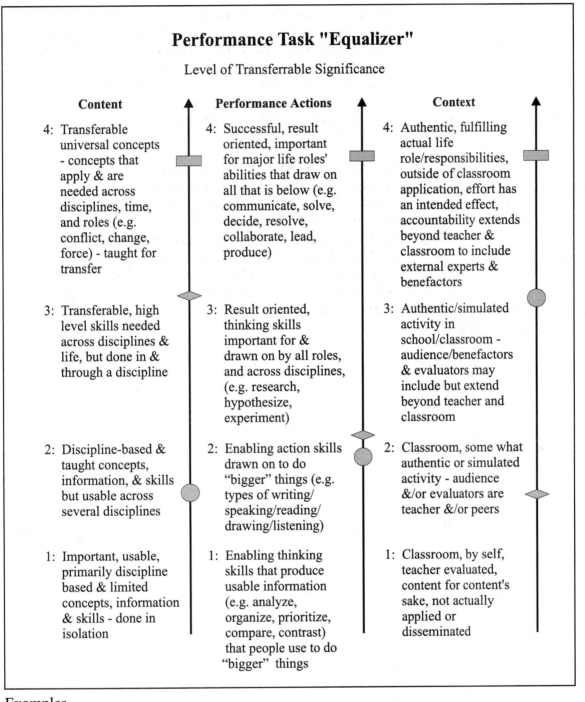

Performance Task "Equalizer"

Level of Transferrable Significance

Content	Performance Actions	Context

4: Transferable universal concepts - concepts that apply & are needed across disciplines, time, and roles (e.g. conflict, change, force) - taught for transfer

4: Successful, result oriented, important for major life roles' abilities that draw on all that is below (e.g. communicate, solve, decide, resolve, collaborate, lead, produce)

4: Authentic, fulfilling actual life role/responsibilities, outside of classroom application, effort has an intended effect, accountability extends beyond teacher & classroom to include external experts & benefactors

3: Transferable, high level skills needed across disciplines & life, but done in & through a discipline

3: Result oriented, thinking skills important for & drawn on by all roles, and across disciplines, (e.g. research, hypothesize, experiment)

3: Authentic/simulated activity in school/classroom - audience/benefactors & evaluators may include but extend beyond teacher and classroom

2: Discipline-based & taught concepts, information, & skills but usable across several disciplines

2: Enabling action skills drawn on to do "bigger" things (e.g. types of writing/ speaking/reading/ drawing/listening)

2: Classroom, some what authentic or simulated activity - audience &/or evaluators are teacher &/or peers

1: Important, usable, primarily discipline based & limited concepts, information & skills - done in isolation

1: Enabling thinking skills that produce usable information (e.g. analyze, organize, prioritize, compare, contrast) that people use to do "bigger" things

1: Classroom, by self, teacher evaluated, content for content's sake, not actually applied or disseminated

Examples

▨ The students identify and work to resolve community issues.

◇ The students write a persuasive essay that is turned in to the teacher for grading.

● The students develop an educational game which they use to present subject matter information to a class of younger students.

Chapter 10

LAUNCHING INITIATIVES & STAYING AFLOAT: PRACTICAL TIPS FOR GETTING STARTED & CONTINUING TO SUCCEED

Introduction

The purpose of this chapter is to provide a wealth of concepts/tips for successful implementation of performance learning. The primary focus of the tips will be at the classroom level. We sincerely believe that no educational initiative will ever be successful unless it can be done successfully in the classroom. That is not to say that there are not major system issues to address for any reform effort to be successful – because reform of a system will not be successful unless it is approached systemically by the system. A part of reforming the system, however, is to be certain that the people in the classrooms and schools have the knowledge and skills necessary to use any new approaches successfully *and to earn support for them.*

The tips that are provided in this chapter are based on practices that have worked successfully for many educators and non-educators alike. The basis for these ideas can be found in books such as *Principle Centered Leadership* by Stephen Covey and *Enlightened Leadership* by Doug Krug and Ed Oakley. (We highly recommend these two books be added to all educators' libraries. Many other outstanding references are included in Appendix I.)

Often we are asked, "Why do you recommend so many leadership books for teachers to use?" The answer is simple. Sound leadership principles and practices form the basis for inspiring others and creating a context in which people want to excel. Many of the tips do not fit what some of us were taught twenty years ago. However, twenty years ago the emphasis was not on educating all students to the highest levels. These tips have worked for many of us and are much more consistent with the writings of people we consider to be experts in the field of creating contexts conducive to high performance. We could list lots of references, but we believe we can serve every one better by just strongly urging you to acquire and study …

- everything you can that has been written by Dr. William Glasser;
- the book, *Enhancing Adult Motivation to Learn* by Dr. Raymond Wlodkowski, (Josse-Bass Publishers, 1991) (an outstanding resource which is applicable working with young people also);

- the book, *Diversity and Motivation* by Dr. Raymond Wlodkowski and Dr. Marjorie Ginsberg (Josse-Bass Publishers, 1991); and

- the book, *Motivation & Learning: A Teacher's Guide to Building Excitement for Learning and Igniting the Drive for Quality* by Spence Rogers, Shari Graham, and Jim Ludington (Peak Learning Systems, 1997).

It is important to note that the tips presented within this chapter are like tips presented anywhere – they need to be selected and implemented appropriately for the context and in a manner consistent with the principles on which they are based. Research and common experience have shown that tips and strategies applied in isolation or in inappropriate ways do not make a difference at best, or at worst, cause undesired results.

Underlying Principles

The following are principles on which the following tips are based.

- "Seek first to understand, then to be understood."
  — *Dr. Stephen Covey*

The deeper one understands this principal, the more powerful a principle it becomes. The answers we seek to questions regarding how to improve learning for all students are out there – we need only listen.

- "Treat others as you would have them treat you."

So often resentment and anger builds because of the way people believe they are being treated. However, quite often these very same people are treating others the way they themselves resent being treated. It is so easy to wish that our superiors were treating us one way, while we're treating others a different way.

- Constantly build and pursue a vision that is based on the ideal.

It's important to clarify what you're trying to achieve as much as possible before beginning an endeavor. We refer to this as "creating a vision." However, a vision is not a picture – there is a difference. If we paint a detailed picture, we can become locked into our thinking, and if we've never been where we're trying to go, we need to be able to make adjustments along the way.

- Commit to continuous improvement.

As many of us were growing up, we had pictures of one day having it all figured out. Unfortunately, everything is so complex and is changing so quickly, that will probably never happen. Dr. W. Edward Deming brought to all of us the concept of continuous improvement. When we are committed to continuous improvement, we have accepted in our hearts that whatever we do, we will study it, determine appropriate improvements, and act on our findings. And then, do it again – study what has happened, determine improvements, and act on our findings. Another way of looking at continuous improvement is, if what you're getting isn't the best you can imagine, refine, or change completely if necessary, what you're doing. When one is in a continuous improvement mindset, the destination is a never ending, continuously improving journey.

- Operate on a sound set of principles and values.

Honesty, integrity, trust, commitment and hard work. How can you go wrong? Aren't these the values that great civilizations like ours have held dear for so long? Aren't these what many of us have always thought were important to model and expect in a classroom?

Underlying Beliefs

As teachers strive to increase learning in the classroom, their efforts impact several major groups,

- students,
- parents,
- other teachers,
- administrators, and
- community members.

Our actions will have different effects on the members of each of these stakeholder groups. One way to picture this is to picture a ball of putty made up of several different colors that are predominantly separate, yet still interwoven. Now picture someone squeezing this putty ball. Whenever it's squeezed in one place, it bulges out somewhere else. A similar phenomena occurs when working with people. Depending on the effects, we will either encounter support or resistance from our stakeholder groups.

The tips included in this chapter are sorted based on various stakeholder groups. The acceptance and successful use of the tips are dependent on the following beliefs as they relate to the specific stakeholder groups.

Beliefs about everyone …

- People will do, take risks for, or support whatever they believe is valuable enough.

- People want to feel safe from physical or emotional harm.

- People want to feel "free to be themselves."

- People want to think they are smart and capable.

- People want to feel loved and valued.

- People want to enjoy themselves.

Beliefs about parents …

- Parents greatly value their children.

- Parents want and will work hard to get the best for their children.

- Parents will protect their children from what they perceive as harmful.

Beliefs about a teacher's role …

- As teachers, our work is with children and for the benefit of children.

- As teachers, we report to the administration, which reports to the Board of Education, which reports to the parents and other community members. Therefore, teachers work for the community members and provide their service by working with the children.

Whatever someone's beliefs are, they tend to be either based on experience or they have been proven to that person through experience. Therefore, if a belief is not truly accurate, then it is very difficult for the belief to be changed without experience that supports a different belief.

General Tips for Building Success

1. "Think big, but start small." is something we first heard Dr. Tom Guskey (University of Kentucky) say to a group over six years ago. Vision is essential to forward movement, but so too is an appropriate infrastructure that supports and provides reasonable steps and directions for people. Too often ambitious hopes have failed to become reality because lessons taught to us by stories such as *The Tortoise and The Hare* have been forgotten.

2. Never quit doing anything which stakeholders value until you have something else up and running that is as good or better in the eyes of the stakeholders (most particularly parents and students but also teachers). This implies that dual systems may need to be operating (i.e., traditional report cards continue while portfolios and student-led conferencing are introduced).

3. Do not become driven by exceptions – focus on the rule, but support the exception.

4. Be certain that parents' needs with respect to their children are met ...

    -   their children's health and safety are protected;
    -   their right to have and maintain their family values is protected;
    -   their children are taught the essential academics;
    -   their children are not experimented with;
    -   their children get the best possible education that is not adversely effected because of others; and
    -   their children are treated with fairness.

5. Put your energies and resources where it will make the greatest difference. Remember that in any organization and with any initiative, people tend to fall into five broad, but rapidly shifting categories of attitudes and associated actions. There are *explorers, pioneers, settlers, suburbanites*, and *the unhappy*. With any initiative, *pioneers* and *explorers* run with the concepts as fast as they can. One danger they may create is that they may attempt reforms without adequate expertise or support to be successful. The *settlers* and *suburbanites* do not rush to try the initiative, but if they are provided with adequate training,

support, and safety nets, they may try. They need *high* levels of support, intensive staff-development, and whatever resources and supplies may be necessary. *The unhappy* not only don't try anything, they work hard to convince the settlers and suburbanites that the initiative won't be adequately supported and therefore, can't be done. Therefore, be certain that the settlers and suburbanites receive the support and protection they need, or your efforts will most likely not succeed.

6. Determine and track the indicators of a successful schooling effort that your stakeholder groups value. These include standardized test results, drop-out rates, grades, college admissions, etcetera.

7. Value and hang on to standardized tests. Even though standardized tests seem to always be in our way, they do provided evidence of learning that most of the outside of school stakeholders value and understand.

8. Use block schedules as appropriate to support more authentic learning and assessment experiences. Be certain to provide adequate staff-development to support teachers' needs in learning how to best use the extra time provided by the new schedule.

9. Institute peer review and outside auditing of designs to support improvement efforts and maintain confidence levels with various stakeholder groups.

10. Limit performance unit implementation to one to four per year per teacher. Quality designs require tremendous energy. In addition, working through implementing changes is exhausting. Focus on high quality, continuous, forward movement. Remember the story of the tortoise and the hare.

11. Utilize dictionaries and other expert resources. As sophisticated, performance design efforts progress, it is essential to strive for rigor, validity and reliability in addition to engaging activities. For years, many of us have been creative in our use of language, which can sound nice in conversation, but too often is confusing at best in performance design and assessment. Quite often words like describe, explain, present, express, and convey are mistakenly used almost interchangeably in assignments. These words have very different meanings that need to be modeled, taught, and used. Take the time to

be certain of the distinctions that exist between various concepts and competencies to create the quality, long-term impact that can be supported now and in the future.

12. Fix the educational reform pendulum – get it swinging again. For years we have jumped from one reform idea to another. For example, whole group instruction isn't doing all we want, so let's abandon it and individualize. Clocks only work when their pendulums swing from side to side including each point along an arc. So too for education. Education best serves its learners when the pendulum swings from side to side continuously and smoothly including all the great ideas as they are needed. The issue isn't whole group, small group, or individualized. Nor is the issue whole language or phonics. And the issue is not performance-based or non-performance-based. The issue is simply what needs to be done so each learner learns what is needed for success during school and after graduation.

Tips for Success with Students

1. Adhere to the Principles and Standards for a motivating environment. (Refer to the book *Motivation & Learning*, published by Peak Learning Systems of Evergreen, Colorado 1998.)

2. Involve students in …

   - making as many decisions as is possible and reasonable;
   - developing the rubrics;
   - developing performance options;
   - determining and developing valid ways to demonstrate essential content standards;
   - developing and refining performances that are aligned with the required standards;
   - establishing classroom rules and procedures;
   - locating outside experts;
   - developing and using criteria for credit;
   - presenting to their parents at open house what they are accomplishing; and

- conferencing with parents to show what they've accomplished, what their strengths are, where they are struggling, and how they're improving.

3. Provide for alternative choices as to how the students may demonstrate knowledge, skills, or conceptual understanding. Choices can be based on multiple intelligences.

4. Teach decision making, problem solving, and consensus building for use in applying the content standards and to facilitate the students' involvement in making solid decisions within the classroom environment.

5. Develop criteria up-front before the work begins. As much as possible, include the students in the determination of the criteria.

6. Stay firm on the expected learning results (content standards); be flexible on the means to getting there.

7. Engage students early on in researching the abilities or skills required for careers of their choice. Help them make connections between these abilities or skills and performance abilities that are a part of well structured performances (build shared visions).

8. Provide an audience other that yourself and/or the class whenever possible.

9. Have students maintain growth portfolios in which they chart and document their improvement with specific criteria.

10. Make certain that there is little to no likelihood that students will be embarrassed through public display of significant lack of knowledge or skills.

11. Do not create situations in which students will be expected to divulge anything about their families or other close relationships that they (or their families) might consider embarrassing or inappropriate.

12. Make certain that nothing about students' families or other close relationships that they might consider embarrassing will be divulged by others.

13. Utilize outside experts as resources with instruction to lend freshness and new insights.

14. Connect the subject matter to universal concepts whenever possible.

15. Design and conduct lessons through which students build on prior learning.

16. Avoid the creation of "in groups" and "out groups."

17. Regularly provide evidence for the students of their mastery or progress. People tend to perform better and persevere longer when they have regular evidence of their progress. Dieters and athletes have used this trick successfully for a long time.

18. Provide numerous, fairly distributed, meaningful response opportunities on a daily basis.

19. Provide clear and precise statements as to the content standards or other learning goals. Use effective strategies for building conceptual understanding of them.

20. Maintain the highest standards for level of achievement and or progress (static and dynamic criteria).

21. Engage students in the process of developing the highest standards that result from comparing and evaluating exemplary work. (See *the eight step process for developing rubrics* in Chapter 7 of this book and numerous other strategies included in the book *Motivation & Learning: A Teacher's Guide to Building Excitement for Learning and Igniting the Drive for Quality.*)

22. Develop and use both static (level) and dynamic (progress) criteria.

23. Establish and use solid "scaffolding" for student success in meeting standards such as …

   - involvement in criteria development;

   - continued strategies that increase conceptual understanding of criteria;

   - regularly scheduled checkpoints with self, peer, and/ or other assessment for feedback and improvement before scoring; and

   - "dress rehearsals" with feedback and refinement.

24. Provide for "dress rehearsals" with opportunities for self, peer, and other assessment (specific, supportive, feedback on ways to improve) before final scoring of the performances.

25. For each performance, determine whether the most important criteria is …

- meeting timelines;
- the quality of the students' performance; or
- some combination of the two.

In the world outside of school, each of the above is more true in some cases then others. Be certain that the emphasis you select is most appropriate for the event, and if the emphasis selected is a combination, that it's not conflicting. If a high quality performance is most critical, then the adherence to a non flexible due date will not work. If *the students completing their work on time* is most critical, then expecting a maximum quality performance from all will lead to disappointment.

26. Utilize best known practices regarding what is known about how people learn.

27. Adhere to best research on establishing and maintaining a motivational environment.

28. Design learning experiences so outside knowledge, skills, or references are obtained and used by the students.

29. Begin the school year with "Personal Posters" (described completely in *Motivation & Learning*, 1997) to begin establishing a community of learners and a quality mindset.

30. Model, Model, Model – always provide models. To avoid students just copying your model, provide three, diverse models and have the students determine and use the common characteristics as the criteria.

31. Involve students in evaluating the effectiveness of any new procedures. Solicit their suggestions for refinements that will result in improved learning and attainment of standards.

32. Operate from an *"I know you can do it perspective."* Be certain that signs, posters, grading procedures, etcetera convey that conviction.

33. Build and maintain a total community of learners in which you are also a member.

34. Subscribe to and use relevant resources such as *Education Leadership*, appropriate journals for your grade level or discipline area, and newsletters that target particular interests such as problem-based learning.

35. Earn the respect and support of students, parents, administrators, community members, and colleagues. Respect needs to be earned; it is not a right.

Tips for Success with Parents

1. Function as if you are "working for the parents" and therefore "accountable to them."

2. Work to earn the respect and support of the parents – this can no longer just be expected.

3. Work to earn the respect and support of the students – this too can no longer just be expected.

4. Involve parents in efforts establishing curriculum.

5. Involve parents as outside experts to support learning in the classroom.

6. Involve parents as audiences for student performances.

7. Involve parents as members of assessment teams similar to the teams of judges that are used at the Olympics.

8. Engage parents in discussions at open house as to what skills, abilities, and knowledge they depend on for their success. Solicit their support in teaching those along with the established content standards.

9. Avoid phrases that can terrify parents (and other community members also) that want the most for their kids such as, "Less is more." We know what we mean; it's an excellent slogan and rallying call for us, but parents hear something very different than what is meant. To many of them it sounds like their children will be leaning less, but it will be called more. Try "Learn More Through Higher Standards."

10. Remember, "The schools worked for us." Focus on building on what's been good, rather than tearing down the only thing parents have known.

11. Focus on basic values of hard work, high standards, honesty, and integrity. They've become what many consider the basic values that have made us great.

12. Be successful in visibly increasing learning with their children - and prove it with measures they understand and value.

13. Engage students in sharing their portfolios and other

evidence of high quality performance achievement, and/ or progress.

14. Involve parents rather than informing them whenever the decision will impact on anything the parents want or need. Inform them of changes in the daily schedule, but involve them in changes in the reporting procedures. In the words of Doug Krug and Ed Oakley in their book *Enlightened Leadership*, "Ask– don't tell."

15. When making significant changes in anything important to the parents, even if a parent committee has developed and endorsed the change, maintain the old and the new until the new is working successfully in the eyes of the parents.

16. Listen to parents and their concerns until you have really heard what they're saying and can help them.

17. Utilize best information regarding people and change.

18. Be able to clearly articulate the specific knowledge, skills, and content standards that are being addressed in performances, how they're being addressed, and what the convincing evidence is that proves those essentials are being learned.

19. Eliminate educational jargon from communication with parents. Jargon is essential for enabling precision in communication between experts. It is inappropriate for use with others. If you can't say it in five minutes, or explain it on a sheet of note paper (in plain, everyday "street" language), it probably won't work anyway. Don't try something until you can explain it in simple language and/or express it on a 3x5 card.

20. Every document going to parents needs to be done correctly. Proof read for one another – use spell and grammar checkers.

21. "Keep it simple, smarty!" Sometimes we let our level of sophistication get in the way. Ask the parents what their students need to learn, and guarantee that in their language. Don't bombard them with theory and fancy labels.

Tips for Success with Colleagues

1. Invite other teachers and administrators to be outside experts in your classroom. Teachers don't have to have all

the answers. After all, how do a lot of people feel about someone who has all the answers?

2. Invite administrators and other teachers and/or their students to be audiences for your students' performances.

3. Involve the administrative team in what you're doing and what you're planning. Don't leave them in the dark – they need to know what you're doing in order to support you. Besides, they're experts in addressing parents' needs and concerns. A teacher needs the support of the administration and the parents both in order to be successful with the students.

4. Invite administrators to assist as members of evaluation teams similar to the teams of judges in the Olympics.

5. Invite other teachers to assist as members of evaluation teams similar to the teams of judges in the Olympics.

6. Avoid "soap-boxing." Share your successes but be careful – no one enjoys a *reformed person* who wants to change the world to be just like them.

7. Avoid inconveniencing others for your endeavors.

8. Solicit team efforts.

9. Maintain flexibility.

10. Adhere tightly to best known practices regarding changes within an organization.

11. Solicit input.

12. Avoid creating or fostering "in group" and "out groups."

13. Devote the first five to ten minutes of faculty meetings to teachers sharing success stories regarding initiatives and reaching standards.

14. Expect people to build on their strengths.

15. Don't be an expert – be a "guide on the side."

16. "Lead from behind." Christine Neal, Superintendent, Lockport City School District, Lockport, New York.

17. Create a regular forum for teachers and administrators to air and resolve their concerns.

18. Maintain a regular supply budget to support classroom reform efforts.

Appendices

Appendix A

PRODUCT AND PERFORMANCE FORMAT IDEAS

Advertisements

Analogies

Anecdotes and Stories

Art Exhibits

Art Fairs

Articles (Journals, Magazine, Newspaper, etc.)

Audio Tapes

Autobiographies

Ballads

Banners

Biographical Sketches

Blueprints

Book Jackets

Book Reviews

Brochures

Bulletin Board Displays

Bumper Stickers

Cartoons

Cartoon Strips

Case Studies

Charts

Children's Books

Classified Ads

Clothes Design

Coat of Arms

Collages

Comic Books

Commentaries

Commercials (Radio & TV)

Computer Discs (CD's)

Computer Programs

Concept Maps

Conventions

Dances

Debates

Demonstrations

Depictions

Diaries

Dioramas

Documentaries

Dramatic Presentations

Dramatic Readings

Drawings

Editorials

Essays

Ethnic Dishes or Meals

Exhibitions

Fact Sheets

Fairy Tales

Family Trees

Fishbone Charts

Flags

Flow Charts

Folk Tales

Games

Globes

Graphs

Graphic Organizers

Graffiti Wall

Guess Who or What Descriptions

Hieroglyphics

Historical "You Are There" Scenes

Home Pages

Hyperlearning Stack

Icons

Illustrations

Instructions and Advice

Interviews

Journals

Lab Reports

Last Will and Testaments

Lectures

Letters (Personal & Professional)

Limericks

Logos

Logs

Magazines

Maps (Geographic, Weather, & Treasure)

Matrices

Memos

Metaphors

Models

Mobiles

Mock Trials

Monologues

Montages

Mottos and Slogans

Movies

Murals

Museum Displays
Music Videos
Musical Composition
Newsletters
Newspapers
Notes
Nursery Rhymes
Obituaries
Oral Presentations
Outlines
Paintings
Pamphlets
Panel Discussions
Pantomimes
Parodies
Patterns:
    Descriptive
    Cause/Effect
    Generalization
    Sequence
    Solution
Photo Displays
Photo Journals with Captions
Pictographs
Pictorials
Plans
Plays
Poems
Political Rallies
Pop Up Books
Portfolios
Poster Displays
Presentations (Formal & Informal)
Proposals
Puppet Show

Puzzles
Quizzes
Radio Broadcasts
Recipes
Recitals
Reenactments of Historical Events
Reports
Research Papers
Resumes and Cover Letters
Reviews (TV, Movie, etc.)
Role Plays
Schedules
Science Fiction
Science Demonstrations
Science Projects
Scrapbooks
Scripts
Scrolls
Sculptures
"Show and Tell"
Short Stories
Set Designs (TV & Theater)
Simulations
Sketches
Skits
Slide Shows
Soap Operas
Software with Documentation
Songs
Sonnets
Speech (Formal & Extemporaneous)
Spread Sheets
Story Boxes
Story Maps

Story Problems
Summaries
Surveys
Talk Shows (TV & Radio)
Teaching Lessons
Technical Reports
Telegrams
Thumbnail Sketches
Time Capsules
Timelines
Trade Shows
Travel Guides
Tribute or Eulogy
T-shirts
TV Programs
Venn Diagrams
Videos
Voter's Guides
Wall Hangings
Webs
Web Pages
Web Sites
Work Samples
Word Searches

Appendix B

PERFORMANCE VERBS & DEFINITIONS

Acquisition	Interpretation	Production & Creation	Dissemination &/or Utilization	Evaluation & Improvement
Access	Analyze	Apply	Act	Amend
Ask	Apply	Build	Announce	Appraise
Assess	Appraise	Compose	Apprise	Assess
Canvass	Assess	Construct	Articulate	Check
Elicit	Categorize	Create	Broadcast	Critique
Examine	Check	Depict	Communicate	Elevate
Explore	Combine	Design	Convince	Evaluate
Fact-find	Compare	Develop	Debate	Gauge
Feel	Conceive	Draft	Describe	Grow
Gather	Contrast	Draw	Dialogue	Improve
Inquire	Critique	Editorialize	Disclose	Judge
Inspect	Decide	Fabricate	Discuss	Plan
Interview	Deduce	Fashion	Display	Rate
Investigate	Deliberate	Form	Disseminate	Test
Listen	Determine	Formulate	Distribute	Value
Look-up	Disentangle	Frame	Divulge	Weigh
Observe	Evaluate	Generate	Elaborate	
Probe	Gauge	Invent	Elucidate	
Pursue	Generalize	Make	Explain	
Question	Imagine	Manufacture	Express	
Read	Imply	Originate	Inform	
Recollect	Infer	Paint	Interact	
Reflect	Integrate	Picture	Mime	
Research	Interpret	Plan	Perform	
Review	Judge	Produce	Persuade	
Scrutinize	List	Shape	Portray	
Search	Organize	Work out	Present	
Seek	Picture	Write	Pronounce	
Smell	Prioritize		Publish	
Study	Rate		Relate	
Survey	Reason		Report	
Taste	Resolve		Reveal	
	Synthesize		Share	
	Weigh		Show	
			Sign	
			Sing	
			Teach	
			Tell	
			Transfer	
			Transmit	

Appendix B

Performance Verbs & Definitions Continued

The following definitions are to help ensure precision with language and consequently assessment validity. The definitions are based on numerous dictionaries currently available and in common use.

access	to obtain access to (information, skills, processes, or concepts).
assess	to estimate, set or determine the value, extent, significance, or amount of something.
analyze	to determine the parts or basic principles of something in order to determine the nature of the whole.
apply	to use, put, or adapt for a specific use.
categorize	to classify or to put into categories.
compare	1. to represent as similar, equal, or analogous; or 2. to determine similarities and/or differences.
communicate	to make known, clear, or understood.
contrast	to set in opposition in order to show or emphasize differences.
convince	to persuade through argument.
create	to cause to exist.
define	to state the precise meaning of.
defend	to support, justify, or argue on behalf of.
describe	to give a verbal description, to give an account of or tell about in detail.
determine	to establish, fix or settle conclusively.
develop	to elaborate, expand, or enlarge; to bring gradually to a fuller, greater, or better state.
discuss	to speak with others about; to examine in speech or writing.
disseminate	to distribute; spread abroad; promulgate widely.
evaluate	to determine the value or worth of something.
explain	to make clear, plain, or comprehensible.
express	to set forth in words or by symbol or gesture.
formulate	to put into formula or systemic terms or concepts; to devise.

Appendix B

PERFORMANCE VERBS & DEFINITIONS CONTINUED

frame	to construct by putting together the various parts of; to build; formulate or conceive; to fashion.
generalize	to infer from many particulars; to reduce to a general form, class, or law.
illustrate	to clarify by use, examples, comparisons, or the like.
interpret	to determine, explain, present the meaning of something.
investigate	to examine systematically by observing or inquiring into detail.
justify	to demonstrate or prove something to be just, right, or valid.
observe	to watch attentively or to make a systematic or scientific observation of.
organize	to pull or put together into an orderly, functional, or structured whole; to arrange in a desired pattern.
outline	to give the main points, important characteristics, or general principles of a given subject.
persuade	to win over (someone) to a course of action by reasoning or argument; to convince.
plan	to formulate a scheme or program of action for the accomplishment or attainment of something.
portray	to depict or represent pictorially; depict or describe in words; represent dramatically.
present	to offer to view; to display; or to offer for consideration.
prioritize	to put in an order of importance or urgency.
produce	to create by mental or physical effort; cause to occur or exist.
reflect	to think or consider seriously.
report	to make or present an account of (something).
research	to study thoroughly.
resolve	to reach a decision about or find a solution to.
review	to look over, study, or examine again; consider retrospectively.
summarize	to restate briefly; to make a summary.
support	to furnish evidence for; corroborate or substantiate.
synthesize	to combine so as to form a new.
teach	to impart knowledge or skill to others.

Appendix C

Performance Ideas

This appendix contains performance ideas that vary from quite basic to many that are extensively developed. For easy accessing, the ideas are divided into discipline-based categories, however, most of the ideas can be adapted or modified to be used across subject areas and grade levels.

How to use this resource

Most of the performance ideas included in this appendix can be adapted to any almost any grade level or discipline area. Most of them can be used for interdisciplinary projects. We urge scanning all the ideas when looking for one. However, if time is short, search for ideas in the following order:

1. the first section, *Performance Ideas for All Areas,* which contains ideas easily used in all areas & grade levels;

2. the section for your specific discipline focus;

3. the numerous sections containing performance ideas for your discipline area in combination with others; and then

4. the section of the appendix which contains performance ideas for major interdisciplinary efforts.

Performance Idea Sections

1. Performance Ideas For All Areas and Grade Levels
2. Interdisciplinary
3. Language Arts
4. Social Studies
5. Language Arts & Social Studies
6. Language Arts, Social Studies, & Math
7. Technology
8. Technology & Social Studies
9. Technology & Science
10. Technology, Science, & Language Arts
11. Science
12. Science & Language Arts
13. Science, Language Arts, & Social Studies
14. Math
15. Math & Science
16. Math & Language Arts
17. Math & Technology
18. Math, Science, & Technology
19. Math, Science, Technology, & Social Studies
20. Math & Social Studies
21. Math, Social Studies, & Science
22. Business & Technology
23. Business & Economics
24. World Languages
25. World Languages & Social Studies
26. Health & Physical Education
27. Fine Arts

Appendix C

PERFORMANCE IDEAS CONTINUED

1. Performance Ideas for All Areas & Grade Levels

1. Design, construct, and use a teaching museum.

2. Develop "How to ....." manuals and handbooks.

3. Write a note to a friend explaining or describing a concept or skill.

4. Develop a supported projection as response to, "What would happen if ...?"

5. Explain or describe something through metaphor. Defend your metaphor based on similarities of multiple characteristics and functions.

6. Create and use an educational game to teach significant information.

7. Create simulations showing real-life applications of a concept or competence.

8. Create and defend concept maps and/or other organized charts and patterns.

9. Explain/describe a complex concept - checking and adjusting to be certain the audience understands.

10. Determine or choose ill-defined problems - determine best possible solutions.

11. Analyze attributes of famous people in your discipline - then create and role play a great person showing how he/she has/can benefit others.

12. Find, portray, and explain applications of concepts, procedures, or processes in your community.

13. Build and use a diorama to teach a meaningful concept.

14. Create and use depictions of complex concepts, issues, connections.

15. Create questions, tasks, and rubrics that will prove someone can do or understand something. Use them for self and/or peer assessment.

16. Design role plays and simulations for a purpose relevant to others.

17. Design and build models for a purpose relevant to others.

18. Create and lead self-assessment conferences (student-led conferences) based on portfolios showing evidence of status and growth with specific outcomes.

19. Design, do, and defend quizzes, tests, assessments, and performances.

20. Explain/describe the process for something.

21. Create and present a personal poster showing who you are, what you're proud of, and what your goals are.

22. Design and do a research project for a relevant purpose.

23. Write songs that convey significant messages.

Appendix C

PERFORMANCE IDEAS CONTINUED

24. Maintain portfolios showing evidence of self-assessment, best work, and/or growth.

25. As a class, develop quality standards for work and behavior based on a careful study of exemplary models.

26. Analyze for commonalties and differences - draw conclusions based on findings.

27. Find and disprove misperceptions.

28. Regularly summarize into sentences "most significant or usable learnings."

29. Create and explain a flow chart for important procedures or processes.

30. Develop, defend, and respond appropriately to questions that are appropriate differentiators for Advanced Placement Exams or other standardized exams.

31. Design and display a mural/billboard to … Explain and justify your work.

32. Teach significant concepts to others (e.g., parents, younger students, peers, etc.).

33. Identify community and/or environmental problems - then research or design experiments to determine and justify best possible solutions.

34. Design, create, and publish a study guide.

35. Develop and use consensus building skills in authentic situations.

36. Determine how subject matter is used by local professionals and present to younger students.

37. Find and present applications of what is being taught in the physical world.

38. Document the improvement in your _____ efforts in a portfolio that includes specific evidence of your performance levels over the last 8 weeks. In a letter to your portfolio reader, identify the specific evidence in your portfolio that shows the improvements you have achieved.

39. Based on at least three sources, develop and share a report on a given topic for the purpose of informing others.

40. Create and publish a newsletter with reflections and predictions.

41. Create an advertising campaign.

42. Work through a given problem of procedure, being careful to show each step. Write a description of each step and explain why you did it. Justify the reasonableness of your answer.

43. Discern patterns, explain or describe them, and explain how they can be used.

44. Using a current issue, research the quality of information available on the Internet. Make justified recommendations to a curriculum committee.

Appendix C

PERFORMANCE IDEAS CONTINUED

45. Create an interactive Worldwide Web Site to provide reliable, usable, and significant information on a specific topic.

46. Investigate causes of accidents on the playground. Propose solutions to reduce these accidents.

2. Major Interdisciplinary Performances

1. Collect news reports from overseas, and in groups work to produce an international newspaper that reflects the perspectives represented by different countries. When possible, compare and contrast the perspectives in foreign countries with those in the United States.

2. Produce a well supported recommendation to consumers based on a study of "truth in advertising."

3. Write and share or perform stories/plays around real-world problems and solutions.

4. Based on a survey of at least 20 students and 10 parents of children between the ages of 5 and 10, determine the predominant position in your sample toward regulating violence in cartoons on Saturday mornings. Develop and present a position paper to be presented to your local television station that represents this predominant position and supports it using the constitution and recent court rulings.

5. Create and operate a micro-society.

3. Language Arts

1. Produce an orientation video for new students.

2. Use writing, speech, music, and photos to present family folklore.

3. Develop and share children's stories that convey a relevant message.

4. In writing or speech, summarize a piece of significant nonfiction writing in order to convey the essential points to a specific audience.

5. Select a particular topic and find examples of presentations in different media concerning that topic. Identify the media that you feel best serves the topic and justify your selection.

6. Develop and explain a visual which compares/contrasts characters in literature with people you actually know.

7. Research children's literature in order to identify the salient characteristics. Interview young children to identify what they like about professionally produced children's books. Then, create an original children's story that adheres to the findings of your research. Share your story with young readers and if possible have them either illustrate your story or at least help you with the illustrations.

Appendix C

PERFORMANCE IDEAS CONTINUED

8. Develop and present a visual biographical timeline.

9. Create an audio tape of the most important sounds in your life. Write a narrative describing the sounds and exploring their importance to you.

10. Write a descriptive essay about a family heirloom or tradition of special significance. Include your selection in the class book entitled *What It Means To Be A Family*.

4. Social Studies

1. Publish and distribute a voter's guide.

2. Create simulations of historical/cultural interactions, problems, and solutions. Share supported conclusions that are still relevant today.

3. Create and perform a "You Are There" program conveying supported recommendations based on past and present connections.

4. Prepare for and conduct a trial regarding a current issue.

5. Identify the information about the city in which you live that would be most important or of great interest to someone considering moving into your area. Create a pamphlet that highlights your information, and share it with members of city government in hopes that they might officially distribute it through their office.

6. Develop and display an historical depiction of your town using letters, interviews, photographs, researched text, and other documents.

7. Research and present how a conflict (such as in the Middle East) is affected by culture, ethnicity, economics, and geography. Select a state and create a public service presentation. The purpose of this project is to encourage people to come to your state to vacation or to do business. Your presentation should highlight information about the state that you deem important and should be supported with appropriate visuals.

8. Research a topic related to immigration and present a display representing your findings to an appropriate audience.

9. Describe how to locate a place on a map/globe when given longitude and latitude.

5. Incorporating Language Arts and Social Studies

1. Put a famous person in history on trial in light of what is known today (e.g., Harry Truman).

2. Develop a position and support it with music, art, an historical event, and poetry.

3. Take famous quotes and explain why they are still important.

Appendix C

PERFORMANCE IDEAS CONTINUED

4. Identify and research a famous historical personality in order to role-play that person. Write a biographical entry and present yourself to your classmates/parents. Clearly portray your historical contributions. Identify what have been significant effects of your life's contributions on today's society – explain and justify your thoughts.

5. Write a modern day myth that incorporates what we have learned in our study of mythology. Then explain what your myth reveals about mankind and society today.

6. Research a current topic, write an article that accurately reflects your findings, write an editorial, and draw an editorial cartoon.

7. Using published cartoons as a central vehicle, present a position and support for it.

8. Use at least 5 persuasion techniques in either writing or speaking to endorse a position; assess the effectiveness of your efforts and explain why you used the techniques the way you did based on the conditions inherent in the task.

9. In writing or speech, express a conclusion regarding an issue based on the results of comparing, contrasting, and evaluating the points of view of two authors or speakers.

10. Recreate an historical period. (Identify and explain connections - then make predictions based on patterns.)

11. Compare a literary representation of an historical period to actual documented information. (e.g., *The Grapes of Wrath* - The Great Depression)   Present your supported opinions as to why there is or is not a discrepancy concerning …

12. "Create an original drama showcasing the dominant philosophies, artistic works, occupations, and social class distinctions of an historical period." State of Minnesota

13. Compare/Contrast information about an event in the news with information about the same topic from a different medium such as magazine, documentary film, or Internet. (e.g., the attack by the United States on Iraq in September, 1996) Support your conclusions regarding similarities and differences.

14. Studying a period in history through the eyes of a child can present a very interesting and sometimes very surprising point of view. Become a child during WWII and write a diary in which you record how and why the events of the war affected your life. A few perspectives that might prove interesting are children in the Resistance, children of Oriental heritage living in California, children living in Pearl Harbor, Hiroshima, or London during the bombings.

15. Assume the role of a newspaper reporter in 1862. You have been given the assignment of interviewing one of the women or men who have journeyed westward and settled in the new territories. The newspaper wants you to submit a "human interest" article by describing what life was like for these people and by sharing your conclusions about gender roles during westward expansion.

Appendix C

Performance Ideas Continued

6. Incorporating Language Arts, Social Studies, and Math

1. Publish a newsletter portraying inaccurate perceptions being created currently through misuses of statistical procedures.

2. Study a wide range of magazines, newspapers, televised commentaries, and the like. Identify several issues of interest, watch and read widely about these issues, chart the various viewpoints on each issue, and discuss the information supporting each. Prepare a media guide for one of the issues.

7. Technology

1. Develop, draw, and model ideas for the use of space in a mode of living that is out of the ordinary - a tree house, a space station, an underwater dwelling, etcetera.

2. Research and evaluate ideas for an "adaptive devices" that can make life easier for persons with disabilities. Based on your findings, make recommendations for improvements to the device or ways to extend its usefulness.

3. Provide evidence showing a specific technological innovation has impacted on the environment.

4. Construct a model of a technological device or system and describe how it has contributed to and hindered human progress.

5. Develop applications for available software and/or other technologies.

6. Use the documentation for a software package to learn how to use a procedure. Provide evidence that you learned the procedure and how to apply it. The procedure needs to be one NOT taught in class or previously known.

7. Develop and implement a plan to reduce water and energy consumption in your classroom or home.

8. Research your city plat documents, select a specific, available site, and design a house that meets all applicable codes and that aesthetically complements the landscape.

8. Incorporating Technology and Social Studies

1. Create and produce a segment for a TV commentary that compares information about a specific time period in a social studies textbook with information contained in diaries from the same period. (e.g., Civil War, WW II, Depression, etc.)

2. Select several specific places in the world and research how architecture reflects the geographic locations. Present your findings with appropriate visuals.

3. Research your city's past urban design and create a model that accurately depicts your findings. Gather information about your city's present urban plan and compare this with

Appendix C

PERFORMANCE IDEAS CONTINUED

your model. Based on the results of your comparison, write an article for the local paper that predicts what the city's urban design will look like in 75 to 100 years. Support your predictions using trends in your area and elsewhere.

9. Incorporating Technology and Science

1. "Compile a case study of a technological development that has had a significant impact on the environment and report the findings to an appropriate audience." (New York State Department of Education)

2. "Choose materials based upon their acoustic properties to make a set of wind chimes." (New York State Department of Education) Explain your design and material selection.*

3. Build a model to test an hypothesis.

10. Incorporating Technology, Science, and Language Arts

1. "Describe through example, how familiar technologies can have positive and negative impacts on the environment and on the way people live and work." (New York State Department of Education) Make recommendations based on the findings.*

11. Science

1. "Relate physical characteristics of organisms to habitat characteristics (e.g., long hair and fur color change for mammals living in cold climates.)" (New York State Department of Education)

2. Identify and describe applications of physics principles in everyday life.

3. Build "models" in the community that teach difficult to perceive subject matter to the public. For example, build a scale representation that shows distances within the solar system. Develop and present supporting information that explains and justifies what has been built.

4. Design, execute, document, and report on an experiment.

5. Teach middle school students about chemical reactions using information and examples that are relevant to early teens.

6. Develop a landscape plan for a member of the community. The plan must be based on the expressed tastes, needs, and resources of the person and on the environmental needs and conditions of the region.

7. Design an experiment to show at what angle a three foot ramp should be placed to cause a marble that rolls down it to then roll the greatest distance across the floor. Describe, conduct, and report on your efforts.

8. Create a life form (simulated) for a given environment. Justify your conclusion.

Appendix C

PERFORMANCE IDEAS CONTINUED

9. Acting in the role of a particular species (e.g., grizzly bear), publish a newsletter that reports regularly on different regions and the advantages and disadvantages to you of living in or visiting these places.

12. Incorporating Science and Language Arts

1. Develop, through research, a proposal to test a hypothesis of a given concept. Submit the proposal to an appropriate panel of judges who will rate the proposal on clarity, appropriateness, and feasibility.*

2. Research a planet and create an imaginary life form that could exist in that environment. Interview the "creature" about life on the planet and write an article for the human interest section of the Sunday paper.

13. Incorporating Science, Language Arts, and Social Studies

1. Adopt an endangered species and develop and share an analysis of the advantages and disadvantages of protecting and not protecting it.

2. "Investigate the effects of alterations on cultural and/or physical landscapes (e.g., construction of a mall, changes in local traffic patterns, rezoning from residential to commercial, etc.) in order to develop recommendations for how to maximize benefits and minimize disadvantages." State of Minnesota

14. Math

1. Design a cardboard package that is most economical for given dimensions and weights of the intended contents. Justify your design.

2. Determine with justification whether contestants on "Let's Make a Deal" should stick with their first choice or switch to a new door after they are shown what's behind one of the doors.

3. Examine and analyze tabularly presented data in order to create representative graphs - then make and defend predictions based on the trends in the data.

4. The school is interested in knowing exactly how much tile it will take when the floor is retiled. Determine the square footage necessary, and the number of nine inch square tiles that will be needed if there is about a 2 % waste factor. Use written text and diagrams to describe your procedures.

5. Postal rates have been figured by the ounce since July 1, 1885. Here are the rates for the past 62 years: . . . Based on the postal rates since 1932, predict the cost of mailing a one ounce first class letter in 2001. When if ever do you think the cost will be $1.00? Explain your reasoning.

Appendix C

Performance Ideas Continued

6. Assuming the earth's population will continue to increase at the same rate it is today, how long will it be until the earth will probably not be able to produce enough food for everyone? Present your findings in the form of a school science advisory.

7. Use a motion detector and a TI 82/83 calculator to develop graphical representations showing the relationships between distance, rate, and time.

8. Estimate the number of blades of grass in your lawn using appropriate statistical procedures.

9. Design and produce a quilt pattern and describe its symmetry. Put all of the class patterns together and display your quilt in an appropriate area.

10. Determine how many people are in attendance at a major event by sampling areas within a photograph.

15. Incorporating Math and Science

1. Many people believe J.F. Kennedy was shot by someone on the "grassy knoll." Prove or disprove the "shot from the grassy knoll" theory using physics, mathematics, and publicly available archives.

2. Make a record of reported earthquakes and volcanoes during the past 20 years. Identify and interpret the pattern formed worldwide. Report your findings and interpretations through the use of appropriate graphics. Make predictions based on observed trends.

16. Incorporating Math and Language Arts

1. Given data on graphs, write a story that represents the data or graph.

2. Given headlines or claims with background data, explain whether or not the claims are reasonable.

17. Incorporating Math and Technology

1. "Build a city skyline to demonstrate skill in linear measurements, scale drawing, ratio, fractions, angles, and geometric shapes." (New York State Department of Education)

2. For actual maintenance projects being planned at your school, research the projects in order determine the specified amount of materials and resources necessary to complete the projects.

3. Plan a city including efficient road networks, garbage collection and mail routings, plans for voting processes and equitable precincts. Develop and present a paper that explains the mathematics and design decisions. The paper is also to provide rationale to support the selection of your plans by a company wishing to construct a planned community.

Appendix C

PERFORMANCE IDEAS CONTINUED

18. Incorporating Math, Science, and Technology

1. Find places in our community where the concepts we have been studying are being used or exist. Determine why each of the concepts was used the way it was or why each is an example of the concept. Put together a picture/drawing album showing the application and the reason why it is an application. Use your album to teach younger students the reasons why what we're learning is important.

2. Given trends or sample data, make and justify predictions.

19. Incorporating Math, Science, Technology, and Social Studies

1. Given multiple or competing interpretations of given data, justify each interpretation.

2. Make predictions based on the identification and analysis of trends.

20. Incorporating Math and Social Studies

1. Refer to the attached charts and graphs distributed by various political candidates. Determine how the charts actually misrepresent the data. In writing, explain how the misrepresentations are created. Also, describe how the charts should be done to accurately reflect the data. Explain the potential disadvantage to the voters in inaccurately interpreting the data.

21. Incorporating Math, Social Studies, and Science

1. Use sampling to determine, track, and predict the population of a targeted entity within an environment.

22. Incorporating Business and Technology

1. Create, produce, and market a product.

2. Interview people in the community about job possibilities and responsibilities. Create a database of careers in your community and present to an appropriate audience.

23. Incorporating Business and Economics

1. Analyze, interpret, and evaluate family financial structures and procedures in order to create and defend a family financial structure and the procedures by which it will function.

2. "Compare several retirement investment strategies and propose with justification the one you think is most appropriate for an adult you know." State of Minnesota

3. Compare and contrast marketing in a traditional store with a discount store. Present your findings to a board of local business people.

Appendix C

Performance Ideas Continued

24. World Languages

1. Use your knowledge of one language to interpret common written communication in another, unknown language.

25. Incorporating World Languages and Social Studies

1. Create Travel brochures including recommendations for inter-cultural interactions.

2. Portray conditions, issues, or recommendations in a target language.

3. Select a country and do research on the customs and beliefs of that country. Examine official tourist brochures and articles containing interviews with different classes of residents. Then produce a report that compares and contrasts the different views.

4. Simulate functioning effectively under contextual conditions within a single culture or between multiple cultures.

5. Your family has been selected to serve as a host family for a student from ___. Research the country and the specific area where your exchange student lives. Also, identify and study specific cultural items you think you and your family need to know before your new "family member" arrives. Put your findings along with supported recommendations into a written report for your family.

26. Incorporating Health and Physical Education

1. Develop a diet for a particular person that utilizes best available information.

2. Design and implement a personal wellness program.

3. Design a research supported wellness program that is custom tailored for a relative. In your plan, address fitness, exercise, nutrition, and motivation.

4. Create a presentation about the correlation between employee fitness to job performance, absenteeism, and emotional stability. Present your findings to the appropriate audience, being sure to include viable recommendations and plans for a healthier work environment.

5. Create a public service video that promotes positive behavioral choices concerning drugs, alcohol, and/or tobacco.

6. Investigate an important health issue and evaluate its impact on members of your community. (e.g., contamination of the city water supply)

Appendix C

PERFORMANCE IDEAS CONTINUED

27. Fine Arts

1. Use the fine arts to raise local awareness of current issues.

2. Use the fine arts to convey or persuade.

3. Tell a story through an original dance sequence.

4. Research logo and flag design. Develop a logo and flag for your cooperative team. Present your designs to the class and justify your design rationale.

5. Investigate an art object or a piece of architecture and explain how the artist/architect used design elements or principles to express an idea or feeling.

6. Design a statue, monument, or piece of art for a specific public space and a specific purpose. Explain your choice of media, imagery, purpose, and location.

7. Create a mural that shows ways people demonstrate friendship. Write a narrative that describes what has been depicted in the mural.

Appendix D

Transferable Performance Frameworks

If the purpose of performances and projects is to prepare students for complex tasks in life, then performance designs should replicate the basic patterns found in life's tasks. The following are 14 basic patterns that can be found in life's tasks. Complex performances for students can be designed around any of these at different grade levels and across different disciplines.

1. Solve a complex problem. Defend your solution.
2. Find, clarify, and solve real-life problems.
3. Study the way experts do something in order to plan for and perform as well or better.
4. Teach others information, skills, or concepts and/or their application.
5. Compare past and present conditions and trends in order to make predictions and recommendations for the future.
6. Analyze relationships and interactions to draw usable conclusions.
7. Discern patterns and use what you find to make predictions or draw conclusions.
8. Discover commonalties, differences, and connections in human experiences in order to make usable recommendations.
9. Create and use effective depictions of concepts.
10. Function effectively in real-life scenarios that demand skills, abilities, and decisions.
11. Independently and/or collaboratively learn and apply a significant competency or concept.
12. Reflect over personal performance, then determine and implement plans for improvement and application in other contexts.
13. Gather, interpret, and effectively present/teach needed information and concepts.
14. Evaluate options in order to make recommendations.

Appendix E

AUTHENTIC PERFORMANCE CONTEXTS

Accounting	Culture	Geography	Marketing	Relationships
Adolescence	Dance	Geology	Medicine	Religion
Advertising	Death	Geriatrics	Metallurgy	Research
Aeronautics	Defense	Government	Metaphysics	Retail
Agriculture	Design	Health	Meteorology	Retirement
Archeology	Drama	Health Care	Music	Revolution
Architecture	Ecology	Heritage	Mythology	Royalty
Art	Economics	Heroism	Navigation	Science
Astronomy	Education	Historical	Nutrition	Service
Athletics	Electronics	Homelessness	Oceanography	Social Service
Beauty	Emigration	Horticulture	Optometry	Society
Biology	Engineering	Immigration	Parenting	Sociobiology
Business	Entertainment	Institutions	Pediatrics	Sociology
Careers	Environment	Instruction	Penal System	Space
Cartography	Exploration	Interior Design	Philanthropy	Sports
Chemistry	Fashion	Industry	Philosophy	Systems
Child Care	Film	Investments	Physical Rehabilitation	Technology
Communications	Financial	Journalism	Physiology	Television
Commerce	Financial Planning	Justice	Politics	Theater
Communism	Fine Arts	Land Development	Production	Theology
Computer Science	Fitness	Law Enforcement	Public Relations	Tourism
Construction	Forestry	Law	Radio	Transportation
Consumerism	Genealogy	Literature	Radiology	Youth
Cosmetology	Genetics	Magnetism	Recreation	Zoology
Cryptography		Manufacturing		

Appendix F

PERFORMANCE ROLES BY CAREER CATEGORY

Performance authenticity and relevance is enhanced by designing performances around actual life-roles. Role performances are those performances in which the students are asked to carry out tasks and functions that are consistent with the identified roles.

Advertising and Public Relations

Advertising Art Director
Advertising Developer
Conflict Consultant
Event Organizer
Facilitator
Marketing Manager
Motivational Speaker
Public Relations
Publicity Director
Welcome Committee

The Arts

Actor
Artist
Cartoonist
Composer
Critic
Dancer
Director (TV & Movie)
Graphic Artist
Illustrator
Lyricist
Musician
Painter
Producer (TV & Movie)
Sculptor
Singer
Supporter of the Arts

Business & Economics

Accountant
Actuary
Auditor
Banker
Board Member
Bookkeeper
Boss
Chairman of the Board
Consultant
CPA
Economist
Entrepreneur
Financial Planner
Fund Raiser
Game Developer
Hotel Manager
Investment Counselor
Loan Officer
Owner of Company
Manufacturer
Manufacturer's
   Representative
Market Analyst
Restaurant Manager
Retirement Planner

Communications

Author
Biographer
Desktop Publisher
Editor

Editorial Cartoonist
Interpreter
Journalist
Newscaster
Photo Journalist
Publisher
Reporter
Speech Writer
Talk Show Host
Technical Writer
TV Anchor

Computer Science

Computer Salesperson
Computer Service Technician
Desktop Publisher
Programmer
Software Developer
Systems Analyst

Conservation & Environment

Environmentalist
Farm Worker
Farmer
Florist
Forest Ranger
Game Warden
Gardener
Hazardous Waste
   Management Technician

Appendix F

PERFORMANCE ROLES BY CAREER CATEGORY CONTINUED

Horticulturist
Landscape Architect
Park Ranger
Rancher
Surveyor

Design

Architect
City Planner
CAD Specialist
Fashion Designer
Interior Decorator
Interior Designer
Jewelry Designer
Set Designer

Legal & Political

Activist
Ambassador
Attorney/Lawyer
Candidate
City Council Member
Defendant
Diplomat
Emissary
Governor
Judge
Juror
Legislator
Lobbyist
Mayor
Paralegal
Plaintiff
Political Candidate
President
Prime Minister

Prosecutor
Representative
Secretary of (Defense,
  Education, etc.)
Senator

Medical Technology & Health Care

Aerobics' Instructor
Alcohol & Drug Abuse Counselor
Chiropractor
Dental Assistant
Dental Hygienist
Dentist
Dietitian
Emergency Medical
  Technician
Fitness Counselor
Geriatric Expert
Health Inspector
Home Health Aide
Medical Researcher
Nurse (R.N. & L.P.N.)
Nurse's Aide
Nutritionist
Optician
Personal Trainer
Pharmacist
Physical Therapist
Physician
Podiatrist
Psychiatrist
Psychologist
Radiologist
Recreational Therapist
Retirement Planner

Speech Therapist
Surgeon
Veterinarian

Science & Engineering

Archeologist
Astronaut
Astronomer
Biochemist
Biologist
Botanist
Chemist
Entomologist
Geneticist
Geologist
Inventor
Engineer
  Aeronautical
  Biological
  Environmental
  Structural
  Civil
Laboratory Technologist
Marine Biologist
Meteorologist
Myrmecologist
Navigator
Nuclear Physicist
Oceanographer
Physicist
Physiologist
Zoologist

Services

Cabinet Maker
Candle Maker
Carpenter

Appendix F

PERFORMANCE ROLES BY CAREER CATEGORY CONTINUED

Caterer
Chef
Contractor
Cosmetologist
Craftsperson
Electrician
Event Planner
Grocer
Hair Stylist
Information Broker
Insurance Agent
Insurance Investigator
Maintenance Engineer
Mason
Meat Processor
Mechanic
Mortician
Pest Controller
Photographer
Plumber
Printer
Real Estate Agent
Repair Person
Retirement Planner
Sales Person
Secretary
Shop Keeper
Taxidermist
Volunteer

Social Service

Child Care Worker
Corrections Officer
Curriculum Director
Detective
Fire Investigator
Fire Person
Guidance Counselor

Librarian
Missionary
Police Person
Postmaster
Prison Warden
Professor
School Administrator
Social Worker
Teacher
Tutor

Miscellaneous

Athlete
Cartographer
Coach
Concerned Citizen
Consumer
Cryptographer
Curator
Emigrant
Explorer/Trail Blazer
Factory Worker
Family Members (Parents,
   Grandparents, Siblings, etc.)
Famous Person
Flight Attendant
Flight Scheduler
Friends
Futurist
Genealogist
Guide
Historian
Homeless Person
Immigrant
King/Queen
Literary Critic
Mathematician
Miner

Museum Docent
Museum Curator
Personal Shopper
Pilot
Pioneer
Researcher
Senior Citizen
Settler
Ship's Captain
Sociologist
Sports Fan
Sports Figure
Statistician
Students (Peer, Younger,
   Older, New)
Team Owner
Theologian
Tour Director
Tourist
Travel Agent

Appendix G

AUDIENCES FOR STUDENT PERFORMANCES

The following is a list of potential audiences for student performances. For more specific potential audiences, refer to the performance roles in Appendix F.

Accountants
Actors
Actuaries
Advertising Developers
Airline Personnel
Archeologists
Architects
Artists
Astronomers
Athletes
Attorneys
Authors
Bankers
Biochemists
Biologists
Botanists
Business Owners
Candidates
Cartographers
Cartoonists
City Planners
Classmates
Coaches
Composers
Computer Analysts
Construction People
Corrections Personnel
Cosmetologists
Dancers
Designers
Doctors
Economists
Editors
Emigrants

Engineers
Entomologists
Entrepreneurs
Farmers
Financial Planners
Fire Personnel
Flight Scheduler
Florists
Forest Rangers
Game Wardens
Geneticists
Geologists
Government Officials
Grandparents
Graphic Artists
Grocers
Historians
Hotel Managers
Illustrators
Immigrants
Insurance Experts
Investment Counselors
Journalists
Librarians
Lobbyists
Marketing Managers
Mechanics
Medical Technicians
Meteorologists
Museum Personnel
Musicians
Navigators
Nurses
Oceanographer

Other Classes
Painters
Parents
Performing Artists
Pharmacists
Photographers
Physicist
Physiologists
Pilots
Plumbers
Police Personnel
Professors
Programmers
Prosecutors
Radio Personnel
Realtors
Restaurant Personnel
Sales People
School Administrators
Scientists
Sculptors
Secretaries
Siblings
Social Service Personnel
Surveyors
Teachers
Technicians
Television Personnel
Theologians
Therapists
Veterinarians
Woodworkers
Zoologists

Appendix H

UNIVERSAL CONCEPTS

Universal concepts are those concepts that transcend time, traditional disciplines, and contexts.

Aging	Death	Force	Maturation
Attraction	Degradation	Growth	Opposition
Balance	Dependence	Improvement	Power
Change	Destruction	Inception	Production
Conception	Energy	Inclusion	Reduction
Conflict	Equality	Independence	Repulsion
Construction	Evolution	Interdependence	Systems
Creation	Expansion	Iteration	Variation
Cycle	Extinction	Life	

Appendix I

ASSESSMENT AND SELF-ASSESSMENT PROMPTS

Use these prompts before, during, or after important learning situations to foster self-assessment and improvement. Responses can be requested verbally, on "Door Passes" (a strategy included in *Motivation and Learning: A Teacher's Guide to Building Excitement for Learning and Igniting the Drive for Quality)*, and in journals and logs.

Prompts for self-extending learning

1. How might I apply this learning, connection, or application to a new context?
2. How might I use what I have learned in the future?
3. I can use what I have learned to do when I …
4. I used to think … but now I know …
5. I was on the right track with my idea about … but what I didn't know was …
6. What will be the benefits of continuing to use what I have learned?
7. What might happen if …?
8. A question I am curious about and want to find the answer to is …
9. One thing I am not sure of …
10. Three things I wonder about …
11. What am I curious about and/or what am I confused about?
12. What I really want to learn is …
13. What have I learned that I can continue to use?
14. The new questions that arose during today's lesson or activities are …

Prompts for enhancing performance assessments

(Several of the prompts in this section were contributed by John Booth of the Glendale Union High School District in Glendale, Arizona.)

1. Explain why you used the procedures you did.
2. Describe the process you used.
3. Explain how you …?
4. Explain why you …?
5. Support your decision/conclusion/recommendation.

Appendix I

ASSESSMENT AND SELF-ASSESSMENT PROMPTS CONTINUED

6. What conclusions can be drawn from your work? Justify your conclusions.

7. What predictions can be made based on your work/findings? Justify your findings.

8. What recommendations can be made based on your findings? Support your recommendations with a convincing argument.

9. Explain why your findings are what they are.

10. How can what you've done in this situation be used in ____ (another similar situation? Explain how and why.

11. What might happen differently if … ?

12. How can you conclude that … ?

13. Explain how _____ (situation) is similar to _____ (a similar situation).

14. Propose an alternative, but rational, procedure for solving a given problem. Which procedure is best and why?

15. Present another problem that could be solved by the process you used. Explain how you would use it and why it is appropriate.

16. How would/might it have turned out differently if …? Support your conclusion?

17. How do you know that … ? (… is the best? … is the worst? …is the most likely? … is a sound conclusion? … is reasonable? … is true?)

Prompts for self-assessing what's been learned

1. How accurate is the information I have found?

2. I use what I've learned to do to …

3. What more information do I need in order to …?

4. What did I learn to do this week?

5. What did I learn well enough to teach a friend?

6. The skills I need to refine are …

7. I refine my _____ skills by …

8. One thing I learned today was …

9. What did I learn to do from what I did?

10. What did I learn to do that I did not know before?

Appendix I

ASSESSMENT AND SELF-ASSESSMENT PROMPTS CONTINUED

11. What is the most important learning, connection, or application I gained during this lesson or unit?
12. Today my thinking is like the animal … because both …
13. Today my thinking is like the color … because both …
14. How can what I learned benefit me now?

Prompts for self-assessing learning behaviors

1. What skills do I need in order to …?
2. What were the effects of what I did?
3. What were the effects of what I did best?
4. How did I approach this new learning situation in order to maximize my learning?
5. How did I do it?
6. How well did I do … and how can I do even better?
7. It was hard for me to learn …
8. When I get stuck _____ (reading, writing, adding, spelling, etc.), I …
9. The most important thing I have learned about learning this week is …
10. What caused me to achieve this learning, connection, or application?
11. What caused or aided in my learning?
12. What do I do when I think about my thinking?
13. What helped me to learn _____ was …
14. I adjusted for how I learn best by …

Prompts for self-assessing work with others

1. What did I do to be a good listener?
2. What did I do when I worked with others to better the group effort?
3. What can I do to work better with others?
4. When I worked with others, what I did best was … I know this because …

Appendix I

ASSESSMENT AND SELF-ASSESSMENT PROMPTS CONTINUED

Prompts for self- assessment and improvement

1. How have I modeled the characteristics of a self-directed learner?
2. How will I show that I have kept my promise to do even better next time?
3. What can I celebrate?
4. What caused my success?
5. What will I promise to myself to help me do even better in the future?
6. The ways I have improved are …
7. How close did I come to reaching my goal?
8. What have I done to try and improve in my goal area?
9. Is it necessary to make adjustments in my goals? Why or why not?
10. My greatest strength in the area of _____ is … (support with specific examples)
11. My greatest weakness in the area of _____ is … (support with specific examples)
12. This is an explanation of how I did my work …
13. I planned what I did by …
14. I used the feedback I received throughout the process by …
15. I did my best work today when I …
16. I know my work was done well because …
17. The best part of my work is … The evidence I have to support this is …
18. I am most proud of _____ because …
19. How effective was it when …?
20. How efficient was it when …?
21. I know _____ is excellent because …
22. What more needs to be done?
23. I can make my work even better by …
24. If I were going to do this again, the changes I would make are … because …
25. My _____ would be more logical if I …
26. My _____ would be more convincing if …
27. In order to be more persuasive, I could …
28. In order for my _____ to be more complete and thorough, I need to …

Appendix I

ASSESSMENT AND SELF-ASSESSMENT PROMPTS CONTINUED

29. If I could revise _____, I would …

30. How can I _____ more effectively next time?

31. How can I _____ more efficiently next time?

32. In order to be more effective, it is necessary to …

33. In order to be more efficient, it is necessary to …

34. In order to be more solution oriented, I could …

35. In order to get better results next time, I will …

Appendix J

ADDITIONAL RESOURCES

Airasian, P.W. *Classroom Assessment*. New York: McGraw-Hill, 1991.

Airasian, P. W., and Madaus, G. F. "Linking Testing and Instruction: Policy Issues." *Journal of Educational Measurement*, 1983, *2*, 103-118.

Alverno College Faculty. *Assessment at Alverno College*. (Rev. ed.). Milwaukee, WI: Alverno College, 1985.

American Psychological Association. *Standards for Educational and Psychological Testing*. Washington, DC: American Psychological Association, 1985.

Archbald, D. A., and Newmann, F. M. *Beyond Standardized Testing: Assessing Authentic Achievement in the Secondary School*. Reston, VA: National Association of Secondary School Principals, 1988.

Atwell, N. C. *In The Middle*. Portsmouth, NH: Heinemann, 1987.

Austin, A.W. *Assessment for Excellence: The Philosophy and Practice of Assessment and Evaluation in Higher Education*. New York: American Council on Education/ MacMillan, 1991.

Belasco, J. A., and Stayer, R. C. *Flight of the Buffalo: Soaring To Excellence, Learning To Let Employees Lead*. New York: Warner Books, 1993.

Berk, R.A. (Ed.). *Performance Assessment Methods and Applications*. Baltimore, MD: John Hopkins University Press, 1986.

Block, J. *Mastery Learning: Theory and Practice*. New York: Holt, Rinehart, and Winston, 1971.

Bloom, B. S., Madaus, G. F., and Hastings, J. T. *Evaluation To Improve Learning*. New York: McGraw-Hill, 1981.

Bloom, B. S., Hastings, J. T., and Madaus, G. F. *Handbook on Formative and Summative Evaluation of Student Learning*. New York: McGraw-Hill, 1971.

Bloom, B. S., Madaus, G. F., and Hastings, J. T. *Evaluation to Improve Learning*. New York: McGraw-Hill, 1981.

Blum, R. E., and Arter, J. A. (Eds.). *A Handbook for Student Performance Assessment in an Era of Restructuring*. Alexandria, VA: Association for Supervision and Curriculum Development, 1996.

Bonstingl, J. J. *Schools of Quality: An Introduction to Total Quality Management in Education*. Alexandria, VA: Association for Supervision and Curriculum Development, 1992.

Bonstingl, J. J. "The Total Quality Classroom." *Educational Leadership*, 1992, *49*, 6:67.

Boyer, E. L. *High School: A Report on Secondary Education in America*. New York: Harper and Row, 1983.

Brown, F. G. *Principles of Education and Psychological Testing* (3rd ed.). New York: Holt, Rinehart, and Winston, 1983.

Appendix J

ADDITIONAL RESOURCES

Canady, R. L., and Rettig, M. D. *Block Scheduling: A Catalyst For Change In High Schools.* Princeton, NJ: Eye On Education, 1995.

Carlson, S.B. *Creative Classroom Testing: 10 Designs for Assessment and Instruction.* Princeton, NJ: Educational Testing Service, 1985.

Carnegie Corporation of New York. *Turning Points: Preparing American Youth for the 21st Century.* Report on the Carnegie Task Force on the Education of Young Adolescents. New York: Carnegie Council on Adolescent Development, 1989.

Conley, D. T. *Road Map to Restructuring: Policies, Practices and the Emerging Visions of Schooling.* Eugene, OR: ERIC Clearinghouse on Educational Management, 1993.

Covey, S. R. *Principle Centered Leadership.* New York: Summit Books, 1991.

Covey, S. R. *The Seven Habits of Highly Effective People.* New York: Simon and Schuster, 1990.

Department of Labor. *What Work Requires of Schools: A SCANS Report for America 2000.* Washington, DC: U.S. Government Printing Office, 1991.

Diez, M. *Essays on Emerging Assessment Issues.* Washington, DC: American Association of Colleges for Teacher Education, 1993.

Dunn, S., and Larson, R. *Design Technology: Children's Engineering.* New York: The Falmer Press, 1990.

Educators in Connecticut's Pomperaug Regional School District 15. *A Teacher's Guide to Performance-Based Learning and Assessment.* Alexandria, VA: Association for Supervision and Curriculum Development, 1996.

Educational Leadership: Redirecting Assessment. Alexandria, VA: Association for Supervision and Curriculum Development, 1989.

Erickson, H. L. *Stirring the Head, Heart, and Soul: Redefining Curriculum and Instruction.* Thousand Oaks, CA: Corwin Press, Inc., 1995.

Fiske, E. B., Reed, S., and Sautter, C. *Smart Schools, Smart Kids.* New York: Simon & Schuster, 1991.

Fullan, M. *Change Forces Probing the Depths of Educational Reform.* Bristol, PA: The Falmer Press, 1993.

Gardner, H. "Assessment in Context: The Alternative to Standardized Testing." In *Report to the Commission on Testing and Public Policy.* B. Gifford (Ed.), Boston: Kluwer Academic Press, 1989.

Gardner, H. *Frames of Mind: The Theory of Multiple Intelligence.* New York: Basic Books, 1985.

Gardner, H. *Multiple Intelligences: The Theory in Practice.* New York: Basic Books, 1993.

Appendix J

ADDITIONAL RESOURCES

Gardner, H. *The Unschooled Mind: How Children Think and How Schools Should Teach*. New York: Basic Books, 1991.

Glasser, W. *Schools Without Failure*. New York: Harper and Row, 1969.

Glasser, W. *Stations of the Mind*. New York: Harper and Row, 1981.

Goleman, D. *Emotional Intelligence: Why It Can Matter More Than IQ*. New York: Bantam Books, 1995.

Good, T. L. "How Teachers' Expectations Affect Results." *American Education*, 1982, *18*, 10:25-32.

Goodlad, J.I. *A Place Called School: Prospects for the Future*. New York: McGraw-Hill, 1984.

Guskey, T. R. (Ed.) *ASCD Year Book - 1996: Communicating Student Learning*. Alexandria, VA: Association for Supervision and Curriculum Development, 1996.

Haney, W. "Making Testing More Educational." *Educational Leadership*, 1985, *43*, 2:4-13.

Haney, W. "Testing Reasoning and Reasoning About Testing." *Review of Educational Research*, 1984, *54*, 4:597-654.

Haney, W., and Madaus, G. F. "Searching for Alternatives to Standardized Tests: Whys, Whats, and Whethers." *Phi Delta Kappan*, 1989, *70*, 9:683-687.

Hart, D. *Authentic Assessment: A Handbook for Educators*. New York: Addison-Wesley Publishing Company, 1994.

Herman, J. L., Aschbacher, P. R., and Winters, L. *A Practical Guide to Alternative Assessment*. Alexandria, VA: Association of Supervision and Curriculum Development, 1992.

Hirsch, E. D. *Cultural Literacy: What Every American Needs To Know*. Boston: Houghton Mifflin, 1987.

Jacobs, H. H. *Interdisciplinary Curriculum: Design and Implementation*. Alexandria, VA: Association for Supervision and Curriculum Development, 1989.

Johnson, D., Johnson, R., Roy, P., and Holubec, J. *Circles of Learning: Cooperation in the Classroom*. Alexandria, VA: Association for Supervision and Curriculum Development, 1984.

Johnson-Laird, P. N. *Mental Models*. Cambridge, MA: Harvard University Press, 1983.

Jones, B. F., Palincsar, A. S., Ogle, D. S., and Carr, E.G. *Strategic Teaching: Cognitive Instruction in the Content Areas*. Alexandria, VA: Association of Supervision and Curriculum Development, 1987.

Jones, F. H. *Positive Classroom Instruction*. New York: McGraw-Hill, Inc., 1987.

Jorgensen, M. "The Promise of Alternative Assessment." *The School Administrator*, December 1993, 17-23.

Appendix J

Additional Resources

Kagan, S. *Cooperative Learning*. San Juan Capistrano, CA: Kagan Cooperative Learning, 1992.

Linn, R. L. "Educational Assessment: Expanded Expectations and Challenges." *Educational Evaluation and Policy Analysis*, 1993, *15*, 1-16.

Linn, R. L. *Educational Measurement*. (3rd ed.). New York: American Council on Education/ Macmillan, 1989.

Linn, R. L., Baker, L., and Dunbar, S.B. "Complex, Performance-Based Assessment: Expectations and Validation Criteria." *Educational Researcher*, 1991, *20*, 15-21.

Lynch, D. and Kordis, P. *Strategy of the Dolphin: Scoring a Win in a Chaotic World*. New York: Ballantine Books, 1988.

Madaus, G. F., and others. *From Gatekeeper to Gateway: Transforming Testing in America*. Chestnut Hill, MA: National Commission on Testing and Public Policy, Boston College, 1990.

Marzano, R. J. *A Different Kind of Classroom: Teaching with Dimensions of Learning*. Alexandria, VA: Association for Supervision and Curriculum Development, 1992.

Marzano, R. J., Brandt, R. S., Hughes, C. S., Jones, B. F., Presseisen, B. Z., Rankin, S. C., and Suhor, C. *Dimensions of Thinking: A Framework for Curriculum and Instruction*. Alexandria, VA: Association for Supervision and Curriculum Development.

Marzano, R. J., Pickering, D. J., and McTighe, J. *Assessing Outcomes: Performance Assessment Using Dimensions of Learning*. Alexandria, VA: Association for Supervision and Curriculum Development, 1993.

McCombs, B. L., and Pope, J. E. *Motivating Hard to Reach Students*. Washington, DC: American Psychological Association, 1994.

McTighe, J., and Ferrara, S. "Assessing Learning in the Classroom." *Journal of Quality Learning*, December 1995, 11-28.

McTighe, J. and Lyman, F. T., Jr. "Cueing Thinking in the Classroom: The Promise of Theory Embedded Tools." *Educational Leadership*, 1988, *45*, 18-25.

Mitchell, R. *Testing for Learning: How New Approaches to Evaluation Can Improve America's Schools*. New York: Free Press/ MacMillan, 1992.

Mitchell, R., and Neill, M. *Criteria for Evaluation of Student Assessment Systems*. Washington, DC: National Forum on Assessment, 1992.

Murphy, J. *Restructuring Schools: Capturing and Assessing the Phenomena*. Nashville, TN: National Center for Education Leadership, Vanderbilt University, 1991.

National Center for Fair and Open Testing. *Implementing Performance Assessments – A Guide to Classroom, School, and District Reform*.

Appendix J

ADDITIONAL RESOURCES

National Council on Education Standards and Testing. *Raising Standards for American Education.* A Report to Congress, the Secretary of Education, the National Education Goals Panel, and the American People. Washington, D.C.: U.S. Government Printing Office, Superintendent of Documents, Mail Stop SSOP, 1992.

National Education Association. *Student Portfolios.* Washington, DC: author, 1993.

Neill, D. M., and Medina, N. J. "Standardized Testing: Harmful to Educational Health." *Phi Delta Kappan*, 1991, *73*, 688-697.

Newmann, F. M. "Linking Restructuring to Authentic Student Achievement." *Phi Delta Kappan*, 1991, *72*, 458-463.

Newmann, F. M., and Wehlage, G. G. "Five Standards of Authentic Instruction." *Education Leadership*, April 1993, 8-12.

Nitko, A.J. *Educational Tests and Measurement: An Introduction.* New York: Harcourt Brace Jovanovich, 1983.

Novak, J. D., and Gowin, D. B. *Learning How to Learn.* New York: Cambridge University Press, 1984.

Oakley, E., and Krug, D. *Enlightened Leadership: Getting to the Heart of Change.* New York: Simon & Schuster, 1991.

Peters, T. *In Search of Excellence.* New York: Harper and Row, 1982.

Paul, R. *Critical Thinking: What Every Person Needs to Survive in a Rapidly Changing World.* (2nd ed.) Santa Rosa, CA: Foundation for Critical Thinking, 1992.

Paul, R. "Critical Thinking: Fundamental to Education for a Free Society." *Educational Leadership*, 1984, *42*, 1:4-14.

Perkins, D. N. "Creativity By Design." *Educational Leadership*, 1984, *42*, 18-25.

Perkins, D. N. *The Mind's Best Work.* Cambridge, MA: Harvard University Press, 1981.

Perrone, V. (Ed.) *Expanding Student Assessment.* Alexandria, VA: Association for Supervision and Curriculum Development, 1991.

Quellmalz, E. "Developing Criteria for Performance Assessments: The Missing Link." *Applied Measurement in Education*, 1991, *4*, 4:319-332.

Resnick, D. P., and Resnick, L. B. "Standards, Curriculum, and Performance: A Historical and Comparative Perspective." *Educational Researcher*, 1985, *4*, 5-21.

Resnick, L. B. *Education and Learning to Think.* Washington, DC: National Academy Press, 1987.

Ridley, D. S., and Walther, B. *Creating Responsible Learners.* Washington, DC: American Psychological Association, 1995.

Appendix J

Additional Resources

Rogers, S. T., and Dana, B., "Outcome-Based Education: Concerns and Responses." *Phi Delta Kappa Fastback 388*, 1995.

Rogers, S. T., and Graham, S. K., "Performance Design and Implementation – Having It Your Way." Submitted for publication in *Educational Leadership*, December, 1996/January, 1997.

Rogers, S. T., Graham, S. K., and Ludington, H. J., *Exceeding Standards: Powerful Ways to Increase Student Motivation and Learning*. Peak Learning Systems, 1996.

Scates, D. E. "Differences Between Measurement Criteria of Pure Scientists and of Classroom Teachers." *Journal of Educational Research*, 1943, *37*, 1-13.

Schafer, W. D., and Lissitz, R. W. "Measurement Training for School Personnel: Recommendations and Reality." *Journal of Teacher Education*, 1987, *38*, 3:57-63.

Schlechty, P. C. *Schools for the Twenty-First Century: Leadership Imperatives for Educational Reform*. San Francisco, CA: Jossey-Bass, 1991.

Senge, P.M. *The Fifth Discipline: The Art and Practice of the Learning Organization*. New York: Doubleday, 1990.

Shepard, L. "Why We Need Better Assessments." *Educational Leadership*, 1989, *46*, 7:4-9.

Sizer, T.R. *Horace's Compromise: The Dilemma of the American High School*. Boston: Houghton Mifflin, 1984.

Sizer, T.R. *Horace's School: Redesigning the American High School*. Boston: Houghton Mifflin, 1991.

Slavin, R. E. *Cooperative Learning*. New York: Longman, 1983.

Smith, M.L. *The Role of High Stakes Testing in School Reform*. Washington, DC: National Education Association, 1993.

Spady, W. G. *Outcome-Based Education: Critical Issues and Answers*. American Association of School Administrators, 1994.

Stiggins, R. J. "Assessment Literacy." *Phi Delta Kappan*, 1991, *72*, 534-539.

Stiggins, R. J. *Evaluating Students by Classroom Observation: A Study Guide on Achievement Assessment via Observation and Judgment*. West Haven, CT: National Education Association, 1989.

Stiggins, R. J. *Opening Doors To Excellence In Assessment*. Portland, OR: Assessment Training Institute, Inc., November 1995.

Stiggins, R. J. *Student-Centered Classroom Assessment*. Upper Saddle River, New Jersey: Prentice Hall, Inc., 1997.

Stiggins, R. J., and Conklin, N. *In Teacher's Hands: Investigating the Practices of Classroom Assessment*. Albany, New York: State University of New York Press, 1992.

Appendix J

ADDITIONAL RESOURCES

Stiggins, R. J., Quellmalz, E., and Rubel, E. *Measuring Thinking Skills in the Classroom*. West Haven, CT: National Education Association, 1988.

Stockwell, T. *Accelerated Learning in Theory and Practice*. Liechtenstein: author, 1992.

Sylwester, R. *A Celebration of Neutrons: An Educator's Guide to the Human Brain*. Alexandria, VA: Association for Supervision and Curriculum Development, 1995.

Testing in American Schools: Asking the Right Questions. Washington, DC: Congress of the United States. Office of Technology Assessment, 1992.

Wheatley, M. J. *Leadership and the New Science: Learning about Organization from an Orderly Universe*. San Francisco, CA: Berrett-Koehler, 1992.

Wiggins, G. P. *Assessing Student Performance: Exploring the Purpose and Limits of Testing*. San Francisco, CA: Jossey-Bass Publishers, 1993.

Wiggins, G. P. "Creating Tests Worth Taking." *Educational Leadership*, 1992, *49*, 8:26-33.

Wiggins, G. P. "Rational Numbers: Scoring and Grading that Helps Rather Than Hurts Learning." *American Educator*, Winter 1988, 20-48.

Wiggins, G. P. "Standards, Not Standardization: Evoking Quality Student Work." *Educational Leadership*, 1991, *48*, 18-25.

Wiggins, G. P. "Teaching to the (Authentic) Test." *Educational Leadership*, 1989, *46*, 7:41-47.

Wiggins, G. P. "A True Test: Toward More Authentic and Equitable Assessment." *Phi Delta Kappan*, 1989, *70*, 703-713.

Wlodkowski. R. J. *Enhancing Adult Motivation to Learn: A Guide to Improving Instruction and Increasing Learner Achievement*. San Francisco, CA: Jossey-Bass, 1993.

Wlodkowski, R. J., and Ginsberg, M. B. *Diversity and Motivation: Culturally Responsive Teaching*. San Francisco, CA: Jossey-Bass, 1995.

Wolf, D. P. "Opening Up Assessment." *Educational Leadership*, 1987/1988, *44*, 24-29.

Wolf, D. P. "Portfolio Assessment: Sampling Student Work." *Educational Leadership*, 1989, *46*, 37:5-39.

Wolf, D. P., LeMahieu, P. G., and Eresh, J. "Good Measure: Assessment as a Tool for Educational Reform." *Educational Leadership*, May 1992, 49, 8:8-13.

Worthen, B. R. "Critical Issues That Will Determine the Future of Alternative Assessment." *Phi Delta Kappan*, February 1993, 444-454.

Appendix K

GLOSSARY OF TERMS

Technical Jargon or Communication?

We all learned from our teachers that it is important to write or speak in a manner that works for our intended audience. Though as educators we have proven our ability to teach this concept, we have often failed to hold ourselves to it in our communications within our ranks and with the community at large.

Words are very important in both written and oral communication in that they are used as representations of concepts. Consequently, it is crucial that we use words in ways that *convey* what is intended. Therefore, when engaged in communication about education, it is important that we use words that are heard or read by the receivers in the way they are meant. Two of the traps we tend to get caught in as educators are:

1. using words that our students, parents, community members or colleagues don't understand; and

2. assigning to our words in an education context a meaning that is inconsistent with the ways most people interpret those words in their everyday communication.

It doesn't matter whether we fall into the first, second, or both traps, the consequences are the same:

- ineffective communication;
- anger;
- suspicion;
- loss of credibility;
- unnecessary conflicts; and
- potential loss of valuable initiatives.

The purpose of this glossary is to assist educators in their efforts to communicate effectively with their various stake holder groups. Therefore, each word is defined from up to three perspectives – common usage, educational usage, and student usage. When any one of the definitions is out of sync with the others, the results can be much less than those desired.

Appendix K

Glossary of Terms

Glossary Format

Common   A common, street-usage definition for the word or phrase that is supported by several popular current dictionaries.

Education   An "educationaleze" definition for the word or phrase that is consistent with the common definition.

Student   A definition that a student may give if they are in classrooms in which the teachers use the word or phrase consistently with common usage.

Anchor

Common   A heavy object which is lowered by a rope or cable from a boat to secure/attach it to a desired position.

Education   An example of student work that clearly and accurately shows what is meant by a description of a given level of performance in a rubric.

Student   An example that shows me what my work needs to be like to get a particular grade.

Assess

Common   To judge the value or worth of something.

Education   To check for specific criteria in what a student knows or can do in order to make adjustments.

Student   Checking to see what I know or can do.

Assessment

Common   A judgment; an evaluation; a determination of value as in an assessment for taxes.

Education   An event or series of events to determine specifically what a student knows and/or can do according to predetermined criteria and associated levels of quality; and in order to make decisions as to how to improve the performance.

Student   A way to find out what I know and can do.

Appendix K

Glossary of Terms

Assessment, Authentic

Common   (No common definition.)

Education   Assessment in which the student shows what s/he knows or can do in a real world situation.

Student   Showing something I can do that people really do in the real world.

Assessment, Parallel

Common   (No common definition.)

Education   Parallel assessments are assessments that are different but assess the precisely the same target. Parallel assessment are carefully designed to not only have the same target (such as using sampling from a given population to make predictions with respect to the entire population), but to do so with the same level of difficulty.(must be shown to be parallel)

Student   Similar but different assessments that test the same thing.

Assessment, Peer

Common   (No common definition.)

Education   A situation in which one student assesses the performance of another student in order to give meaningful feedback concerning specific criteria.

Student   Kids telling each other what they are doing well and where they can improve.

Assessment, Self

Common   (No common definition.)

Education   A situation in which a student assesses his/her own performance with respect to his/her specific criteria.

Student   Check my own work to determine what I'm doing well and what I need to improve.

Appendix K

GLOSSARY OF TERMS

Benchmark

Common
An important time in one's life; a fixed point for reference - usually a point of excellence that suggests a new phase has begun or a new standard has been set. In business, an exemplary example from outside one's own business to be used as a model.

Education
A key level of a student's knowledge and skills that are assessed according to established high quality criteria.

Student
(No common definition.)

Concept

Common
A general idea or understanding, especially one derived from specific instances or occurrences.

Education
A significant idea that serves as an instructional organizer or focus.

Student
The big ideas.

Content

Common
What something is made of; what is contained in something.

Education
The specific concepts, information, facts and skills included in a subject area, such as fractions in math, genetics in biology, controlled variables in science, or poetry in language arts.

Student
The stuff I'm supposed to learn.

Context

Common
The setting or circumstances in which a particular event occurs; a situation.

Education
The circumstances, challenges, conditions, and settings surrounding learning experiences and demonstrations.

Student
I'm not sure - it's kinda like the conditions in which I have to work - like do I have to give a speech to a small group or to a class of older kids?

Appendix K

GLOSSARY OF TERMS

Cooperative Learning

Common   Students working in groups on a common project.

Education Learning conditions in which a collaborative effort by two or more students is expected. The students are individually and collectively accountable for successful involvement and acquisition of learning goals, objectives and outcomes.

Student   Cooperative learning is when we work with other kids and we all have to do our jobs.

Corrective (see Reteaching)

Criteria

Common   Standards, rules, or essentials on which a judgment or decision can be based.

Education Essential components, attributes, standards or specifications to evaluate student performances, responses, or products.

Student   The things that really count.

Curriculum

Common   What is to be taught in a school, program, course, etc.

Education What is taught in specific programs, courses, and grade levels, stated in specific goals, outcomes, and objectives.

Student   The stuff they teach us.

Curriculum, Integrated

Common   Mixed together, combined into something whole.

Education A curriculum in which the disciplines are taught in combinations that provide meaning and connections.

Student   When I get to learn different subjects all at once.

Appendix K

GLOSSARY OF TERMS

Demonstrate

Common — The act of showing or proving something.

Education — Students doing something which shows they have really learned - proving they don't just know "things," but can do and/or apply them.

Student — Showing or proving what I can actually do.

Enrichment

Common — Improvement; making more valuable or better.

Education — Learning opportunities which provide greater than the normal challenges. In-depth study is expected.

Student — What I get to learn that goes beyond the regular stuff. The more interesting stuff I get to learn after I've got the basics down.

Evaluation

Common — A judgment of the worth or quality of something.

Education — A judgment of the quality or worth of some response, product, or performance based upon established specific criteria and standards, and for the purpose of labeling, grading, and/or documenting achievement or performance.

Student — A check to see how well I am doing.

Exemplar

Common — Something that is worthy of being copied; a model.

Education — A model or example of something that approximates the desired criteria or levels of performance.

Student — A model or example of really good work that I need to use with others as guides.

Expectation

Common — Something that is viewed as likely, certain, reasonable, and/or required.

Education — That which is "believed" to be an appropriate standard for student performance or achievement.

Student — Something that I'm supposed to do in order to say my work is completed.

Appendix K

GLOSSARY OF TERMS

Goal

Common   Something strongly desired; a hope, an aim that may or may not be achieved.

Education   A broad statement of something desired, generally on a district or program level. Goals set direction, facilitate alignment, and inspire.

Student   What I hope to do or accomplish.

Indicator

Common   A sign, token, or symptom.

Education   Specific evidence that students have demonstrated at least one component of an intended, broad goal or outcome.

Student   A specific thing I have to do towards a goal - like a performance, writing a story, building and explaining a model, or making a speech, etc. All can show my growth as a communicator.

Mission

Common   Purpose; the reason someone or some group does what it does; a "calling" in life. Usually based on convictions.

Education   The stated reason for a program, school, or district to exist and what they strive for or strive to be (e.g., it is our mission to continuously improve in equipping our students with the knowledge, skills, and abilities they will need).

Student   An old Spanish church?

Objective

Common   Purpose, aim; something desired and usually worked toward. May or may not be achieved.

Education   A statement saying specifically what students should know or be able to do because of specific learning experiences.

Student   What I am supposed to know or be able to do.

Appendix K

GLOSSARY OF TERMS

Outcome

Common   A result or consequence.

Education   The desired result; an acceptable culminating performance or demonstration or statement of high level ability in which the student is   expected to continuously improve from the day they enter school until the day they graduate and show required ability levels (e.g., communication, thinking skills, collaboration, etc.).

                                        or

              A statement of what the students are expected or required to learn as a   result of some learning experience.

Student   What I'm supposed to be able to do to be done.

Outcome-Based Education

Common   The term is currently being used to describe so many varied approaches to education that there is no common definition.

Education   Basing all curriculum, instruction and assessment on predetermined final learning results.

Student   Knowing what is expected of me to be done and then having to do it.

Paradigm

Common   A pattern, model, or set of rules/regulations.

Education   An understanding; a belief system; a pattern of thought; an expectation of the way things should be (e.g., a room full of desks in rows is the way a classroom should be).

Student   Two dimes?

Performance, Performance Task

Common   The act of doing, carrying out, or accomplishing something.

Education   A demonstration of learning in which students construct a response and/or create a product or performance.

Student   Having to prove I can use what I know.

Appendix K

GLOSSARY OF TERMS

Performance-Based Education

Common   (No common definition.)

Education   An approach to education in which students are taught and assessed for their ability to apply the knowledge, skills, and abilities they've learned.

Student   It means I have to prove I can use what I've learned.

Performance Assessment

Common   (No common definition.)

Education   An assessment in which the students demonstrate their ability to apply their learning through constructing responses, performances and/or products.

Student   Showing I can use what I'm learning.

Portfolio

Common   A collection of accomplishments/"artifacts" used to establish one's qualifications or performance record.

Education   A purposeful, integrated collection of student work showing effort, progress, and/or achievement in one or more areas.

Student   An album or scrapbook of my work to show what I've accomplished or how much I've improved.

Re-teaching

Common   Teaching again?

Education   Offering learning opportunities which are designed to teach something in a way different from the way it was first taught. Re-teaching is done to help a student learn something which was not learned fully the first time around. Re-teaching is often called a corrective.

Student   Having the chance to learn something in a new or different way when I didn't get it the first time.

Appendix K

GLOSSARY OF TERMS

Role Performance

Common A character or part played by an actor in a dramatic performance.

Education A student's demonstration of learning in which the student does what a "real person" does such as acting in the role of a particular kind of scientist, designing and carrying out a scientific experiment to test an hypothesis and then making appropriate recommendations based on the results of the experiment.

Student When I show what I've learned and can do by actually doing what people do in the real world.

Rubric (See also: Rubric, Coaching and Rubric, Scoring)

Common (No common definition.)

Education A well defined set of performance criteria used to evaluate or assess a student's performance in a given area or to guide students to desired performance levels.

Student A sheet of paper that tells us (students) what a really good job looks like. Sometimes they are used for coaching and sometimes for grading.

Rubric, Coaching

Common (No common definition.)

Education The criteria used to guide students until they have completed a task well.

Student A coaching rubric is what we use to tell us how well something has to be done for us to be done with it.

Rubric, Scoring

Common (No common definition.)

Education The criteria that is used to score, label, evaluate the level of quality achieved by a student with a specific task.

Student A scoring rubric is the set of criteria used to determine our grade for something we've done.

Scoring Guide (See Rubric, Scoring)

Appendix K

GLOSSARY OF TERMS

Standard

Common A degree or level or requirement, excellence, or attainment..

Education An established or defined level of quality performance achievement; usually derived from experts, authorities, samples of quality work, or a student's personal best to date.

Student How good something has to be.

> *or*

What I have to do.

Test

Common A check to see if something is operating correctly.

Education A set of questions or situations designed to determine what a student knows or can do.

Student Something that checks to see what I know.

Theme/Thematic Instruction

Common The main point, idea, or message.

Education A central topic or idea that ties different content pieces together (e.g., Ecology and Me, The Westward Movement, Heroes, or Conflict).

Student Learning a whole lot about one main idea.

Universal Concept

Common (No common definition.)

Education A general idea or understanding that is meaningful and/or useful to virtually anyone in any capacity. This concept is general enough that it can be used across disciplines as an organizer for integrated assessments (e.g., conflict, change, force, variables).

Student An idea that connects to a lot of the classes I am taking and is important outside of school as well.

Index

Classroom Performance Assessments, 29-38

Cohen, Allen, 180

Concept, 370

Concepts, Universal, 73, 109-110, Appendix H

Content, 370

Content, Essential Subject Area, 110

Context, 370

Context, Performance, 107-109, 113-114, 120, Appendix E

Continuous Improvement Model, 74-75

Cooperative Learning, 371

Corrective, 371

Covey, Stephen, 316-317

Cordell, Karin, 104

Criteria, 109, 371

Appearance and presentation, 226

Content, 225

Dynamic, 212-213

Essential targets, 224-226

Form, 225

Impact/Effect/Result, 10, 125, 225-226

Process, 226

Static, 212-213

Targets, 224-226

Criteria for Credit, 207, 259

Curriculum, 371

Curriculum, Integrated, 371

D

Declarative & Procedural Knowledge, 181-192

Templates, 184-192

Demonstrate, 372

E

Enrichment, 372

Essential (Focusing) Questions, 73-74, 103, 122-123

Evaluation, 7, 17, 372

Assessment and Evaluation Matching, 25-27

Categories, 19-24

Definition, 16-17, 369

Methods of, 26

Assessment and Evaluation Wheel, 18-19

Selection-Based, 20

Performance-Based, 20-21

Constructed Response, 20-21

Product, 21-22

Performance, 22

Process, 22-23

Personal Communication-Based, 23-24

Multi-Faceted/Thorough Assessment, 11, 17-18

Performance Assessment or Evaluation Task Design Checklist, 55

Performance-Based Assessments and Evaluations, 28-30

Assessing Designs, 306-313

Classroom Performance Assessments and Evaluations, 29-38, 172-177

Example of, 31-34

Templates, 35-38, 175-177

Definition, 20-23

Essential Considerations, 28-29

System Performance Assessments, 39-69

Administration of, 56-69

P

U, V

Understanding, Assessment of, 182-183

Universal Concept, 377

Validations, Multiple, 12, 108

Verbs, Performance - A List & Definitions of,
Appendix B

W, X, Y, Z

Wiggins, Grant, 183

World Language Performance Tasks Ideas, *See*
Performance Task Ideas.

Wlodkowski, Raymond, 316-317

Resources from Peak Learning Systems

The High Performance Toolbox: Succeeding with Performance Tasks, Projects, and Assessments by Spence Rogers and Shari Graham

> Practical, teacher-tested guidelines, templates, strategies, tips and supporting examples for successfully using performance tasks and assessments as a part of a comprehensive approach to student learning and achievement.

Motivation & Learning: A Teacher's Guide to Building Excitement for Learning and Igniting the Drive for Quality by Spence Rogers, Jim Ludington, and Shari Graham

> Over 600 immediately usable strategies and tips with a supporting theoretical foundation to improve the quality of motivation, achievement, and student work.

Teaching Tips: 105 Ways to Increase Motivation & Learning by Spence Rogers and the Peak Learning Systems' Team

> Over 105 brain-compatible tips from teachers to teachers that make teaching easier, increase assessment results, improve work quality, boost memory, reach hard-to-reach students, unlock the five critical keys for improved student attitudes and establish a learning environment for increased student motivation.

Teaching Treasures: 172 Prompt Cards to Make Learning by All a Dream Come True by Spence Rogers and the Peak Learning Systems' Team

> 172 teaching prompt cards with tips and strategies that are fun, practical, and immediately usable in the classroom to enhance student learning and motivation.

Duplicating Masters for The High Performance Toolbox

> Over 50, ready to use duplication masters of critical templates to support individual users of *The High Performance Toolbox* book. Site licenses are available for considerable savings.

Duplication Masters for Motivation & Learning

> Over 40, ready for individual use, duplication masters to support many of the strategies explained in the book *Motivation & Learning*. Site licenses are available for considerable savings.

Workshops and Consulting

> Workshops, consulting, and train-the-trainer sessions by the authors and their colleagues can be scheduled at your site. Each workshop will be custom-tailored to meet your specific needs, and will be conducted consistent with best practices and research.

To order copies of these books or materials, schedule presentations or workshops, or request information about any of the above resources, please call, fax, write, or e-mail Peak Learning Systems.

Telephone	303-679-9780
Fax	303-679-9781
Write	6784 S. Olympus Dr., Evergreen, CO 80439-5312
e-mail	Peaklearn@aol.com
website	www.peaklearn.com

Teaching Strategies & Tips from Peak Learning Systems

More Teaching Strategies & Tips from Peak Learning Systems

ORDER FORM

Purchaser/Shipping Address   Date

Purchaser's Name	

Organization Name	Title/Role

Address	☐ Check if residence ☐ Check if school/business

City	State/Province	Postal/Zip Code	Country

Phone ( )	Fax ( )

How to Order

1. FAX   **(303) 679-9781**
24 hours a day, 7 days a week

2. PHONE **(303) 679-9780**
Or toll free: 877-321-PEAK (7325)
Monday through Friday
7:30 AM-5:30PM (MT)

3. E-MAIL **Peaklearn@aol.com**
24 hours a day, 7 days a week

4. MAIL   Peak Learning Systems
6784 S. Olympus Dr.
Evergreen, CO 80439-5312

Quantity	Description (Please call for current pricing and availability)	Unit Cost	Total

	Item Subtotal	
	Colorado orders only: Enter Tax Exemption # or add 4.3% sales tax	
	Order Subtotal	
	Shipping & Handling (See selections at left)	
	TOTAL in U.S. dollars	

Shipping and Handling   Please Indicate Your Choice of Shipping Method

☐ UPS Ground Service within the 48 contiguous United States: Add $5.00 for the first item, $1.50 for each additional item. Allow 10-15 days for delivery. Orders of 10+ books, please call for shipping quote.

☐ Rush Service Available within the 48 contiguous United States: Please call for pricing.

☐ Other -- Please call for pricing.

Overnight Service available, please call for pricing. Orders for over 10 items, please call for shipping quote.
For shipments to AK, HI, PR, Canada, and other locations outside the contiguous United States - please call for rates.

Payment Information

☐ Cash -- Please do not fax or mail cash orders

☐ Check payable to Peak Learning Systems

☐ Purchase Order Number _____

(Please include a copy of purchase order when mailing or faxing)

☐ Charge my   ☐ MasterCard   ☐ American Express
                      ☐ VISA   ☐ Discover

Exp. Date MM/YY

Signature: _____

Prices & Availability Subject to Change Without Notice.

**Making Learning by All
a Dream Come True**

6784 S. Olympus Dr.
Evergreen, Colorado
80439-5312

**PEAK
LEARNING
SYSTEMS**

phone: 303.679.9780
fax: 303.679.9781
www.peaklearn.com